Forty Seasons of First-Class Cricket.

Photo. by R. Berry, Blackpool, 1908.]

Faithfully Yours
R G Barlow

Forty Seasons of
First-Class Cricket

Being the Autobiography and Reminiscences of
Richard Gorton Barlow,
The ex-professional Lancashire and International Cricketer,
during 40 Consecutive Seasons. of First-class Cricket,
playing and umpiring ;
Together with many curious and interesting Anecdotes
incidental to Cricket,
And valuable Advice to Young Cricketers
on all points of the game.

With Forty-four full-page Illustrations and over
300 Autographs of County Cricketers.

John Heywood, Ltd.,
Deansgate & Ridgefield,
Manchester ;
20, 22, 24, 26, Lamb's Conduit,
London, W.C.

DEDICATION.

This book is respectfully dedicated to my old and highly-esteemed friend and colleague, A. N. HORNBY, Esq., for many years Captain and President of the Lancashire County C.C.

Introduction.

IN making my bow to the cricketing public as an author, I beg at once to cut away the ground from beneath the feet of the critics by making the candid avowal that authorship from a literary standpoint is not my forte. Neither my occupation nor my antecedents have been favourable for undertaking the rôle of writer. I therefore ask to be judged as a cricketer only, on which grounds I am quite fearless as to the result. I have been in the habit of making a note of a point here and an opinion there during my professional career, which covers forty consecutive seasons of first-class cricket. Then my three cricket trips to the Antipodes—included in the above—along with the English teams, provided plenty of unoccupied time for observation and for making jottings. In this way a large quantity of material has been accumulated. Having shown my rough notes to several friends whose opinions carry considerable weight, and having been frequently requested during the past few years to give the many admirers of our national game the benefit of my experience, I have at last ventured into print, and hope to be treated with that indulgence which is always accorded to a first appearance; no matter whether the *début* be made in the cradle or on the stage, in the pulpit or on the platform. My desire, amongst other things, has been to give good practical advice to the young and inexperienced aspirant for cricket fame, though my modesty forbids me being quite certain that even an experienced hand may not secure a wrinkle or two here and there if he will patiently scan what I have written herein.

R. G. BARLOW.

"Glen May,"
    Raikes Parade,
        Blackpool.

List of Illustrations.

Index.

A

* Denotes Australians.

* Denotes Australians.

* Denotes Australians.

H

* Denotes Australians.

J

K

L

* Denotes Australians.

M

N

O

P

* Denotes Australians.

S

T

* Denotes Australians.

* Denotes Australians.

Z

* Denotes Australians.

My Autobiography.

I WAS born at Barrow Bridge, Bolton, Lancashire, on the 28th of May, 1850. I took instinctively to cricket almost as soon as I could walk, and in my early school days often played truant in the afternoons, in order to practice my favourite game. I also persuaded other boys to do likewise, so as to ensure having someone to play with. It is scarcely necessary to add that I was on familiar terms with the schoolmaster's cane, in consequence. I have also heard my mother tell how that sometimes I was allowed to remain at home on the pretext of illness, but that, as soon as the school hour was safely past, I would make a rapid and complete recovery, and sally forth with bat and ball in search of some boy chum with whom to play cricket. I made my own bats and balls in those days; the former out of any piece of wood that came in my way, while the latter were composed of pieces of cloth and string. Then with a few bricks, or our jackets, for the wicket, we were ready for action. My elder brother, Robert, was also an enthusiast at the game as a lad, and I remember how that we two could beat any other two boys in the district. At times we would play three and four boys for a penny or twopence, but we were always on the winning side, and this got to be such a common occurrence that eventually we could not get any of the boys to play against us; consequently, when at practice, I was only allowed to bat for 15 minutes at a stretch, when I had to give my bat up to another boy.

My brother Robert and I, in order to perfect ourselves in the art of catching, were accustomed to practice in a field behind our house, by throwing the ball from one to the other. On one occasion I quite thought I had killed him, as I sent him a high ball which, owing to the sun being in his eyes, he failed to grasp; it slipped through his fingers and fell with great force, on to his nose. He dropped like a stone, and lay prone upon the ground for some little time, the blood streaming from his nose and over his face. In a state of great fright, I ran home and explained to my mother what had occurred. She came at once and took Robert to the doctor, who, upon examining the wound, found that the bridge of the nose was broken. To this day my brother bears in his nose the mark of his accident with the cricket ball. When I was only eleven years old I carried my bat right through an innings for 14 runs, in a school match, "St. George's v. All Saints." Two years later I repeated this feat in another school match at Bolton Park, making 33 runs. In this match I also performed the hat trick—taking three wickets with three successive balls. Again ours was the winning side in each match. At that time I batted, as well as bowled, left-handed; but, acting on the advice of my father, I began to bat right-handed, to avoid the awkwardness and stiffness which left-handed bats so often display. This method I have stuck to ever since, thus presenting the somewhat rare instance of a cricketer batting right-handed and bowling left.

Occasionally, when school was over, I would go to the cricket ground up at Tong Moor when the "Bolton Gents"—the name usually given to the premier Bolton club at that time—were at practice. Some of these gentlemen would give me twopence or threepence for fielding out for them. In this connection I recall the names of Messrs. F. and W. Hardcastle, who were then considered to be very fine cricketers. There were also a Mr. Jones, a Mr. Scott, and a player named Ned Hurley. The professional's name was Smith, a man who often bowled in clogs. I remember the "Bolton Gents" leaving the ground at Tong Moor and going to Back-o'-th'-Bank, where George Parr's old All England XI. played in the Sixties.

At the age of fourteen I left school, and went to work at a printing office, intending to learn the trade of a compositor. This, however, did not suit me, the hours being much too long, thus preventing me from getting my usual cricket practice—which was, of course, something that could not be put up with for long. So, after a few months I left this trade, and became a moulder at the works of Messrs. Dobson and Barlow, at Bolton, until 1865. In this year my parents removed to Staveley, Derbyshire, where I found the same occupation at Staveley Iron Works. Here they had a very good Cricket Club, which enabled me to continue my cricket in good earnest. The first season I played in the 2nd Eleven, and made some good scores. The following season I was drafted into the 1st Eleven, where I remained for several seasons, being successful with both bat and ball. In 1869 I was publicly presented with a bat and ball for my all-round play with the Staveley Works Club during the summer of 1869. The report in the local newspaper reminds me that the chairman, Mr. Fenton, prophesied that I should make one of the finest cricketers in the country. May I say, without appearing vain, that I rejoice in the fulfilment of Mr. Fenton's prediction. Thus, Staveley Works gave me my first present for playing our noble game ; and I have only to add that I have kept the bat and ball to this day. I have never used them, but have kept them as a memento. This occasion was also my first attempt at making a speech.

I made my first century in 1870, when playing for Mount St. Mary's College, against Sheffield Wednesday C.C., at Spink Hill, near Chesterfield. In this match I made 26 and not out 101, and also took six wickets for 18 runs. I usually played for this College team in their matches.

I remember the Staveley Cricket Committee offering a prize in 1869 or 1870, for the one who put in most attendances on practice nights during the season. I easily won this prize, not having been once absent. I usually also paid a visit to the cricket ground each Sunday.

My father was the hon. sec. for the Staveley Works Cricket Club for close on 20 years, and was presented with a gold guard and a marble clock for his good work done for the club. One might have frequently seen at the matches at Staveley, both cricket and football, no fewer than ten members of the Barlow family on the ground at one time. In cricket, my father would be scoring, myself and three brothers playing, and four sisters and my mother watching the match. None of my brothers became county players, though I feel certain that my brother Jack would have made a fine county batsman but for a serious accident to his knee cap, when a young man, which occurred only a fortnight before he received a letter asking him to play for Derbyshire in a county match.

The first big match in which I played was at Staveley, in June of 1871, against the late Geo. Parr's All England XI. ; this match is referred to elsewhere.

The only time that I played *two* matches in one day, was in 1869, one in the morning at a place called Netherthorpe near Staveley, and the other in the afternoon at Staveley; I had to do some rushing about to manage this, I must say. These matches took place on Good Friday, of all days.

The best innings I played for Staveley was against a club called Barlbro, in 1869, when I made 71 runs, against the very fast bowling of George Hibbard, whom I name elsewhere with regard to his fast bowling.

The following is a report of a single-wicket match in which I played whilst at Staveley.

Single-wicket match, five on each side played at Staveley, in 1870, between T. Gee's side and R. G. Barlow's side, which ended in a tie, and caused great excitement :—

R. G. Barlow, bowled Jarvis	2
T. Chambers, bowled Jarvis	1
G. Beresford, run out	0
E. Hall, bowled Jarvis	1
J. Brown run out	1
Total	5

W. Jarvis, caught Brown, bowled Barlow ...	5
J. Doughty, caught Brown, bowled Barlow ...	0
D. Rodgers, caught Hall, bowled Barlow ...	0
T. Gee, caught and bowled Barlow	0
F. Buxton, bowled Barlow	0
Total	5

At one time it looked 100 to 1 on Gee's side winning, as Jarvis had made five runs when I went on to bowl. I, however, took all five wickets for no runs.

My first regular professional engagement was in 1871, at Farsley, near Leeds, which covered two seasons. Batting average 24·50; bowling, I took 84 wickets, average 5·53 per wicket.

Whilst here I played a single-wicket match against Myers, the Yeadon " pro."

Myers was a good cricketer, having since played for Yorkshire on several occasions, and has now a place on the M.C.C. list of county umpires.

This kind of match is never played at the present day, and it should be explained for the information of the tyro, that only two men took part in the match now referred to, the bowler doing all his own fielding, and the batsman having to run to the bowler's wicket and back again to count one run. This match arose through the boasting of the Leeds Clarence Club " pro."—Johnny Smith (" Soldier ")—who, when in the company of some gentlemen friends of the Farsley Club, said he would play any member of the Farsley team for £10 or £20, or would find a Yeadon Club player to do so.

I might say, in passing, that this same Smith had played in several county matches for both Lancashire and Yorkshire.

The gentlemen named thereupon put down £20, which was covered, and the match arranged forthwith—myself being chosen for Farsley, and Myers for the Yeadon Club. I should like to add, in justice to myself, that I was not, nor have I ever been, a betting man; and that I hadn't a single penny laid on the result of this match, though I received several presents for winning it; also that Myers and myself have always been the best of friends. It is not so long ago that we were laughingly discussing this very match at Blackpool, where Myers is an occasional visitor. The following news-cutting well describes the event :—

"CRICKET MATCH FOR £20.

"A single-wicket match, of considerable interest to the cricketing world, was played on the ground of the Yeadon Cricket Club, on Monday and Tuesday, between R. G. Barlow (professional), Farsley, and M. Myers (professional), Yeadon.

"The toss for choice of innings was won by Barlow, who thereupon put his opponent in first, but the fourth ball destroyed the shape of the wickets, and Myers had to retire without scoring. Barlow then assumed the defensive, and completely mastering the bowling of Myers, scored 39, when he hit his wicket, retiring amid great applause. After a short interval, Myers again appeared at the wickets, and when he had scored 10, play was stopped for the day. The game was resumed on Tuesday afternoon by Myers again going in, and when he had scored four more he was bowled by a bailer, Barlow thus winning the match by one innings and 26 runs. The following is the score :—

"Myers, bowled ...	...	...	...	...	0
Myers, bowled ...	...	...	...	...	14
				Total	14
"Barlow hit wicket	...	...	...	...	39
No ball	...	...	...	...	1
				Total	40

"This match was witnessed by a large concourse of people, and much money changed hands over it."

My second professional club engagement was with the Saltaire C.C., near Bradford, and lasted five seasons, 1873 to 1877. My best bowling performance while at Saltaire, was in 1874, against Bradford, where at that time the late Geo. Ulyett (Yorkshire) was engaged as professional. He played against us in this match.

Saltaire made 79, my score being 12 runs. Bradford made 66, and I took nine wickets for 14 runs.

Whilst at Saltaire, I played another single-wicket match in 1873, for a silver cup, value £25, my opponent being a cricketer named J. Burnhill, of Otley, Yorkshire. The following is a newspaper description of this match :—

"On Saturday, a single-wicket match at cricket was decided at the Cardigan Arms ground, Leeds, for a silver cup, value £25, between R. G. Barlow, of Saltaire, and J. Burnhill, of Otley. There was a very large company present, and the betting ruled in favour of Barlow, who, in the first innings made 38 singles, one wide, and one no ball; total 40. Burnhill made six singles and two two's, total 10, when darkness setting in, they agreed to meet on Monday to play it out; but Burnhill failed to show up, and in consequence, Barlow received the cup."

My severance with the Saltaire C.C. was alluded to in a complimentary manner at their annual dinner, as the following report will show :—

"Saltaire Cricket Club Annual Dinner. The committee have pleasure in again meeting the members and friends of the club, and in presenting their report for the past year. Your committee cannot allow the report to pass without expressing their regret that the long connection of years with R. G. Barlow has at last been severed by mutual consent. The committee cannot speak too highly of Barlow's services as professional. The play of most members of the club exhibits traces of his beneficial influence, and every member will admit that his character and conduct have been such as to command the respect of all the members and patrons of the club. The members have rejoiced at his successes and rapid advance to a leading position in the cricketing world, but were sorry for their own sakes to see that frequent engagements in grand matches would eventually prevent his services being of much more use to a local club. The time having arrived, your committee feel that the club collectively, and every member individually, regret its arrival, and wish Barlow every success and continued health.

"The chairman then offered some remarks, and before sitting down, paid a high compliment to R. G. Barlow. 'The report,' he said, 'had not been too strongly worded, for Barlow was one of the honestest and fairest players of cricket they ever met, and his gentlemanly demeanour had been such as to reflect credit upon himself and the club by which he had for the past five years been engaged.'—(Applause)."

Whilst engaged with the Saltaire C.C., I made over the 100 on several occasions.

The following are my averages during my engagement with the club, and I was first each season both in batting and bowling:—
1873. Bowling, 70 wickets for 5 runs per wicket.
1874. Batting, 20·10 per innings. Bowling, 81 wickets for 6·9 per wicket.
1875. Batting, 32-6 per innings. Bowling, 67 wickets for 6 runs per wicket.
1876. Batting, 40·4 per innings. Bowling, 64 wickets for 6·12 runs per wicket.
1877. Bowling, 51 wickets for 5·1 runs per wicket.

As showing the difference in the remuneration of a club professional, between then and now, when £5 and £6 weekly and a benefit are often paid to a good man, I give the salaries which I received as a professional. During my first season's engagement at Farsley in 1871, my salary was 27/- per week, and the second season, 30/-. The following season at Saltaire I received 35/- per week, followed by 40/- and 45/-, and the last season I was with them, in 1877, I was in receipt of 50/- per week.

The committee also gave me leave of absence when I was engaged in any county matches. I have never had a regular club engagement since 1877, as my engagements to play in big matches increased in number every year.

The means of my "discovery," and of my being brought to the notice of the Lancashire County Committee, was a match in which I was playing at Staveley, Derbyshire, in June 1871, against the late Geo. Parr's All England XI. W. Hickton, who was at that time engaged on the county ground at Manchester, was also playing, and hearing that I was a Lancashire-born lad, came and had some conversation with me. He advised me to write to the Lancashire Committee, and promised to back up my application. I therefore wrote to them, and at once received a reply asking me to come over to Manchester for a trial on the Friday afternoon. I accordingly went, and found a good practice wicket ready for me, upon which I was given about half-an-hour's batting against the bowling of Hickton and several other professionals. This was followed by half-an-hour's bowling, and then some fielding and catching practice; so taking it all round, they gave me a very

R. G. BARLOW, 1867.
(First Photo.)

R. G. BARLOW, 1908.
(Last Photo.)

[*Photo. by R. Berry, Blackpool.*]

thorough trial. I must have satisfied my attestors, for in a few days after my return home, I received a letter from the Lancashire Committee, asking me to play against Yorkshire, which match took place at Sheffield on the 17th, 18th, and 19th of July, 1871. Here I made my first appearance in county cricket, not having previously had to play in any Colts' matches.

I am pleased to say that I made a good start for my county, as I went in to bat at the fall of the fifth wicket, and at the close of the day's play was "not out" with 18 to my credit. I was compelled to retire shortly before the drawing of the stumps, owing to Clayton having, with a bumping ball, fractured the little finger of my right hand. On the following day, I continued my innings with my hand bound up, and added 10 to my score, carrying out my bat for 28. I remember at this match that the Yorkshire tail gave us some trouble; West and Iddison had each made over 40 runs, when Mr. Hornby gave me the ball. I think that C. Coward had been suggesting to Mr. Hornby to give me a trial with the ball, for I had been bowling to the former that same morning before the opening of the match. I went on to bowl, and with my very first ball upset West's wicket. I shall never forget how elated I felt.

In the next innings I was put on to bowl first, and secured three more wickets. My analysis for the two innings was: 23 overs, 4 maidens, 44 runs, 4 wickets. I may say that I did not miss many matches after this, and continued to play right on till 1891. So on the whole I think I had rather a long innings, comprising as it did, 21 seasons and three cricket tours to Australia. I played in every match out there, and some of my doings with both bat and ball are given elsewhere.

It is to me very noticeable what a great change has come over the county cricket ground at Old Trafford, Manchester, since I made my début. I well remember that at some of the county matches in the early Seventies I could almost count the spectators around the ground. I often think of the many happy days I have spent on the county ground, and of success after success which the county achieved in the Seventies and early Eighties. We Lancashire professionals were a happy family in those days, and possessed in Mr. A. N. Hornby one of the best captains who ever lived. A thorough gentleman, possessing good qualities all round, Lancashire are not likely ever to look upon his like again.

I am certain that everything to-day is better for the professional county cricketer than it was say 20 or 30 years ago. For one thing the present day professional receives winter pay at the rate of 30/- to 40/- per week, a thing unknown in the old days; then the matches are arranged more conveniently, the players taking a kind of tour through the country instead of having to travel long distances between the matches as formerly. At the same time the cricketers do not in my opinion derive nearly so much pleasure from the game as the old players did.

I consider that several of the counties play too many matches in a season, making it very severe on some of the players, especially the bowlers, on these present-day wickets.

It is a somewhat common occurrence now-a-days for a batsman to make his 1,000 runs, and a bowler to get his 100 wickets in a season. In the 1904 season there were over 50 batsmen who each made their 1,000 runs, and more than 20 bowlers who each took over 100 wickets. Just compare this with the season of 1880, when Barnes, of Notts, was the only batsman to make his 1,000 runs, and Shaw (Notts), Morley (Notts), and Peate (Yorks.), the only bowlers to take over 100 wickets each.

I was singularly fortunate in escaping serious injury during a long career, and was only off playing for a few weeks altogether. The most serious accident befel me—singular to state—in my first county match, when I sustained a fractured finger. This I have already referred to.

During my long career in county and first-class cricket I never acquired a "pair of spectacles." I once had the misfortune to get them, however, in a local match.

I took my benefit on August 5th, 6th, and 7th, 1886, which was described as being the most attractive fixture on the Lancashire card for that season, and it proved a great success. The weather was fairly good the first two days of the match, the third day being spoiled by rain, which continued up to within a few minutes of lunch time. It was computed that over 27,000 persons paid for admission. The match ended in a draw in our favour. Altogether, I made something like £1,000, including gate money and subscriptions. This amount, of course, falls far short of the sums realised at benefit matches of the present day, over £3,000 having been made in two cases. The reason for this difference is not far to seek. County clubs now possess many more members, and far greater numbers attend the matches. Then, again, benefit matches—in the case of "stars"—occasionally take place on Bank Holiday, which always has the effect of running up the figures.

The Manchester press gave me the following complimentary notice :—"This match (Lancs. *v.* Notts) was for the benefit of Barlow, the most popular of all Lancashire professionals, and one of the best all-round cricketers in the world. Barlow's characteristic is steadiness. He probably never really disappointed his admirers during the whole of a match. If he has occasionally failed as a batter, as the best batters sometimes must, he has almost invariably compensated for the disappointment by doing something brilliant with the ball, whilst at point he has few equals in or out of England. The mere chronicle of the 'good things' he has done for his native county would fill a column. Was there ever a more distinguished pair of batters than Barlow and his captain ? The wonderful things they have done between them will never be forgotten whilst Lancashire county cricket has a history. Moreover, as everybody knows, Barlow has for a whole generation been the stone-wall of Lancashire cricket. Many a match has been pulled out of the fire by the mere fact of keeping up his wicket. He simply is a terror to all bowlers when the necessities of the game make this his cue. At the same time, we could name many instances where he has given a good account of himself as a fast scorer. (See averages.) His record is, indeed, one of splendid interest. Personally he has in every way conducted himself in such a manner as to elevate professionalism in cricket."

Following, I give a few of my performances with both bat and ball during my cricketing career, extending from 1871 to 1901.

For Lancashire in first-class matches, from 1871 to 1891, I scored 8,092 runs in 388 innings, which represents an average of 20·6. Bowling, I took 754 wickets. Runs from, 9,986. Average, 13·2 per wicket. I have made three trips with English cricket teams to Australia and other countries, as follow :—

1881-2, with A. Shaw's team, which visited America, Australia, and New Zealand;

1882-3, with the Hon. Ivo Bligh's team, which visited Australia and Tasmania; and in

1886-7, with Shaw and Shrewsbury's team to Australia.

I played in every match during these three trips. My batting average with the 1881-2 team was 30·1 for first-class matches, and for all matches 26·3. Bowling average, 29·2 for first-class matches, and for all matches 9·8 per wicket.

1882-3 team : Batting average in first-class matches, 28·1. Bowling average, first-class matches, 18·3 per wicket.

1886-7 team : Batting average in first-class matches, 20·66, and in all matches, 24·3. Bowling average, first-class matches, 24·11 ; all matches, 10·35.

The *Manchester Guardian* (1902) says : "Always putting the same county matches first-class, as they have done of late years, and all other first-class matches, from 1871 to 1891 Barlow scored over 12,000 runs, and took over 1,000 wickets. This is only excelled by Dr. W. G. Grace in the time named, taking both together, the double feat."

The first time I carried my bat through the innings for Lancashire was at Maidstone, against Kent, in 1874, when I made 26.

I believe I hold the record for batting through the innings, having accomplished the feat about fifty times in first-class cricket and other matches, named elsewhere. My best season in this respect was in 1882—six times—four times in first-class matches, viz., once against the Australians, twice against Notts, and once against Gloucestershire.

In spite of the oft-repeated statement by some that I was a slow scorer, it will be found on glancing over the following scores that I was generally responsible for a large share of the runs :—

1875. Lancashire *v.* Leicestershire, at Manchester, 66 not out.

1875. Lancashire *v.* Kent, at Catford Bridge, 87.

1875. Lancashire *v.* Yorkshire, at Old Trafford, 50 not out.

This season I had the highest batting average in England in first-class matches, viz., 38·8.

1876. Lancashire *v.* Kent, at Gravesend, 36 out of a total of 68 from the bat, on a very bad wicket. The next highest score to mine was 7.

1876. Gentlemen *v.* Players, at Prince's ground, London, 45 not out.

1876. Lancashire *v.* Notts, at Nottingham, 34, and carried my bat through the innings against Shaw and Morley, the great bowlers at that time. This was the first occasion on which I played against them. For this innings I was presented with a few pounds.

1877. North *v.* South, at Hull, 82. My bowling analysis for this match reads : 13 overs, 10 maidens, 5 runs, and 2 wickets, including that of Dr. W. G. Grace. I was presented with £5 at the close of this match.

1877. Lancashire *v.* Kent, at Manchester, 56 out of a total of 114 from the bat.

1878. Lancashire *v.* M.C.C., at Lords, I carried my bat through the innings for 35 out of a total of 99, on a bad wicket, against the bowling of Shaw, Morley, G. G. Hearne, and Mycroft.

1878. Lancashire *v.* Gloucestershire, at Manchester, 40 out of a total of 82 from the bat.

1878. An England XI. *v.* Derbyshire, at Derby, 67 runs, also bowled 5 overs for no runs and took 3 wickets.

1879. Lancashire *v.* Derbyshire, at Derby, 50 out of 148 from the bat.

1881. Lancashire *v.* Surrey, at the Oval, 96 on a very bad wicket. Surrey, 2nd innings, were all out for 81 on the same wicket.

1881. Shaw's English Team *v.* Philadelphia, at Philadelphia, 17 and 59 (top score).

1881. Shaw's Team *v.* New South Wales, at Sydney, 75.

1881. Shaw's Team *v.* 18 of San Francisco and District, at San Francisco, 63.

1881. Shaw's England XI. *v.* South Australia, at Adelaide, 62 1st innings.

1881-2. Shaw's Team *v.* 22 of Orange and District, in New South Wales, on a bad wicket without grass, I carried my bat through the innings for 60 runs, next highest score 24.

The Sydney Mail said : " Barlow thus carried out his bat for 60 after playing one of the best all-round innings, against 22, that has ever been seen, never having given one single chance of any kind." Another newspaper report adds : " Barlow is one of the few batsmen who have assisted in putting over 100 runs on for the first wicket in a test match, England *v.* Australia. Barlow and Ulyett put on 122 runs for the first at Sydney in 1882. Barlow made 62, Ulyett 67."

1882. Lancashire *v.* Notts, at Liverpool, 44 not out, out of a total of 93, on a bad wicket, and 49 run out in the second innings.

1882. Lancashire *v.* Middlesex, at Lords, Mr. Hornby and myself put on 180 for the first wicket.

1882. Lancashire *v.* Notts, at Nottingham, I carried my bat through the innings for 5 runs on an extremely bad wicket.

1882. Lancashire *v.* Australians, at Manchester, I carried my bat through the innings for 66, and was presented with £17 15s.

1882. Shaw's English Team *v.* Australia (Test match), at Sydney, 31 and 62.

1882. Shaw's England XI. *v.* 18 of Canterbury, at Christchurch, New Zealand, 77.

1882. Lancashire *v.* Gloucestershire, at Clifton, carried my bat through the innings for 58 runs.

1882. Hon. Ivo Bligh's English Team *v.* New South Wales, at Sydney, Mr. Leslie and myself put on 224 runs for the second wicket.

1882. Shaw's English Team *v.* Australia (Test match), at Melbourne, 16 and 56.

1882. Hon. Ivo Bligh's English Team *v.* New South Wales, at Sydney, 80.

1882. Shaw's Team *v.* Australians, at the Oval, London, 56 2nd innings.

This year (1882) I made 1,088 runs in first-class cricket, average 27·8. I also took 92 wickets for an average of 10·82 runs. This is my best all-round year, and I was first in batting and bowling averages for Lancashire. Batting, 30·16 per innings. Bowling, 9·61 per wicket. This is a record in Lancashire county matches up to the present time (1908).

Speaking of my 1882 season, the Manchester press said : " If the honours of the season have fallen to an individual, it is to Barlow. That imperturbable cricketer has decidedly increased his previously high reputation, and may claim to be the champion cricketer of the champion county of 1882. His batting average is the highest of the year, his bowling is also the highest, and he is one of the best points in England. Impatient people say his batting is too slow to be good, but those laugh who win, and assuredly Barlow has won."

Another newspaper cutting in 1882 reads : " Barlow, for the fourth time this season, carried his bat right through the innings. I can only say that he did not give a chance, and that he is undoubtedly one of the very best professionals we ever had in this country."

Wisden's Cricket Almanack for 1883 gave the following : " Barlow in batting, as in bowling, is at the top of the tree for Lancashire, and considering how splendidly successful he has been in both departments, he is fairly entitled to be reckoned the best all-round cricketer in England."

1884. Lancashire *v.* M.C.C., at Lords, 117.

1884. Lancashire *v.* Cheshire, at Stockport, 100.

1884. Lancashire *v.* Leicestershire, at Leicester, 119. Also took 7 wickets.

1884. North of England *v.* Australians, at Nottingham, 101, and also took 10 wickets for 48 runs. Was here presented with the full score printed on satin, and a few other presents.

1885. Lancashire *v.* Surrey, at Manchester, 71 and 39 not out. Was presented with £8 for batting.

1885. Lancashire *v.* Gloucestershire, at Manchester, 108.

1885. Lancashire *v.* Essex, at Leyton, 82, and also took 9 wickets for 63 runs.

1885. Lancashire *v.* Cheshire, at Manchester, 71, and took 6 wickets for 39 runs.

1885. Louis Hall's England XI. *v.* Shaw's Australian XI., at Bradford, 34 not out, out of 56 from the bat, 2nd innings; but only a few wickets were down when time was called.

1885. Lancashire *v.* Gloucestershire, at Clifton, I carried my bat through the innings for 62 runs, and also took 7 wickets.

1886. Lancashire *v.* Oxford University, at Manchester, 52 not out, out of a total of 105 from the bat.

1886. England *v.* Australia, at Manchester (Test match), 38 not out, and 30; and also took 8 wickets for 68 runs, and caught 3 other men out.

1886. Shaw and Shrewsbury's Team *v.* 18 of Geelong and District, 108. This was my highest score in Australia, and in first-class matches 86 against Victoria at Melbourne.

1886. Players of England *v.* Australians, at Nottingham, 113. Was again presented with the full score on satin and £5 for this performance.

1887. Shaw's England Team *v.* Australia (Test match), at Sydney, 34 and not out 42.

1887. Lancashire *v.* Cheshire, at Manchester, 59.

1889. Lancashire *v.* Gloucestershire, at Liverpool. The Manchester press said : " R. G. Barlow ought to pat himself on the back. In his weekly notes, Dr. W. G. Grace says that in the Lancashire *v.* Gloucestershire match ' Barlow was, by far, the hardest to play, and bowled splendidly until Briggs missed " W. G." at cover.' The great batsman evidently respects the bowling of ' R. G.,' who has got his wicket pretty frequently."

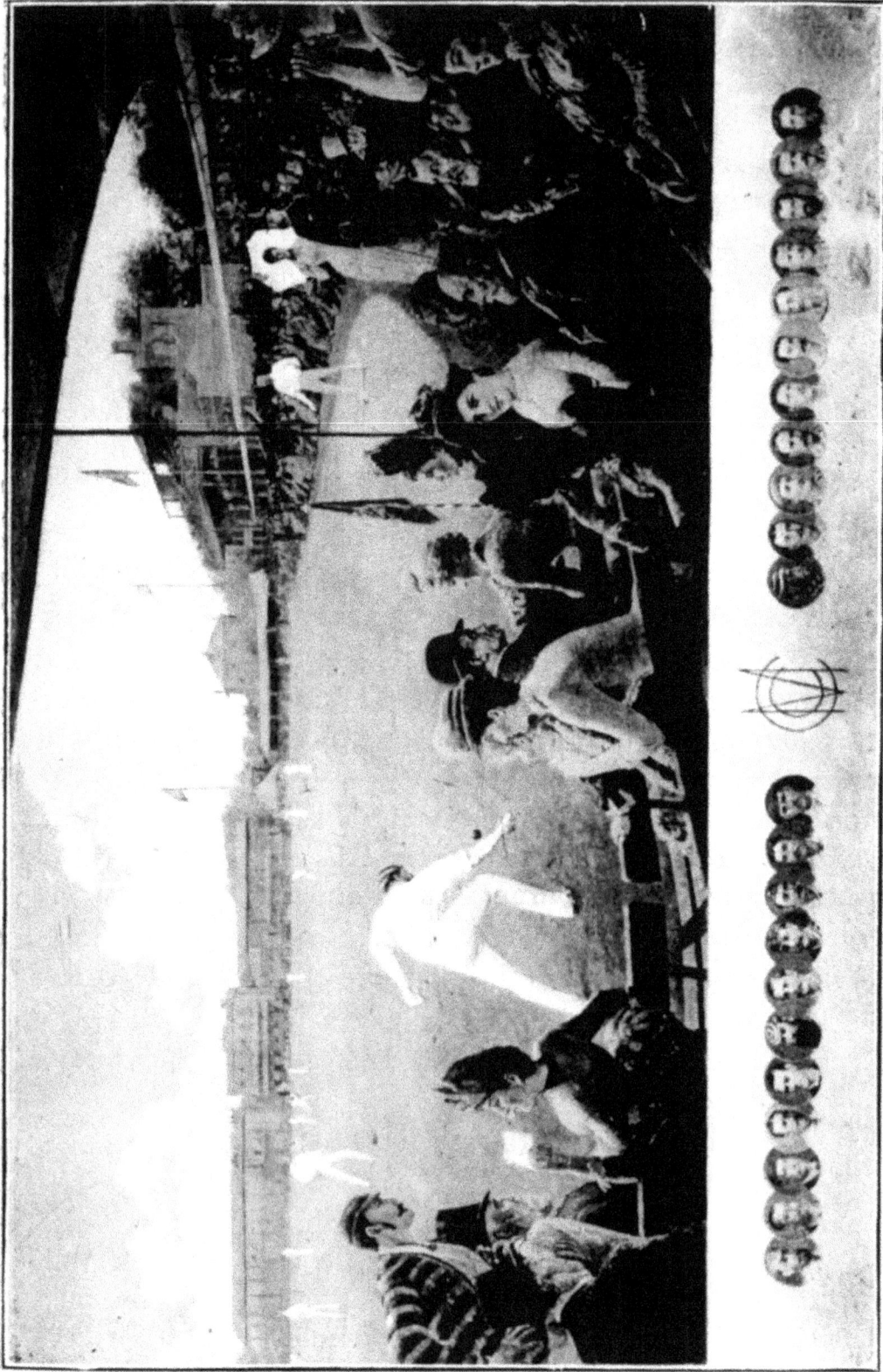

AUSTRALIA v. ENGLAND.—A painting by G. H. Barrable and R. P. Staples, representing an ideal cricket match at Lords in 1887, the centenary of the Marylebone C.C. Ideal teams were chosen with careful attention to possibilities; and without prejudice to the many eminent cricketers, they may be said to fairly represent the best cricket on both sides. The Australian Eleven was selected by Messrs. Spofforth, Scott, and others; the English on the advice of Lord Harris, Messrs. I. D. Walker, V. E. Walker, and others. They are as follows:—English Team: Lord Harris, Hon. A. Lyttelton, Dr. W. G. Grace, W. W. Read, Esq., A. G. Steel, Esq., A. N. Hornby, Esq., A. Shrewsbury, R. G. Barlow, W. Barnes, G. Ulyett, W. Scotton. Australian Team: W. L. Murdoch, Esq., F. R. Spofforth, Esq., G. Griffen, Esq., G. J. Bonner, Esq., J. M. Blackham, Esq., S. P. Jones, Esq., P. S. McDonnell, Esq., G. E. Palmer, Esq., H. J. H. Scott, Esq., T. W. Garrett, Esq., A. C. Bannerman, Esq.

By permission of S. Hildesheimer & Co., Ltd., Manchester, owners of the Copyright.

B

1889. Lancashire *v.* Leicestershire, at Manchester, 35 on a bad wicket. The following is from a newspaper cutting : " The Lancashire innings was not a big one, but it was quite large enough for the purpose. Barlow, who is a wonderful batsman on a bad wicket, scored 35 in capital style."

1889. Lancashire *v.* Dublin University, at Dublin, 81.

1889. Lancashire *v.* Cheshire, at Stockport, 106 runs with the bat. The newspaper report of this match said : " Cheshire looked like making a good stand in their second innings with Lancashire until Barlow was put on to bowl, and the veteran—if he will excuse my terming him one—got 7 wickets for 27 runs. Apparently there is a deal of life in the old man yet. He seemed determined to shine with both bat and ball on Friday and Saturday."

1890. Lancashire *v.* Middlesex. at Lords, 40 in the 2nd innings out of a total of 108 from the bat.

1890. Lancashire *v.* Gloucestershire, at Clifton, 92 and not out 18.

1891. Lancashire *v.* Oxford University, at Manchester, 88.

I have given the foregoing scores partly to show that I was not invariably a "stonewaller" or slow scorer, a statement which has often been made by both press and public alike.

Following, I give a few of my bowling performances in first-class matches :—

1878. Lancashire *v.* Yorkshire, at Huddersfield, 1st innings : 27 overs, 16 maidens, 22 runs, 8 wickets.

1878. Lancashire *v.* Kent, at Manchester, 2nd innings : 9 overs, 7 maidens, 3 runs, 5 wickets.

1878. At Newcastle, against Dr. W. G. Grace's South of England XI., I took 7 wickets for 14 runs, and also scored 42 with the bat.

1878. Lancashire *v.* Kent, at Town Malling, 2nd innings : 39 overs, 19 maidens, 35 runs, 7 wickets.

1880. Mr. C. I. Thornton's England XI. *v.* Cambridge University, 1st innings : 23 overs, 15 maidens, 16 runs, 7 wickets. 2nd innings : I took 6 wickets for 32 runs. Both innings : 66 overs, 48 runs, 13 wickets.

1880. Lancashire *v.* Surrey, at Manchester, 2nd innings : 15 overs, 11 maidens, 12 runs, 5 wickets.

1881. Lancashire *v.* Derbyshire, at Derby : 10 overs, 9 maidens, 3 runs, 6 wickets. I took 3 wickets with 3 balls, and the first 5 wickets were taken without a run being scored off my bowling.

1881. Lancashire *v.* Kent, at Manchester, 1st innings : 30 overs, 15 maidens, 29 runs, 8 wickets ; and in the return match, at Mote Park, Kent, I took 5 wickets for 16 runs, and was top scorer with 61 runs.

1881. Gentlemen *v.* Players, at Lords : 72 overs, 44 maidens, 55 runs, 7 wickets. The seven wickets were Dr. W. G. Grace, Hon. A. Lyttelton, A. N. Hornby, A. P. Lucas, A. G. Steel, A. H. Trevor, and A. H. Evans—a very tough lot, it must be admitted.

1882. Lancashire *v.* Kent, at Maidstone : 18 overs, 7 maidens, 20 runs, 6 wickets.

1882. Lancashire *v.* Somerset, at Taunton : 8 overs, 5 maidens, 7 runs, 4 wickets.

1882. England *v.* Australia (Test Match), at the Oval, 1st innings : 31 overs, 22 maidens, 19 runs, 5 wickets.

1882. Lancashire *v.* Cambridge University, at Manchester : 30 overs, 26 maidens, 13 runs, 5 wickets.

" Mr. A. G. Steel, the Lancashire and International cricketer, thinks Barlow was at that time (1882) the best all-round cricketer in England."—*Vide Press.*

1883. Hon. Ivo Bligh's English Team *v.* Australia (Test Match), at Sydney, 2nd innings : 34 overs, 20 maidens, 40 runs, 7 wickets. For my bowling in this match I received over £20 and a silver cup, also a few other presents.

1883. Lancashire *v.* Gloucestershire, at Manchester : 22 overs, 15 maidens, 10 runs, 5 wickets.

1884. An England XI. *v.* Australians, at Birmingham, 1st innings : 17 overs, 9 maidens, 31 runs, 7 wickets.

1884. Lancashire *v.* Yorkshire, at Sheffield, I took 13 wickets for 66 runs.

1884. Gentlemen *v.* Players, at the Oval, I took the wickets of Dr. W. G. Grace, Messrs. W. W. Read and J. Shuter, with three successive balls. I was captain for the Players in this match, and am pleased to say that we won.

1884. This season I took 130 wickets in first-class matches, at an average per wicket of 15·9 runs. Only one other cricketer took more wickets than myself this season, viz., the late E. Peate, who took 137 wickets. I might add here that there were only eight bowlers in England who took their hundred wickets during the season just named ; last season (1907) there were 22. This will show that very many more matches are played now than 20 years ago.

1885. "Extraordinary bowling. Lancashire v. Sussex, at Manchester. Barlow bowled for an hour, and had only one run scored off him. The first 31 overs were 28 maidens, 6 runs, 5 wickets."—*Vide Press.*

1886. England v. Australia (Test Match), at Manchester, 2nd innings : 52 overs, 34 maidens, 44 runs, 7 wickets. Also scored 38 not out, and 30. I was here presented with £5 and several other small gifts.

1886. Lancashire v. Notts, at Manchester (my benefit match), I made just 50 with the bat, and also took 3 wickets with 3 successive balls, viz., those of Shacklock, Sherwin, and Shrewsbury, being the last two balls of the first innings and the first ball after I went on bowling in the second, Notts having had to follow on.

1886. Lancashire v. Sussex, at Manchester : 32 overs, 16 maidens, 39 runs, 9 wickets, and the tenth batsman was missed off my bowling.

1886. England v. Australia (Test Match), at Lords : 24 overs, 20 maidens, 12 runs, 2 wickets. Two other batsmen were also missed off my bowling in this innings.

1886. Lancashire v. Cheshire, at Manchester (2nd innings) : 11 overs, 8 maidens, 7 runs, 4 wickets. I also made 71 runs with the bat.

1886. Lancashire v. Warwickshire, at Birmingham : 16 overs, 10 maidens, 14 runs, 5 wickets.

1887. Lancashire v. Surrey, at the Oval (1st innings) : 14 overs, 7 maidens, 11 runs, 5 wickets.

1887. Lancashire v. Notts, at Manchester : 26 overs, 17 maidens, 25 runs, 8 wickets.

1887. Lancashire v. Kent, at Gravesend. In the 2nd innings I took 6 wickets for 28 runs.

1888. Lancashire v. Gloucestershire, at Liverpool (both innings) : 36 overs, 19 maidens, 42 runs, 6 wickets.

1888. Lancashire v. Kent, at Manchester : 1st innings, 36 overs, 24 maidens, 27 runs, 3 wickets ; 2nd innings, 31 overs, 21 maidens, 18 runs, 3 wickets.

1888. Lancashire v. Yorkshire, at Manchester (2nd innings) : 11 overs, 5 maidens, 14 runs, 3 wickets.

1888. Lancashire *v.* Gloucestershire, at Gloucester: 26 overs, 16 maidens, 13 runs, 5 wickets (including Drs. W. G. Grace and E. M. Grace).

1888. Lancashire *v.* Gloucestershire, at Liverpool:—" R. G. Barlow was probably well satisfied with what he did against Gloucestershire, at Liverpool. One little feat is worth a line all to itself—

    Dr. W G. Grace, b Barlow... 4   b Barlow...16

Rather curiously, E. M. Grace was also caught off him in both innings for 8 each."—*Vide Press.*

1888. Lancashire *v.* Sussex, at Brighton (1st innings): 57 overs, 43 maidens, 27 runs, 4 wickets.

1889. Lancashire *v.* Cheshire, at Stockport (2nd innings): 17 overs, 7 maidens, 27 runs, 7 wickets.

1889. Lancashire *v.* Oxford, at Oxford (2nd innings): 10 overs, 5 maidens, 12 runs, 4 wickets.

1889. I bowled very little this season, owing to a sprained leg.

My last first-class County match for Lancashire was at Manchester, against Yorkshire, in 1891. I made nine runs, and did not bowl at all. It is a coincidence that my first County match was also against Yorkshire, in 1871.

My last County match for Lancashire was at Manchester, against Cheshire, in 1892. I was caught at the wicket for six. I did not bowl. This was counted as second-class.

In 1893 I played in my last match against a first-class team. This was for Sixteen of Blackpool and District against the Australians, at Blackpool. I made 15 and 13, and in the first innings bowled 19 overs, 7 maidens, 23 runs, 4 wickets.

I always considered, like a great many more, that I was left out of the County team much too soon. As Dr. W. G. Grace remarks, in his book on Cricket, " Barlow was left out of the Lancashire team long before he had lost his form."

" From 1875 to 1891 Barlow has scored more runs and taken more wickets than any other cricketer, taking both departments together, in first-class cricket, with the exception of Dr. W. G. Grace."—*Vide Press.*

" Between 1881 and 1890 Barlow scored close upon 7,000 runs, an average of 21 runs per completed innings, and took 714 wickets at an average cost of 14 runs apiece, only seven cricketers capturing a larger number of wickets in that period, in first-class cricket."—*Vide Press.*

" We may safely make the general statement that Barlow has got the champion's wicket (Dr. W. G. Grace) as often and as cheaply as any bowler he ever met, even in the very zenith of his fame. Barlow is the only representative cricketer in England, in International matches v. Australia, who has first been selected to bat and bowl in the same match, and for the Players v. Gentlemen, same season. Also in County matches, he has been selected to bat and bowl first in the same match more times than any other living cricketer."—*Vide* "*Manchester Guardian.*"

" It is remarkable how very unsuccessful Dr. W. G. Grace has invariably been against Lancashire on Lancashire grounds, and also how often Barlow has brought about the downfall of this great batsman."—*Vide Press.*

SOME OF MY ACHIEVEMENTS IN LOCAL CRICKET.

A few of my achievements in local cricket, both batting and bowling, will be found in the following list :—

1870. Mr. B. Rogers' team v. R. G. Barlow's team, 12 aside, at Staveley. I took 10 wickets, and caught the eleventh from George Hay's bowling.

1871. Farsley v. Manningham, at Farsley : 50, out of a total of 94 from the bat.

1872. Farsley v. Manningham, at Manningham : 52, out of a total of 92, from the bat.

1872. Farsley v. Morley Nelson (a good local club). I bowled right through the innings for 3 runs, and took 4 wickets with 4 successive balls.

1879. G. F. Grace's United South of England XI. v. Eighteen of Leicester and District, at Leicester : 1st innings, 34 overs, 21 maidens, 19 runs, 6 wickets ; 2nd innings, 32 overs, 20 maidens, 21 runs, 8 wickets.

1879. G. F. Grace's United South of England XI. v. Twenty-two of Kidderminster, including Bates, Ulyett, Hill, and Lockwood, at Kidderminster : 36 overs, 22 maidens, 40 runs, 10 wickets, including the wickets of the above-named four Yorkshire County players for 6 runs.

1879. G. F. Grace's United South of England XI. v. Twenty-two of Birmingham, at Birmingham : 1st innings, 35 overs, 17 maidens, 32 runs, 11 wickets ; 2nd innings, 34 overs, 18 maidens, 16 runs, 8 wickets.

The above were the Yorkshire Team which made the record score in any first-class County Match, viz.: 887 against Warwickshire, at Birmingham, in May, 1896.

Barlow (Umpire).   Hirst.   Wainwright.   Denton.   Hunter.
Tunnicliffe.   Hon. F. S. Jackson.   Lord Hawke.   F. W. Milligan.
Brown.   Peel.   Moorhouse.

Four separate hundreds were scored: Lord Hawke 166, Hon. F. S. Jackson 117, Wainwright 126, and Peel 210 not out. Being one of the Umpires in this match I must say that the batting, bowling, and fielding were all excellent, but the wicket was too good and easy for any bowler.—R.G.B.

[Photo. by Messrs. Whitlock & Sons, Birmingham.]

I played for Mr. G. F. Grace's United South of England XI. a few times this season, as will be seen by the foregoing matches.

1879. United North v. Eighteen of Leeds and District, at the Horticultural Gardens, Leeds. The Press said: "The feature of the second innings of the 'United' was that Barlow went in first and came out bat in hand for 41, out of a total of 103 from the bat; a wonderful innings, considering the dangerous state of the wickets."

I remember being hit on the head twice, the ball on each occasion going to the boundary for four. These were, of course, put down as leg byes. Our opponents included Mr. Motley and a professional named Blackburn, two very good and fast bowlers, the other professional bowlers being Gilbert, Skinner, Littlewood, and Louis Hall (the old Yorkshire player). How I managed to stay in batting so long on such a bad wicket, I do not know. Alec Watson, the old Lancashire player, always said, and will have it to this day, that this innings was the most wonderful he ever saw on such a wicket.

1880. G. F. Grace's United XI. of England v. Eighteen of Bedminster, including Drs. W. G. and E. M. Grace, at Bedminster. I got Dr. W. G. Grace's wicket (caught) for 6 in the 1st innings, and bowled him for 10 in the 2nd innings.

1880. Rishton v. Enfield, at Rishton: 45 not out, out of a total of 84.

1880. Renishaw v. Manvers Main, at Renishaw: 42 not out, out of a total of 75 from the bat.

1881. United England XI. v. Eighteen of Nuneaton and District: 30 overs, 22 maidens, 15 runs, 10 wickets.

1882. Dukinfield v. Meltham Mills, at Dukinfield: 67 not out, out of a total of 108 from the bat.

1882. Dukinfield v. Bentfield, at Dukinfield: 15 overs, 9 maidens, 15 runs, 7 wickets.

1883. Lancashire v. Twenty-two Colts, at Manchester: 32 runs, out of a total of 66.

1883. Dukinfield v. Birch, at Dukinfield. I took 6 wickets for 7 runs, and made 28 out of a total of 38.

1884. Lancashire v. Eighteen of Crewe and District, at Crewe: 13 overs, 5 maidens, 20 runs, 10 wickets.

1884. Ramsbottom *v.* Oldham, at Ramsbottom : 58 not out, out of a total of 84.

1884. Ramsbottom *v.* Rishton, at Rishton : 80 runs, out of a total of 151 from the bat.

1885. Lancashire *v.* Twenty-two of Nantwich, at Nantwich (2nd innings) : 33 overs, 20 maidens, 24 runs, 10 wickets.

1885. Ramsbottom *v.* Bacup, at Ramsbottom : 18 overs, 10 maidens, 19 runs, 6 wickets.

1885. Ramsbottom *v.* Keighley, at Ramsbottom : 26 not out, out of a total of 49.

  For two seasons (1884-5) I played for Ramsbottom C.C. on all my spare Saturdays. My 1884 batting average was 36 per innings, and bowling 7·30 per wicket, which headed the list both in batting and bowling averages. My 1885 batting average of 16·7 per innings, and bowling average of 5·5 per wicket, were both again first in the averages.

1885. Castleton Moor *v.* Lydgate, at Castleton : 43 runs out of a total of 86 from the bat ; and also took all five wickets that were down, for 14 runs.

1886. Cheetham *v.* Denton, at Cheetham : 7 overs, 2 maidens, 7 runs, 6 wickets.

1887. Lancashire *v.* Eighteen of Colne and District. I took 12 of the 14 wickets down, for 29 runs.

1887. Lancashire *v.* Twenty of Nantwich and District, at Nantwich (2nd innings) : 9 wickets for 19 runs, and also performed the " hat trick."

1887. Lancashire *v.* Sixteen of Leyland and District, at Leyland : 69 runs, out of a total of 155 from the bat, and 24 not out, 2nd innings.

1887. Lancashire *v.* Eighteen of Bolton and District, at Bolton : 14 wickets for 51 runs.

1887. Lancashire *v.* Eighteen Colts, at Manchester (2nd innings) : 23 overs, 11 maidens, 25 runs, 10 wickets.

1887. Dukinfield *v.* Moorside, at Dukinfield : 6 wickets for 12 runs (and scored 87 runs for them against Castleton Moor the following week).

1888. East Lancashire *v.* Burnley, at Blackburn : 5 wickets for 13 runs, including F. Sugg's, who played for Burnley.

1888. Rochdale *v.* Ashton-under-Lyne, at Rochdale : 71 runs; also took 6 wickets. Several pounds were collected and given to me for my all-round play in this match.

1889. Mr. A. N. Hornby's Team *v.* Eighteen of Church Minshull, at Parkfield, Nantwich. I made 60 runs.

1889. Barlow's Lancashire Team *v.* Twenty of the Isle of Man. I made 58 runs, and took 8 wickets for 24.

1889. Dukinfield *v.* Saddleworth, at Dukinfield. I made 41 runs, and took 6 wickets for 15.

1890. Stalybridge *v.* Barnsley (with Bagshaw and Bennett). I had the following extraordinary bowling average—23 overs, 20 maidens, 7 runs, 7 wickets. The Barnsley score was 60. I bowled throughout the innings.

1890. Stalybridge *v.* Moorside, at Moorside. I made 28 runs, and took 7 wickets.

1891. Royton *v.* Littleborough, at Littleborough : 9 wickets for 15 runs, and caught the 10th.

1891. Royton *v.* Crompton, at Royton : 8 wickets for 23 runs.

1891. Royton *v.* Padiham, at Padiham. I took 8 wickets, and made 50 not out.

1891. My averages for Royton this season were 24 runs per innings with the bat, and I took 55 wickets for 6 runs each. I was second on the list for both batting and bowling.

1892. Mr. A. N. Hornby's Team *v.* Rossall School, at Rossall : 96 runs.

1892. Royton *v.* Stalybridge, at Stalybridge : 52 not out, out of a total of 122 from the bat.

1892. Royton *v.* Bury, at Royton : 7 wickets for 16 runs.

1892. Royton *v.* Friarmere, at Royton : 6 wickets for 4 runs.

1892. Royton *v.* Padiham, at Padiham : 42 runs, and took 5 wickets for 14 runs.

1892. Royton *v.* Padiham, at Royton. I carried my bat through the innings for 25 runs out of a total of 51, and took 7 wickets for 24 runs.

1892. Royton v. Stalybridge, at Royton : 51 not out.

1892. " Besides occasionally officiating as umpire in the big matches, R. G. Barlow is still doing good work for the Royton Club, and on Saturday, playing against Milnrow in a League match, he took 6 wickets for 7 runs, in addition to scoring 46. As Barlow also performed ' the hat trick,' we should think he would be very well satisfied with the afternoon's proceedings. He has still a lot of cricket left in him, and he might do worse than shave off his beard and come out as a Colt in the match at Old Trafford, on Bank Holiday."—*Vide Press.*

1892. Averages for this season for Royton: Batting, 30·11 per innings; bowling, 61 wickets for 6·54 per wicket. First in both batting and bowling.

1893. Royton v. Walsden, at Royton: 51 runs, and took 4 wickets for 16 runs.

1893. Royton v. Heywood, at Royton: 57 runs.

1893. Royton v. Heywood, at Heywood: 8 wickets for 19 runs.

1893. Royton v. Milnrow, at Royton. Carried my bat through the innings for 26 runs, and took 4 wickets.

1893. Averages this season for Royton: Batting, 18·10 per innings; bowling, 85 wickets for 7·78 per wicket. First in bowling, second in batting.

1894. Royton v. Milnrow, at Royton. I took 3 wickets with three successive balls, and with each ball bowled the middle stump. Also made 46 runs, and took 6 wickets for 7 runs, including the above.

1894. Royton v. Radcliffe, at Radcliffe. I carried my bat through the innings for 13 runs, out of a total of 30 from the bat, and took 4 wickets for 23 runs.

1894. Dr. Fergusson's Team v. Burnley St. Andrew's (including Forbes), at Burnley. I carried my bat through the innings for 60 runs, and took 6 wickets for 33.

1894. Averages this season for Royton: Batting, 24·4 per innings; bowling, 35 wickets for 5·32 per wicket. First in both batting and bowling.

"Barlow was before Briggs both in batting and bowling for Royton this season. They had almost the same number of innings, and almost the same number of overs and wickets. Briggs averaged in batting 15·2 per innings, and 7·18 per wicket in bowling. Barlow and J. Briggs were both engaged for Royton this season for all their spare Saturdays."—*Vide Press.*

1895. Royton v. Bacup, at Royton: 15 runs, and took 7 wickets for 13 runs.

1895. Royton v. Littleborough, at Littleborough. I carried my bat through the innings for 11 runs out of a total of 34, and took 5 wickets.

1895. Royton v. Milnrow, at Milnrow: 51 runs, and took 5 wickets.

1895. Royton v. Darwen, at Royton: 50 runs, and took 5 wickets.

1895. Averages this season for Royton: Batting, 18·9 per innings; bowling, 65 wickets for 7·40 per wicket. First in both batting and bowling.

1896. Royton v. Rochdale, at Royton: 19 runs, and took 6 wickets.

1896. Royton v. Walsden, at Walsden. I carried my bat through the innings for 50 out of a total of 106 runs from the bat, and took 4 wickets for 29 runs.

"GOOD PERFORMANCE BY A VETERAN.—In a match between Royton and Walsden, in the Lancashire Central League, on Saturday, R. G. Barlow, the old Lancashire County professional, playing for Royton, carried his bat through an innings of 119 for 50. This performance makes over fifty times that Barlow has carried his bat through an innings in county and local matches. In this match he also took 4 wickets for 29 runs."—*Vide Press.*

1896. Averages this year for Royton: Batting, 21·5 per innings; bowling, 38 wickets for 8·28 per wicket. First in bowling, and second in batting.

1897. Royton v. Crompton, at Royton: 51 not out, and took 5 wickets.

1897. Royton v. Walsden, at Royton: 45 runs, and took 7 wickets for 34 runs.

1897. Averages this season for Royton: Batting, 20·33 per innings; bowling, 65 wickets for 8·55 per wicket. First in bowling and second in batting.

All Royton matches are Central Lancashire League.

With the 1897 season, my connection with the Royton Club came to a termination. During my engagement with them I received from the secretary the following kind letter of appreciation:

ROYTON CRICKET CLUB.
56, Church Street, Royton, Sept. 22, 1897.

Dear Sir,

I have been requested by my Committee to tender you their thanks for the services you have rendered to our Club during the seven seasons you have been connected with us.

You have given the greatest satisfaction, not only to the Committee, but to every member of the Club, for the excellent manner in which you have assisted the team, as we feel sure that you have been the means of achieving many a victory, which we should not otherwise have done, without your help.

With the exception of a few weeks at the commencement of the season just ended, your form has been most consistent, and you come out at the finish with splendid averages. Your bowling analysis is indeed a grand performance, and is a proof that you are far from being played out; and I feel certain you are still worthy of a place in the County Eleven.

I sincerely hope you may still devote several years to your favourite game of cricket, a sport you have already done so much for; and I trust we may again have the pleasure of seeing you in our team, as we may rest assured that whenever you play you will try with all your might to help the team to victory.

Thanking you once more, I am, yours sincerely,

JAS. MORTON, Hon. Secretary.

Mr. R. G. Barlow, Blackpool.

Royton was a good club, and occupied a high position in the Central Lancashire League.

1898. Mr. A. N. Hornby's Team v. 15 of Wigan, at Wigan: I took 6 wickets.

"Visitors to the new cricket ground of the Wigan Cricket Club, on Saturday last, saw a sight that would doubtless carry the minds of some of those present back a good few years. Before many of our present-day players knew much about cricket, the names of A. N. Hornby and R. G. Barlow were as familiar as household words. As a pair they have done many wonderful deeds, opening the Lancashire batting for season after season almost without a break. Indeed, so inseparable did they become, that at last, when Lancashire were once playing Yorkshire at Huddersfield, a Yorkshire critic alluded to Barlow as Mr. Hornby's 'Man Friday,' and for many a day afterwards 'R. G.' was known far and wide by that name."—*Vide Press.*

1898. Mr. A. N. Hornby's Team v. Nantwich, at Nantwich: 16 runs, and took 5 wickets for 18 runs.

1898. Ramsbottom v. Colne, at Colne (Lancashire League match): 50 not out, and took 3 of the 6 wickets that were down.

1898. Ramsbottom v. Burnley, at Burnley (Lancashire League match): 7 wickets for 23 runs.

1898. Blackpool v. Lytham, at Lytham: 63 not out.

1898. Blackpool v. Leigh, at Blackpool: 55 runs, and took 4 wickets for 13 runs.

1898. Averages for Blackpool this season: Batting, 41·4 per innings; bowling, 5·13 per wicket. First in both batting and bowling.

1898. Averages for all matches this season against such clubs as Bury, Leyland, Wigan, Burnley, Lytham, Colne, Bacup, and East Lancashire Wanderers: Batting, 27·4 per innings bowling, 44 wickets for 5·3 per wicket.

"Cricketers generally, and Lancashire men especially, will be glad to hear how well he has gone through the season, and shows better results than for many years past. Mr. R. G. Barlow, whom Blackpool now claims as a townsman, is one of the finest exponents of England's favourite summer pastime the world has ever seen, and few men keep their form the number of years he has done. He can still bat, bowl, and field wonderfully well, as recent performances testify."—*Vide Press.*

1899. Blackpool v. South-East Manchester, at Blackpool : 51 not out

1899. Blackpool v. Clifton, at Blackpool : 45 not out, and took 8 wickets for 28 runs.

1899. Average for Blackpool this season : Batting, 37·2 per innings; bowling, 9 runs per wicket. First in bowling, and third in batting.

1900. Blackpool v. East Lancashire Wanderers, at Blackpool : 20 runs, and took 6 wickets.

1900. Blackpool v. Burnley St. Andrew's, at Blackpool : 55 runs, and took 3 wickets.

1900. Averages for Blackpool this season : Batting, 16.9 per innings; bowling, 10·1 per wicket. Second in both batting and bowling.

1901. Blackpool v. Lytham, at Lytham : 10 runs, and took 5 wickets for 30 runs.

1901. Blackpool v. Paddock, Huddersfield, at Blackpool : 29 and 33 not out.

1901. Averages for Blackpool this season : Batting, 12·4 per innings; bowling, 10·1 per wicket. First in bowling, and eighth in batting.

These last few seasons I could not get much practice, owing to my many umpiring engagements. I had also reached the age of 51 years. All things considered, I decided to give up match playing at the end of season 1901. This was therefore my last cricket season.

"OLD EBOR'S" OPINION OF THE AUTHOR.

The following talk is reproduced (by permission) from "Old Ebor's" (Mr. Pullen's) book on "Old English Cricketers."

R. G. BARLOW.

"The writer seriously doubts if there is a man living so thoroughly devoted to cricket as R. G. Barlow. Cricket is not

GROUP OF PRESENTATION BATS, BALLS, AND WICKETS.

The bat on left was given for the first batting average in England in first-class cricket, 1875, viz.: 38·8 runs. The right hand bat was presented on the memorable occasion when Mr. Hornby and Barlow put on 148 runs against Yorkshire in 1875, and won the match for Lancashire without being separated. One of the two balls is a memento of the season 1882, when Barlow held the first bowling average for Lancashire, viz.: 9 runs per wicket. The second ball and a bat were presented to him by the Staveley C.C. for his excellent batting and bowling during the season, 1869.

merely Barlow's profession, it is his one object in life. He lives, as it were, in an atmosphere of cricket, all his surroundings are reminiscent of bat and ball. You immediately identify his residence, ' Glen May,' Raikes Parade, Blackpool, by the cricketer's armorial bearings above the doorway—bat and wickets in terra cotta. In the vestibule door you see a coloured-glass representation of Mr. A. N. Hornby and the owner of the house at the wicket, and of the late Richard Pilling in the act of keeping wicket. The hall lamp reflects the names of A. G. Steel and other famous cricketers. In the front sitting-room a new and practical version of 'Cricket on the Hearth' is given by a representation of Lord Sheffield's ground in coloured tiles, with portraits (also in tiles) of Mr. Hornby and Barlow on the one side, and Pilling on the other. Throughout the house is a profusion of cricket portraits and sketches, for when on cricketing tours abroad Barlow made it his practice to obtain photographs of nearly all the principal places he visited, and players he became acquainted with. Cricket trophies and presents innumerable, mementoes of great performances on the field, are tastefully displayed. But what Barlow probably most values is the array of bats which hang on the bath-room wall. With one of these, now broken-faced and splintered, he scored over 4,000 runs. In 1882, he played six times through an innings with it. He has taken it with him round the world, and when in its present battered condition he scored 44 runs with it at Melbourne against Victoria. No wonder, therefore, that Barlow thinks it 'a record bat.'

" It is not possible to do justice to Barlow's career, or to produce more than a tithe of his voluminous reminiscences, within the compass of this ' Talk.' The famous Lancashire cricketer has gone through the world with his wits about him. He has during his career collected material from which a most interesting book could be written. At present he is half inclined to put this material to its legitimate use. The other half of the inclination will probably soon be forthcoming.

" What Barlow did in first-class cricket from his initiation down to his retirement in 1891, a period of 21 years, it is not the writer's province to narrate in detail. To do so would involve the publication of a vast array of figures, and statistics are not talks. It must be sufficient to state that he had 388 innings for Lancashire, scored 8,092 runs with an average of 20·6 per innings. In bowling he took 754 wickets for 9,986 runs, an average cost of 13·2 per wicket. If all the counties he played against were classified first-class as now, he would have the record of over 12,000 runs, and more than 1,000 wickets.

"Barlow has made three trips with English cricket teams to Australia. The first was with Shaw, Shrewsbury, and Lillywhite's team in 1881-2. The second with the Hon. Ivo. Bligh's team in 1882-3; and the third with the team organized by the triumvirate first-named in 1886-87. Beyond all other recollections of these trips across the water, an experience on ship-board with the Hon. Ivo. Bligh's team, has impressed itself most vividly on Barlow's mind. There was a collision at sea, which, as by a stroke of Providence, just escaped adding a ghastly contribution to the great wrecks that mark the pathways of British maritime commerce, and form the 'price of Admiralty' of which Rudyard Kipling so stirringly sings.

"The journey out on the 'Peshawur' was interesting and pleasant enough up to a certain point. It enabled the team to see the effects of the bombardment of Alexandria. Their ship was the first to call there after the war, and Bates, Barlow, and others found the opportunity to go on shore and see the havoc wrought four months earlier by the 'Alexandra,' the 'Monarch,' the 'Invincible,' *inflexible*, the 'Penelope,' the 'Condor,' and other mighty engines of naval warfare. 'It was a grand sight,' says Barlow, when he now recalls it; from which the reader will assume that the ruin was great. On ship-board Barlow showed his athletic versatility by carrying off the first prizes for the 100 yards' scratch race, the hurdle race, and the egg and spoon race, besides being second in the high jump. The trip, in short, was pleasantness itself, until one night, on the open sea, a big black hull, with sails full set to the breeze, shot suddenly out of the gloom and crashed amidships into the 'Peshawur.' Then came terror, confusion, despair—and after all a great thankfulness. But Barlow must tell this thrilling experience himself.

"We were about 350 miles out of Colombo, and had not seen another ship. It was Sunday night, about nine o'clock, and church service had just concluded. I was looking over the side of our vessel, in company with W. W. Read, Fred Morley, and others of our party, when I saw in the near distance a full-rigged ship coming before a brisk breeze straight towards us. I looked a moment, then exclaimed, 'My word, she's coming too near to be pleasant; there's going to be an accident, if they don't mind.' I had scarcely got the words out of my mouth when the prow of the vessel crashed into our steamer, near the engine-room, tearing her plates and leaving an ugly gap large enough to drive a coach and pair through. Then she sheered off and lay to.

"What my sensations were I cannot describe. Inwardly I bade everyone at home good-bye. Ladies were fainting and praying, passengers and crew rushed hurriedly about, while the captain called calmly for 'the boats.' I seized and donned a life-belt; others did the same. The lifeboat and other small boats were launched, and preparations were made to leave, as it was thought, the sinking ship. But the ship was not sinking. By the mercy of Providence the great rent in her side stopped about half a yard above the water-line. The sea, too, was as calm as a mill-pond, and remained so during the four days that it took us to put back to Colombo.

"We had 400 souls on board, the sea was infested with sharks, and one shudders even now to think what would have happened had the blow gone below the water-line, or had the collision occurred in a stormy sea. The ship that collided with us was the 'Glen Roy,' about 1,500 tons burthen, and we towed her back to Colombo. We were detained there nearly a week for repairs. A vote was taken by the passengers as to whether we should wait for the ship to be made seaworthy again, or go by another boat, and we decided to wait.

"'That collision practically finished poor Fred Morley. He had several ribs broken when the "Glen Roy" struck us, but the nature of his injuries was not known until we got to Melbourne. One day I found him crying like a child in his bedroom. When asked what was the reason he said, "I don't know what is the matter with me, but there is something seriously wrong somewhere." I spoke to Mr. Bligh, and he had Morley examined, with the result that the fracture of the ribs was discovered. We missed his bowling sadly during the tour. But the effect was much worse than that. The accident laid the seeds of a fatal illness. Morley did not live long after his return to England.'

"The Colombo experience was not the only narrow escape Barlow had. 'On the 1881 trip, we had been out to supper across the river at Sydney, and being detained, just missed our boat. It was moving off when we reached the wharf. We were annoyed at our ill-luck. But that boat never reached its destination. It was split open in a collision and sent to the bottom, and several of those on board found a watery grave. I think Providence must have been watching over us on that occasion also.'

" In his three trips to Australia, Barlow never missed a match ;
that is to say, he played in every game in which the three teams
took part. It is probable that no other Anglo-Australian cricketer
can say the same. In one of the last matches he hurt his foot
badly, and had a man to run for him. He wished to be able to say
he had played in all matches, otherwise he would have stood out.

" The 1881 trip was made via San Francisco. It was there
that a celebrated baseball-pitcher pitched the team out for a small
score in the first innings. The late Ed. Peate and George Ulyett,
in their ' Talks ' mentioned that in the second innings, so far from
objecting to the style of the ' pitcher,' they hoped he would be kept
on throughout, and the pitcher 'nearly pitched his arm off,' while
Ulyett and Barlow were making 166 runs. Of that incident
Barlow says :—

" 'Ulyett and I took twenty half-crowns to one that we would
not put 100 on in the second innings before we were parted. We
won the bet easily enough ; before I left, the score was 166. On
that tour, when at Sydney, playing against the combined eleven of
Australia, there was another curious batting success. When Ulyett
and I went in to open the second innings, George said, " Now, Dick,
I'll be Mr. Hornby ; let's see if we can't put 100 on before we are
parted." " Right," said I, " we will." And we did ; the score was
122 when the first wicket fell. Ulyett made 67, and myself 62.'

" 'The first eleven-a-side match I played in, in Australia,
commenced on December 9th, 1881, against New South Wales, and
I was batting for about four hours for 75—the top figure on our
side. As I was walking back to the pavilion, a gentleman stepped
over the rails, and with ceremonious politeness handed me an old
cricket-belt with the remark, " I thought we had the champion
sticker in Alec. Bannerman, but you win the belt. Take it." I
took it, and have it to this day.'

" Barlow considers his best bowling feat in Australia, was at
Sydney, on January 30th, 1883, when England won the rubber.
The Australians had to go in at the finish to score 153 to win the
match. Barlow and Morley were the bowlers. Alec. Bannerman
and G. Giffen had 20 minutes batting against them over-night, and
not a run could be scored. The next day Murdoch and his men
were got out for 83, and England won by 69 runs. Barlow's
analysis worked out to the following remarkable figures : 34·2 overs,
20 maidens, 40 runs, 7 wickets. ' For this feat,' says Barlow, ' I
was presented with a silver cup, and other mementoes, and some

enthusiastic admirers of the old country carried me shoulder high off the ground, and collected over £20 for me. This was very kind of them, though the " chairing " business is rather embarassing.'

" Of the famous seven runs' defeat of England by Australia at the Oval on August 29th, 1882, Barlow has an explanation which has not previously been given to the world. He says :—

" 'I admit England ought to have got the runs at the finish, but in my opinion they ought not to have had even so many as 85 to get. Mr. Hornby was our captain, and he went out in my judgment a bit too soon on the second day. The ground was wet, and Peate and I could not stand, while the ball was like soap. I had to get the groundsman to fetch a spade to get the mud out of the bowling-holes, so that I could fill them up with sawdust. In the first innings of the match my analysis was 31 overs, 22 maidens, 19 runs, 5 wickets. In the second, 27 runs were hit off me, and I could not get a wicket. I ground my teeth with vexation time and time again ; and if ever I swore in a match—to myself—it was then. There was some nervousness on the English side at the finish. But I was not nervous. Even though Spofforth did bowl me for a duck. This match, by the way, enables me to make a statement— not boastfully, but as a fact of interest. I was selected to both bat and bowl first for England (also for the Players v. Gentlemen the same year). That is what no other representative English cricketer has been called upon to do in England.

" 'Next to Alf. Shaw, I am entitled to say I have clean bowled Dr. Grace more frequently than any other bowler did up to 1895. The feat, I may tell you, is richly coveted by bowlers, for " W. G." was such a champion. In 1888 at Liverpool, I bowled him twice— for four in the first innings, and 16 in the second. I remember that in this match a gentleman who had come from Manchester to see the match, bet me a new hat to a shilling, after I had bowled " W. G." in the first innings, that I did not repeat the feat in the second. I took the bet, and won it.'

" Most cricketers have good umpiring stories to tell when they can think of them. This of Barlow's is one of the best :—

" 'The 1886-87 team to Australia played against 22 of Cootamundra on November 29th and 30th of the former year. The Mayor of the place stood as one of the umpires. One of the local batsmen hit the ball to Johnny Briggs at cover-point, and he, whipping it back with his usual deftness and accuracy to Sherwin, the other batsman who had thrown in his bat was easily run out

OLD TRAFFORD CRICKET GROUND, MANCHESTER.

Lancashire v. Australians, June 5th, 6th, 7th, 1884.

But he made no effort to go, though Sherwin said, " Out, my dear fellow, out." No one had dreamed of appealing to the umpire, but at last we did so. All the answer that could be got from his worship was, " D—d good bit of fielding that, wasn't it ? " This novel reply produced a convulsion of merriment ; and Shaw generously allowed the batsman to have another innings.'

" Barlow formerly had an athletic business at Manchester. One day when in that establishment a man came up and asked him if he kept a full supply of cricket requisites ? ' Certainly,' was the response. ' Then,' gravely demanded the man, ' wrap me up a bottle of arnica, a paper of court plaster, and an arm-sling, ' I am going to play in a cricket match this afternoon against Jack Crossland.'

" Here is another good Crossland story :—Some years ago at Nantwich, Mr. Hornby's Eleven were playing against a local eighteen. Crossland was bowling, and on one of the local batsmen coming in, the first ball struck him on the knee. The next hit his finger. The batsman dropped his bat and walked away to the pavilion. ' You're not out,' was the remark made to him as he left. ' No,' was the reply, ' but I know if I stop there I soon shall be out, so I'm off,' and off he went.

" ' In 1878, in the Lancashire v. Yorkshire match at Huddersfield, Bates was bowling to me, and he would have Hall to field close-in at " silly mid-on." He told the Batley man to " get in—Barlow won't hurt you ! " Before long, Bates gave me one that I let go at, and the ball hit Hall full on the head. Louis spun round like a top, and dropped ; I thought I had killed him. Fortunately, the injury was not so serious as it looked, but Hall said he would not field at " silly mid-on " again either for me or anyone else.

" ' As a set-off to this, I may say that in 1888 poor George Ulyett caught me close-in, off Peel at point. He seemed to take the ball almost off the edge of the bat. In the second innings " Happy Jack " again came close-in, so I remarked, " Now, George, I should not like to kill you ; I shall be hitting one very hard to the off if one comes that way." " Well, Dick," was the reply, " if you do, I shall be the first that you have killed by hard hitting." However, in the next over, Ulyett brought off another catch almost off the bat, and I retired with the remark, " You are my master this match, George ! "

" ' Against Leicestershire I once went through an innings for 29, compiled in about three hours. There was a dinner and a jollification at night, and being called upon to sing, I gave them

" You'll remember me," quite unconsciously of any humour in the selection. A few minutes afterwards one of the speakers said he did not know whether I had sung that song with a special meaning, but after the innings of that day, he could give an assurance that they were not likely to forget me." '

" W. G. Grace has never captured a ' pair ' in first-class cricket ; Richard Barlow can make the same boast ; but he admits he has been very near it, and adds that ' Dr. W. G. Grace ought to have had the " specs." once in a match, England v. Australia, at the Oval. He got a cipher in the first innings, and was missed easily at point before scoring in the second.'

" Cricketers well know that Mr. Hornby and Barlow had a weakness for running each other out. As bearing on these little escapades, Barlow is fond of telling the following stories :—

" ' I remember walking round the ground in one of the matches against Middlesex at Old Trafford, and overhearing a conversation between two Lancashire men. Said one of them, " Tom, who dost loike to see bat ? " " Oh, I loike to see 'Ornby an' Barla'." " Ah, I can do wi' Mester Hornby, ony he's too keen, an' runs Barla' out. I'm all on the fidgets when he's there." People used to bet pretty freely, too, on the probability that one of us would run the other out.

" ' There was one curious instance at Old Trafford. Two Oldham men were talking together, and one of them said, " Jim, dost know who's won t' toss ? " " Ai, Bill, Lancashire has done it." " All right then, I'll see t'owd Boss bat, and when he gets out I'll go in teown till lunch-toime. I'll tak two bob to one as Barla's in when I coom back." The bet was taken, and at lunch-time I was " not out." A friend of mine who had heard the previous conversation saw the man return, and went up to hear what he had to say. After considering the matter over in his mind for a few minutes, the Oldham man said, " Coom neow, lads, I'll tak another bet of five bob to one that they woan get Barla' out to day." He again won his rash bet, for at 6-30 I was " not out " for 103.'

" One item more, and this desultory ' Talk ' must close :—

" ' In 1889 we had here at Blackpool the most extraordinary exhibition of cricket I have ever seen. It was a match, Barlow's Eleven v. Twenty-Two of Blackpool. My team included Mr. A. N. Hornby, Mr. J. Eccles, Frank Sugg, F. Hearne, G. G. Hearne, Pougher, Albert Ward, Watson, Pilling, Nash, and myself. We were all out for 15 runs, and this to local bowling! Nevertheless, we won the match, which was a most exciting one.' "

Barlow's batting and bowling averages for Lancashire during fifteen of his best seasons :—

BATTING.			BOWLING.		
1871	...	18·1	1871	...	10-5*
1875	...	38·8*	1873	...	10·1
1876	...	20·4	1875	...	15·2
1877	...	18·15	1878	...	10·27
1878	...	21·11	1879	...	10·21*
1879	...	20·6	1880	...	11·4
1881	...	26·19	1881	...	9·14*
1882	...	30·16*	1882	...	9·61*
1883	...	26·1*	1883	...	13·59
1884	...	18·9	1884	...	10·24*
1885	...	30·1*	1885	...	15·24
1886	...	19·20	1886	...	11·83
1887	...	20·13	1887	...	16·29
1889	...	31·18	1888	...	13·21
1890	...	21·8	1889	...	9·8*

* Best for the county this season.

All the above are first-class, except the bowling for 1889, which is for all Lancashire matches during that season.

I was first in batting in England in 1875, with an average of 38·8—first-class cricket. In 1885 I was ninth on the list with 29·4.

In bowling, I was second in England to Alfred Shaw in 1880, with an average per wicket of 10·29.

In 1881 I was 4th, with an average per wicket of 11·70.
,, 1882 ,, 4th, ,, ,, ,, ,, 10·82.
,, 1883 ,, 8th, ,, ,, ,, ,, 15·7.
,, 1884 ,, 9th, ,, ,, ,, ,, 15·3.
,, 1886 ,, 7th, ,, ,, ,, ,, 14·55.

R. G. Barlow's averages during the three Australian tours :—

SHAW'S TEAM, 1881-2.

3rd in batting, first-class matches	...	30·1
2nd ,, all matches	...	26·13
5th in bowling, first-class matches	...	29·2
5th ,, all matches	...	8·13

Including the few matches in America.

Ulyett (Yorkshire), Bates (Yorkshire), and R. G. Barlow were the only three to get 1,000 runs with the bat on this tour.

HON. IVO BLIGH'S TEAM, 1882-3.

3rd in batting, first-class matches ... 28·1
3rd in bowling,   „   „   ... 18·3

SHAW AND SHREWSBURY'S TEAM, 1886-7.

5th in batting, first-class matches ... 20·66
3rd   „   against odds ... ... 27·31
6th in bowling, first-class matches ... 24·11
2nd   „   against odds ... ... 5·56

The following is from the *Manchester Evening News* of January 18th, 1907 :—"A correspondent writes—'The death of Alfred Shaw, the famous cricketer, leaves R. G. Barlow, of Blackpool, the celebrated "stonewaller" of cricket, the sole survivor of a powerful combination of notable players who toured America, Australia, and New Zealand under Shaw's captaincy exactly a quarter of a century ago. It may be interesting to recall their names. They were Alfred Shaw, Arthur Shrewsbury, W. Scotton, and J. Selby (Notts), George Ulyett, W. Bates, Tom Emmett, and E. Peate (Yorkshire), W. Midwinter (Gloucestershire), and R. Pilling and R. G. Barlow (Lancashire), with J. Lillywhite (Sussex) as umpire. A generation ago these names were most familiar in cricket circles throughout both hemispheres, but to-day the only one still alive is R. G. Barlow, to whom also belongs the melancholy distinction of being the sole survivor of the quartette of professionals who comprised part of the Hon. Ivo Bligh's team during the Australian tour of 1882-3.'"

During the three tours I played in every match.

The following is a complete list of the matches in which I carried my bat through the innings. In the three matches marked with an asterisk I went in to bat at the fall of the first wicket :—

St. George's School *v.* All Saints', in Bolton Park ... 14, in 1861
St. George's School *v.* All Saints', in Bolton Park ... 33, in 1863
Staveley Works C. C. *v.* Selston, at Staveley ... ... 14, in 1867
Moulders *v.* Officials, at Staveley ... ... 26, in 1868
Mount St. Mary's College *v.* Sheffield Wednesday
     Club, at Spinkhill... ... ... 101, in 1869
R. G. Barlow's Team *v.* G. Hay's Team, at Staveley... 27, in 1869
Chesterfield *v.* Sheffield Wednesday Club, at Bramall
     Lane, Sheffield ... ... 52, in 1870
Staveley *v.* Chesterfield, at Chesterfield ... ... 58, in 1870
Mr. T. Spencer's Team *v.* Mr. J. Nicholson's Team, at
     Staveley ... ... 36, in 1870

Bramley v. Dudley Hill, at Bramley ... ... 53, in 1871
Saltaire v. Baildon Green, at Baildon ... ... 41, in 1874
Lancashire v. Kent, at Mote Park ... ... 26, in 1874
Lancashire v. Leicestershire, at Manchester ... ... 66, in 1875
Baildon Green v. Morley, at Baildon ... ... 50, in 1875
Saltaire v. Harrogate, at Saltaire ... ... 115, in 1875
Saltaire v. Bradford Albion, at Saltaire... ... ... 55, in 1875
*Players v. Gentlemen, at Princes Ground, London ... 45, in 1876
Lancashire v. Nottinghamshire, at Nottingham ... 34, in 1876
Saltaire v. Spen Victoria, at Spen, near Bradford ... 9, in 1877
Idle Lillywhite C. C. v. Eccleshill, at Idle ... ... 51, in 1877
Mr. W. Jarvis's Team v. Mr. R. Pearson's Team, at
    Renishaw ... ... 24, in 1878
George Kay's Team v. R. G. Barlow's Team, at
    Staveley ... ... 26, in 1878
Lancashire v. M.C.C., at Lords... ... ... 34, in 1878
Chesterfield v. Derby Midland, at Chesterfield ... 77, in 1879
United North of England v. 18 of Leeds and District,
    at Leeds ... ... 41, in 1879
Renishaw v. Manvers Main, at Manvers Main ... 42, in 1880
Rotherham v. Chesterfield, at Chesterfield ... ... 25, in 1880
Rishton, near Blackburn, v. Enfield, at Rishton ... 45, in 1880
Nelson v. Burnley, at Burnley ... ... 63, in 1880
Lancashire v. Yorkshire, at Manchester ... ... 10, in 1880
Staveley v. Brimington, at Staveley ... ... 52, in 1882
A. Shaw's England XI. v. 22 of Orange, in Australia... 60, in 1882
Lancashire v. Australians, at Manchester ... ... 66, in 1882
Lancashire v Notts, at Nottingham ... ... 5, in 1882
Lancashire v. Notts, at Liverpool ... ... 44, in 1882
Lancashire v. Gloucestershire, at Clifton ... ... 58, in 1882
Ramsbottom v. Keighley, at Ramsbottom ... ... 26, in 1885
Lancashire v. Gloucestershire, at Clifton ... ... 62, in 1885
*A. Shaw's English Team v. Australia, at Sydney ... 42, in 1886
Ramsbottom v. Church, at Church, Accrington ... 49, in 1888
Moss Lane C. C. v. Mr. J. Lyons' Team, Old Trafford 37, in 1889
Lancashire v. Leicestershire, at Leicester ... ... 29, in 1889
Lancashire v. Kent, at Maidstone ... ... 51, in 1889
Lancashire v. Surrey, at the Oval ... ... 29, in 1890
Lancashire v. Notts, at Old Trafford ... ... 29, in 1890
Mr. M'Leod's Team v. a Buxton XI., at Buxton ... 43, in 1892
Royton v. Padiham, at Royton ... ... 25, in 1892

Royton v. Milnrow, at Royton ...	...	...	26, in 1893
Royton v. Radcliffe, at Radcliffe	...	...	13, in 1894
Dr. Fergusson's Team v. Burnley St. Andrew's, at Burnley ...	...	...	60, in 1894
Royton v. Littleborough, at Littleborough	...	...	12, in 1895
Royton v. Darwen 9 men, at Royton ...	...	...	50, in 1895
Royton v. Walsden, at Walsden	...	...	51, in 1895

RUNNING SHORT RUNS.

1889. Lancashire v. Sussex, at Manchester.

"Sussex did not enjoy the barefaced way in which Mr. Hornby and Barlow stole runs on the first day of their match, and the wild way in which several of the Southerners shied at the wicket would have disgraced a four-year-old. The climax was reached when Harry Phillips knocked down Panter, the umpire, who would remember the little incident when he came to sit down to tea."— *Vide Press.*

AN INTERESTING COMPETITION.

In 1886 the *Cricket and Football Field* held a competition, offering a prize for the selection of a team to represent the North of England against the Australians at Manchester, on May 31st and following days of that year. The award was to be made according to the voting of the competitors, and the following is the list which received the prize, with the number of votes which were given to each player. It will be seen that I headed the list with 781 votes :—

R. G. Barlow, Lancashire ...	...	...	781
J. Briggs, Lancashire	...	...	777
G. Ulyett, Yorkshire...	...	...	761
E. Peate, Yorkshire ...	...	...	682
A. N. Hornby, Lancashire ...	...	...	673
A. Shrewsbury, Nottingham	...	...	672
R. Pilling, Lancashire	...	...	637
W. Barnes, Nottingham	...	...	635
W. Bates, Yorkshire...	...	...	615
W. Scotton, Nottingham	...	...	540
A. G. Steel, Lancashire	...	...	454

It will be of interest to my readers to give the names composing the team which was selected by the Lancashire County Committee to meet the Australians on this occasion, and a glance at this list proves that the cricket-loving public are not far out of their reckoning and have a very fair idea of the merits of the different players :

R. G. Barlow, Lancashire.
J. Briggs, Lancashire.
G. Ulyett, Yorkshire.
E. Peate, Yorkshire.
A. N. Hornby, Lancashire.
A. Shrewsbury, Nottingham.
R. Pilling, Lancashire.
W. Bates, Yorkshire.
A. Watson, Lancashire.
W. Gunn, Nottingham.
J. Preston, Yorkshire.

The match ended in a draw.

THE AUTHOR AS A FOOTBALLER.

I have been interested in Association football all my life, and was for many years a player. For several years there were four brothers of us playing for the Staveley Football Club, and I was keeping goal for them when Staveley won the Sheffield Association Challenge Cup at Sheffield in 1880. The two final clubs were Staveley and Heeley, the latter a strong Sheffield club at that time. Staveley won by three goals to one. The late Jack Hunter, the old Blackburn Rovers player and trainer, played against us in this match, and Mr. (now "Sir") W. E. Clegg, brother to the present chairman of the Football Association, was one of the linesmen.

If I remember rightly, the Lancashire Association Challenge Cup was first played for in 1879-80, when Darwen won it. Staveley being the winners of the Sheffield Cup for the same season, two matches were arranged between the two clubs—the first at Staveley, and the return match at Darwen. Both matches ended in a draw. I played on each occasion, and remember that the forwards gave me plenty of work in goal at Darwen. I considered that we had done very well to play two drawn games with Darwen, as they were in those days a very fine team.

I also kept goal a few years later for the North against South at Sheffield. J. Brown, of Blackburn Rovers fame, played centre-forward in this match in first-class style. He was one of the best players of his day, and it would be difficult to find his equal even at the present time. He was almost on a par with Mr. W. N. Cobbold, of the "Corinthians."

I was also goalkeeper for a few years for the Manchester F. C. at the time their ground was situate at Whalley Range, Brooks's Bar, near the old Rugby football ground.

STAVELEY FOOTBALL CLUB.

Winners of the Sheffield Association Challenge Cup, 1879-80.

R. G. Barlow.   D. James.   T. Kenyon.   H. P. Marples.   G. Hay.   G. B. Marples.   E. Widdowson.   J. Till.

W. Young.   W. Wallace.   S. Doughty.   J. Hay.

The Manchester Press, in 1879, said : " R. G. Barlow, that most popular of Lancashire professional cricketers, has come to reside in Manchester, and has joined the only Association football club in Cottonopolis. He kept goal remarkably well last Saturday at Blackburn, and proves, as in cricket, a most stubborn defender. Barlow at goal, and Mr. Hornby at full back, wouldn't be a bad pair at the Association game."

Not many are aware that I have represented my county at football; but such is the case, as I played for Lancashire against Ayrshire at Darwen about the year 1884. The following is the team which played for Lancashire in this match, which unfortunately we lost :—R. G. Barlow, goal; W. Trainer and Mather, backs; W. H. Latham and F. Hargreaves, half-backs; J. Hargreaves, R. Horne, J. Brown, W. M. Brown, T. Bentley, and J. Lonsdale, forwards.

I took to refereeing for some years, and acted in that capacity at Preston in 1887, in the English Cup Tie, when Preston North End made the record score in these matches of 26 goals to none, against Hyde; and I may say that had the Hyde goalkeeper not been in good form, North End would have materially increased their score. I have never seen such splendid passing and shooting in my life. The old Preston North End team would, in my opinion, be at least two goals better than any team in the field at the present day.

Football has made some startling changes since the days when I fought in the cup ties, and I could write, if necessary, at some length on football of to-day as compared with thirty years ago.

When I had finished my county cricket days for Lancashire, several other counties wished me to qualify and play for them, and one county offered me a three-years' engagement on very favourable terms; but I always said that I would never play for any county but the one of my birth. I therefore took to umpiring, and have to thank Mr. A. N. Hornby, and a few others of the Lancashire County Committee, for nominating me and getting me placed on the list of county umpires. I have been engaged each season ever since.

In conclusion, I don't think that any cricketer has enjoyed his cricketing career better than I have done; and if I had my time to come over again I should certainly be what I have been all my life—a professional cricketer. I am only sorry that my " long innings " in first-class cricket will soon be drawing to a close.

I might state that I was the first to introduce the rubber-faced gauntlets, to which I put the late Richard Pilling's name along with my own. Messrs. Page and Co., cricket accessories manufacturers, late of Kennington Park Road, London, paid us a royalty on the sales. After a few years, however, something went wrong, and we lost our rights in them.

I was also the first to bring out the single-strap leg guards. I sold my rights in these to Mr. J. Vickers, manufacturer, of Bolton.

Another idea of my own was the removable cricket spikes, which could be changed in a few minutes, to suit either condition of the ground; but, somehow or other, they did not "take on" very well. The objection to them, I believe, lay in the time occupied in changing; but I used them for years, as did many of my colleagues, and we always found them very satisfactory.

REMUNERATION.

The remuneration I received for my services on the three Australian tours was as follows:—With the Shaw and Shrewsbury team of 1881-2, the sum of £220. With the Hon. Ivo Bligh's team of 1882-3 I received the sum of £220 from the Melbourne Cricket Club, who were the promoters of this tour; but with the Shaw and Shrewsbury team of 1886-7 I received £320. All first-class expenses were paid in each case.

I may mention here that I had an offer about the year 1884, from Major Wardell, of the Melbourne C.C. to go out to Australia as cricket coach to the Melbourne Club. I also had a good offer from the Brisbane (Queensland) C.C., in 1883; but I could not see my way to leave old England.

HEAD BOWLING—LANCASHIRE *v.* SURREY, 1885.

"On ground like the pavement of a racquet court, Barlow's bowling to-day, at the Oval, was a really fine example of the bowler's skill. With a perpetual variation of pace and pitch, he kept the batsmen constantly on the defensive, and the ball with which he bowled W. W. Read (thereby in all probability saving Lancashire a hundred runs) was a perfect specimen of that exact mean between a length to play forward and one to play back, which still remains the most difficult ball a batsman has to meet. Till Barlow was tired out, the game seemed to be in favour of Lancashire; but afterwards the want of another change bowler was severely felt, and Mr. Allan Steel would have been invaluable. Surrey won this very exciting match by one wicket."—*Vide Press.*

DR. GRACE AND " R. G. B."

" The ' Champion,' in his book on ' Cricket,' gives a lengthy list of ' Cricketers whom I have met.' The notices are in the main genial and appreciative, but there is one conspicuous exception, and that is the Doctor's treatment of R. G. Barlow. Now we should probably be accurate in asserting that Dr. Grace for many years must have ' met ' Barlow almost as frequently as he met any English cricketer, and that he must have had reason on many of these occasions to admire his great abilities both with the bat and the ball; and yet, in ' Cricket,' he dismisses the famous Lancashire professional with a shorter notice than he bestows upon that illustrious cricketer, Prince Christian Victor of Schleswig-Holstein, and not one-third the length of his account of Edward Barratt, who was a third-rate bowler and a tenth-rate bat, late of Surrey. In fact, if Barlow's reputation as a cricketer depended on the record in Dr. Grace's book, he would be remembered merely as ' one who has been an exceedingly useful all-round player for his county, and has both batted and bowled with success for the Players v. Gentlemen.' The Doctor has something rather ungenerous to say about Barlow's slowness in scoring. We are all acquainted with Barlow's style, and although we have often found it rather tedious, yet we have reflected that it was a style deliberately adopted by a consummate master of the game, and one that on occasions innumerable has been found to be of immense value to his side. Moreover, we know that on many occasions Barlow has shown that he can hit hard, and with great judgment, as well as defend his wicket with conspicuous skill. Fifty times he has carried his bat right through the innings, and who shall estimate the value of that prolonged and stubborn defence which worries out a bowler almost as much as a succession of boundary hits? Mr. A. G. Steel, we imagine, recognised the value of Barlow's style in the great England v. Australia match, in 1884, at Lord's, when Grace, and Lucas, and Lord Harris, and Ulyett, and Shrewsbury, had done nothing particularly brilliant, and a follow-on seemed probable. At a very critical stage of the game Barlow went in, with orders to ' stop the rot '; and he did stop it. The two famous Lancashire players, amateur and professional, obtained the complete mastery over the bowling of Spofforth, and Palmer, and Giffen; and Barlow's steadiness came in for its due recognition. In 1881 this rather mediocre cricketer, as Dr. Grace evidently regards him, clean bowled the Champion, Mr. Hornby, and Mr. Lucas, in the Gentlemen v. Players match, for 27 runs. In 1882 he was at the top of the tree, both in batting and bowling, for Lancashire; he had a splendid average in his Australian tour; and was pronounced by the editor of *Wisden's Almanac* 'to be fairly entitled to be reckoned the best all-round cricketer in England.' Dr. Grace admits that Barlow 'bowls a good length.' How often that 'good length' has been fatal to the big wicket, it would perhaps be ungenerous to enquire too closely; but we may safely make the general statement that Barlow has got the Champion's wicket as often and as cheaply as any bowler he ever met, even in the very zenith of his fame. Our object in this brief retrospect has been to supply what seems to us an obvious deficiency in a much-lauded book; and we believe the Doctor himself will readily admit that he has not done justice to a player who has been one of the chosen representatives of his country, both at home and abroad, and who has done at least as much to raise the cricketing fame of what has been, and will be again, the foremost of counties, as any other professional that has appeared in its ranks.— *Manchester Guardian.*

Apropos of the above, it will doubtless be interesting to give my readers the occasions (31 in number) on which I was the means of bringing about the dismissal from the wicket of the great "W. G." Naturally, I feel gratified at being able to show such a record, especially when it is remembered that this occurred at the time when this hero of cricket was at his very best :—

1877. North *v.* South, at Hull. Dr. W. G. Grace, c Emmett, b Barlow, 24 (second over I bowled.)

1878. North *v.* South, at Lord's. Dr. W. G. Grace, b Barlow, 77 (my fourth ball).

1878. Gentlemen *v.* Players, at the Oval. Dr. W. G. Grace, leg before wicket, b Barlow, 63 (second over I bowled).

1880. Lancashire *v.* Gloucestershire, at Clifton. Dr. W. G. Grace, c Nash, b Barlow, 106.

1880. United Eleven of England *v.* Eighteen of Bedminster (with Drs. W. G. and E. M. Grace), at Bedminster. Dr. W. G. Grace, c Pooley, b Barlow, 6; 2nd innings, b Barlow 10.

1881. Gentlemen *v.* Players, at Lord's. Dr. W. G. Grace, b Barlow, 2.

1882. Lancashire *v.* Gloucestershire, at Clifton. Dr. W. G. Grace, b Barlow, 86.

1883. Gentlemen *v.* Players, at Lord's. Dr. W. G. Grace, b Barlow, 14.

D

1883. Lancashire *v.* M.C.C., at Lord's. Dr. W. G. Grace, c Haigh, b Barlow, o.

1883. North *v.* South, at the Oval. Dr. W. G. Grace, c Disney, b Barlow, 1 ; 2nd innings, b Barlow 7.

1884. Lancashire *v.* M.C.C., at Lord's. Dr. W. G. Grace, c Watson, b Barlow, 14.

1884. Lancashire *v.* Gloucestershire, at Manchester. Dr. W. G. Grace, b Barlow, 53.

1884. Gentlemen *v.* Players, at Lord's. Dr. W. G. Grace, b Barlow, 21.

1884. Gentlemen *v.* Players, at the Oval. Dr. W. G. Grace, c Ulyett, b Barlow, 66.

1884. Lancashire *v.* Gloucestershire, at Clifton. Dr. W. G. Grace, c Pilling, b Barlow, 31.

1885. Lancashire *v.* Gloucestershire, at Clifton. Dr. W. G. Grace, b Barlow, 49.

1886. Lancashire *v.* Gloucestershire, at Clifton. Dr. W. G. Grace, b Barlow, 23.

1887. Lancashire *v.* M.C.C., at Lord's. Dr. W. G. Grace, c and b Barlow, 1.

1887. Lancashire *v.* Gloucestershire, at Manchester. Dr. W. G. Grace, c Hornby, b Barlow, 41.

1887. Lancashire *v.* Gloucestershire, at Cheltenham. Dr. W. G. Grace, b Barlow, 23.

1888. Lancashire *v.* Gloucestershire, at Gloucester. Dr. W. G. Grace, b Barlow, 1.

1888. Lancashire *v.* Gloucestershire, at Liverpool. Dr. W. G. Grace, b Barlow, 4 ; 2nd innings, b Barlow 16.

1888. North *v.* South, at Hastings. Dr. W. G. Grace, b Barlow, 44.

In the following five cases I caught Dr. Grace when fielding at my usual position at point :—

1879. North *v.* South, at the Oval. Dr. W. G. Grace, c Barlow, b Morley, 21.

1880. Lancashire *v.* Gloucestershire, at Manchester. Dr. W. G. Grace, c Barlow, b A. G. Steel, 3.

1882. Gentlemen *v.* Players, at Lord's. Dr. W. G. Grace, c Barlow, b Bates, 4.

1882. Lancashire *v.* Gloucestershire, at Manchester. Dr. W. G. Grace, c Barlow, b A. G. Steel, 9.

1883. Lancashire *v.* Gloucestershire, at Manchester. Dr. W. G. Grace, c Barlow, b Nash, 13.

"THE SOLE SURVIVOR.

"A correspondent to the *Standard* draws attention to the interesting circumstance that now that Alfred Shaw has passed away there is only one representative living (R. G. Barlow) of the eleven Players who took part in the annual match, Gentlemen v. Players, at Lord's, in July, 1880. On the other hand, the Gentlemen's team is still complete—at least, no obituary notice of any one of them has appeared in any of the cricket annuals since that date. It is remarkable, adds the writer, how many of the leading professionals of 25 years ago passed away in middle life."

The names of the Players who took part in the above-named match were:—

W. Oscroft (Notts)	F. Morley (Notts)
W. Barnes (Notts)	G. Ulyett (Yorkshire)
J. Selby (Notts)	W. Bates (Yorkshire)
A. Shaw (Notts)	T. Emmett (Yorkshire)
W. Scotton (Notts)	R. Pilling (Lancashire)

R. G. Barlow (Lancashire).

I close my autobiography by quoting a tribute to my defensive methods from the *Manchester Guardian*:—"An eloquent appreciation of the valour displayed by the Manchester Regiment during the siege of Ladysmith is contained in an article published by the *Morning Post* from its correspondent, Mr. John Stuart, who incidentally also pays a pretty compliment to our esteemed townsman, Mr. R. G. Barlow, the famous 'stone-waller' of international cricket fame. Says Mr. Stuart:—'It is a great thing to make a regiment that will charge any place on earth; it is a greater thing to have made a regiment that will sit tight like the Manchester under heavy shell fire, cracking "pawky" little north-country jokes that somehow recall the brave days of Hornby, and Barlow, and William Macintyre, and the Crossland throwing controversy, a regiment that won't blaze into the brown unless the brown is worth hitting; privates who will take calm, deliberate aim when anything can be seen that looks like the enemy. Do you remember Dr. Grace's story about an Eleven of Barlow's, and not one of them out? Well, the Manchesters are a regiment of Barlows, and they can open their shoulders when the bowling gets loose. Good luck to them always; you will find regiments as good, but you will go far before you find a better.'"

Umpire Stories.

THE following humorous incident occurred during a match at Staveley. The umpire was a Mr. Riley, and his son, one of the players, was the first batsman. The second ball of the match—a very good ball—took young Riley's wickets, when, to the surprise of everybody, the umpire called " Not out, bowl that ball over again, I did not see the particular pitch." After this the young batsman made 22 runs, which of course highly pleased the old gentleman. To this day I can picture the expression of disgust on the bowler's face ; but the other players had a good laugh over the little incident.

The fallibility of the local umpire is illustrated by the following incident, which happened at a Lancashire League match—Royton v. Radcliffe,—played at Radcliffe some years ago. I was bowling to one of the Radcliffe batsmen, who hit the ball back smartly, it struck the umpire and then continued on its way some few yards further. The batsman seized the opportunity for a short run, but I fielded the ball and threw the wicket down, and the batsman was "run out" some yards. The umpire, without any appeal having been made, called " Not out, the ball was dead after hitting me." This impromptu decision was greeted with much laughter, after which I told him he was entirely wrong, and advised him to read the laws of cricket well over before he went out umpiring again.

UMPIRING AS IT WAS.

In a Lancashire County match, in the year 1888, our umpire had given one or two decisions which had not suited some of our opponents, and at lunch time their umpire was overheard to say that he would try and get straight with his rival before the match was over. We had not resumed play long after lunch when he gave me " run out." I must say that this was a most unfair decision, as I was right up to the wicket when given out. I spoke to him about it after the match, and we had " a few words." In those days, each county had its own umpire, who travelled about with the team. As I have mentioned in another place, all this is now altered, and a very good thing, too. County umpires are selected annually by the county captains at Lord's ; consequently present-day umpires are neutral, and strict impartiality is assured.

AUSTRALIAN CRICKETERS, 1878.

H. F. Boyle.   J. Conway;   G. H. Bailey.   Mr. Gibbs (Agent in Advance).   F. E. Allen.
W. L. Murdoch.   T. Horan.   D. W. Gregory.   A. Bannerman.   F. R. Spofforth.
T. W. Garrett.   C. Bannerman.   J. Blackham.

The above Team of Australian cricketers were the first to visit England in 1878, when they made a great name for themselves in this country by dismissing at Lord's Ground a very strong side of the M.C.C. for 33 and 19, and defeated them in a single day by nine wickets.

A GOOD UMPIRE FOR HIS SIDE.

On the occasion of a match at Oldham, in 1879, one of our players having a bad finger, asked if he might umpire, which was agreed to. The bowler, on bowling his first ball, appealed for lbw. calling out "How's that?" "How's what?" retorted our umpire, "he's only just come in; you get on with your bowling." After this appeal, the batsman put on 20 runs, thus helping his side to win the match. The umpire, whose name I will not divulge, afterwards told me that conscientiously speaking the batsman was out, as the ball was dead on the leg stump all the way. This same umpire resides near to me in Blackpool, and we were discussing this match only recently.

UMPIRE'S REMARKABLE ACCIDENT.

At a match in which I was playing at Burley, Yorkshire, in the Seventies, we had for one of the umpires, a man with a wooden leg. Whilst this umpire was standing at short leg, the batsmen hit a ball with great force in his direction. The umpire was unable to get out of the way quickly enough, and the ball struck his wooden leg, snapping it in halves like a carrot. The man whose support was thus suddenly knocked from under him, immediately toppled over, and some of the players had to pick him up and bear him away to the pavilion, from whence he was sent home in a cab. We were sorry for the poor fellow, but could not help feeling amused at this very peculiar accident. I am pleased to be able to add that the umpire was not hurt by his adventure.

AN UMPIRING MATCH.

In the early Seventies I remember playing at Bramley, near Leeds, and as our umpire did not turn up we decided to wait a little for him. After waiting for some little time, the umpire for the other side, an elderly gentleman, came into our dressing-room, and proposed that he should umpire at both ends. He explained that he knew how to proceed, as he had done the same thing before. We received this unique proposal with an outburst of laughter. One of our players then volunteered to umpire for us, saying that he was not feeling well, and that he thought he would be of more benefit to his side by umpiring than by playing. We accordingly played a man short, and won the match as a matter of course. We concluded that our umpire was about equal to the other in ability, for neither of them knew any more about umpiring than the " man in the moon," and each gave several bad decisions.

AN UMPIRE CAUGHT NAPPING.

This humorous occurrence took place at a match in which I was umpiring at Taunton many years ago—Somersetshire v. —— and concerns my fellow umpire. He lived, like myself, a great distance away, and had been travelling all through the previous night in order to reach the ground in time for the match, and had had no sleep. The first day was very hot, and this, combined with loss of sleep, made the poor fellow exceedingly drowsy, and at times as he stood at his post he found it almost impossible to keep his eyes open. At one point in the game, about four o'clock in the afternoon, he was just dropping off into a doze when the wicket-keeper suddenly startled him into wakefulness by appealing for stumping. Pulling himself together, he promptly replied "Not out." At the close of play, the wicket-keeper came up to him and said, "That was a very near thing, wasn't it, when I appealed?" "Yes," replied the umpire, "you're right, it was; but I thought I'd give the batsman the benefit of the doubt." The funniest part of the story lies in the fact that my friend had really been caught napping, and when the appeal was made had seen neither the ball bowled, nor taken by the wicket-keeper. We were, of course, bound to keep the joke to ourselves, which we greatly enjoyed, and have often since referred to it.

A WOULD-BE DISHONEST UMPIRE.

About 1894, I was umpiring for the "Northern Nomads" against another gentlemen's team, whose name I forget. This was a two-days' match. At lunch time on the second day, my fellow-umpire came to me and said, "Look here, Barlow, this match doesn't look like being over before six or six-thirty, and my train leaves at 6-10. If I miss this, I cannot reach home till midnight." He went on to point out that it depended on our umpiring as to how long the match would last, and asked me to give all doubtful appeals "out," and thus help him to catch his train. I, of course, refused to be a party to anything of the kind, and told him he ought to be ashamed to make such a proposal.

It so happened that there were only one or two appeals made, and the match lasted until 6-15; consequently this would-be smart man missed his train, and he deserved it.

FROM A NEWSPAPER CUTTING, 1891.

"Some of the local clubs were busy on Saturday, and we hear that in one instance at least the eccentric umpire was on the warpath again. R. G. Barlow was batting for his Saturday club—Royton against Littleborough—and the bowler appealed for 'leg before.' 'I didn't see it,' replied the umpire; but the bowler turned to him again and said 'What do you say?' This was too much for the umpire, and he announced his decision in the following words: 'I didn't see it, but I give him out.' This decision is worthy to be bracketted with the famous 'Not out, but don't do it again.'"

ANOTHER UMPIRE STORY.

About the year 1869, I was playing in a local match at Barrow Hill, Staveley, when the umpire was appealed to for "run out." He replied that it was a dead heat, the batsman having put his bat down inside the crease at the identical moment that the ball hit the wickets. When asked again, he gave the same reply, consequently the batsman continued his innings. I, however, bowled him with the very next ball.

THE LATE TOM EMMETT, OF YORKSHIRE, AS AN UMPIRE.

When I was playing with the Shaw and Shrewsbury team in one of their matches in America, in 1881-2, Shaw, our captain, asked Tom to umpire for a short time. His reply was, "No, I shan't stand; there's sure to be an appeal, and I shall make a fool of myself." However, on being pressed, he consented to stand. The late R. Pilling was batting, and, as luck would have it, Emmett soon had a difficult point to decide. Pilling played a ball which either went on the ground or on to the wicket-keeper's foot, whence it bounced to short-slip, who appealed for a catch. Tom was nonplussed. "I don't know," was his reply to the appeal. Then, turning to Pilling, he asked, "What did that do, Dick?" Pilling replied, "It struck the ground, and went to short-slip." "No," interposed the wicket-keeper, "it struck my foot, and went to short-slip." Then Tom said, "Well, Dick, I shall have to give you out." And out he had to go, wild at Emmett for taking the wicket-keeper's word before his own. Tom said afterwards, "I told you all that I should make a silly mess of it. I shall stand as umpire no more on this journey," and he was as good as his word. For some time afterwards we made great fun of Emmett and his umpiring. He often told me that however much practice he had, he would never make an umpire, and that he had more sympathy for umpires after that match than he ever had before, and would never dispute their decisions again. I might add that Tom Emmett was one of the most jovial cricketers who ever lived.

Personal Anecdotes.

A DREAM WHICH CAME TRUE.

AS will be readily understood, I have often dreamed about cricket; but one particular dream was so remarkable in that it was fulfilled to the letter, that it is deserving of a place here.

In 1879, Lancashire was playing Derbyshire, at Derby, and after the first day's play, I ran over to Staveley to spend the night at my parents' home, who were residing there at that time. It was here that I had my dream, which I related to my parents on coming down for breakfast the next morning. I dreamed that I had made 50 runs that day at Derby, and that I was then bowled by Mycroft with a "shooter." This actually came to pass, Mycroft bowling me with a "shooter" when my score had reached 50. I remember telling my dream to a few friends whilst waiting at the station that same morning. They remarked that they hoped my dream would come off, and I replied "the chances are a thousand to one against that."

A CURIOUS DISMISSAL.

The following occurred at a practice game in which I was playing in the early Eighties, near to the Manchester county ground. A batsman played a ball straight back again, very hard, which hit the other batsman's bat, knocking it out of his hand. The ball was then caught by the fielder at mid-on. To be caught out in this way was very hard lines on the batsman.

A CURIOUS INCIDENT DURING FIRST-CLASS CRICKET.

This occurred at a match at Clifton in 1885—Lancashire v. Gloucestershire. During the progress of the game, a seagull came hovering around and above the wicket, and play had to be stopped for some little time. The players occupied the interval in having shots at the bird with both ball and stumps. It can be imagined what fun was caused by this. The bird remained for several minutes, and it was remarkable how it eventually managed to escape unhurt.

INSECTS AND CRICKET.

Another incident, somewhat akin to the foregoing, happened at Cootamundra (Australia), in 1886. During a match—Shaw's XI.

v. twenty-two of Cootamundra—the sky was suddenly darkened by a cloud of locusts which passed over the field ; there were literally millions of them. Some of the local players seeing the approach of these creatures called out to us to lie flat on the ground. The players took the advice, and also many of the spectators, and we remained in this position until the phenomenon had passed. We were afterwards told by the natives that at certain intervals, these insects travel over this part of the Continent in this manner.

I am also reminded of the fact that on several occasions when playing on different grounds in New South Wales, the batsmen were compelled to wear nets over their faces to protect them from the swarms of flies, which otherwise seriously interfered with their movements.

THE RIVER FIELDER.

The above title was earned by a certain player in the following manner : At a match—Staveley *v.* Chesterfield, at Staveley—in which I was taking part, about the year 1868, a batsman named Ben Rodgers, a big hitter, made a great drive into the river which runs alongside the cricket ground. A Mr. Hazlehurst, who was rather short-sighted, and wore spectacles, ran after the ball. Not noticing the water, he went head over heels into the river, getting a thorough ducking, and had to be hauled out. What made it the worse for him he had not a change of clothing with him, and my father, who was the hon. secretary of the Staveley Club, sent for some clothes to his house, which was close at hand ; and which Mr. Hazlehurst was very glad to put on. This little adventure caused great amusement at the time, and for many years afterwards Mr. Hazlehurst was spoken of as " The River Fielder."

HARD LINES.

On one occasion, in my early days of county cricket, I was caught napping. It was during a match at Old Trafford, Lancashire *v.* Kent. The umpire had called " wide " to a certain ball, and the other batsman signalled me for a run. Having my mind so occupied about the " wide," I was not careful to get into my crease. The alert wicket keeper knocked off the bails, and I was given " out." Naturally I felt very foolish as I walked back to the pavilion.

I was also caught napping on one occasion at Lord's, when Lancashire was playing the M.C.C. in the Eighties. I was batting, and played a ball to Mr. J. S. Russell, who was fielding at mid-off. I then went out of my ground a little way to pat the pitch down, expecting the fielder to return the ball to the bowler. He, however, flung it to the wicket-keeper, and before I could get back I was put out. I should have recovered my ground in time, but the pitch being soft I slipped, and was unable to return to my wicket quickly enough.

Another case of "hard lines" occurred in a match at White-haven. The late Mr. G. F. Grace's Eleven v. a local twenty, which included the late J. Platts and myself. When batting, I hit a ball between mid-off and cover point, and whilst running my second run, the bat stuck in the ground, causing me to fall forward on to the handle, from which I received a blow which rendered me insensible. They gave me a little brandy—though I was a teetotaller—and on coming round, the first thing I asked was, " I am not out, am I ? " Imagine my feelings on being told that I was out. This was a case where misfortunes did not come singly.

CRICKET AS A MEDICINE.

At the close of the match Lancashire v. Yorkshire, in 1875, when Mr. Hornby and myself knocked off the required 146 runs without the loss of a wicket, I remember sending my father the result by telegram. He was ill at the time, having been confined to his house for several days. When the wire arrived, he was in the act of retiring for the night, but the news of our achievement had such a tonic effect upon him that he immediately re-dressed and sallied forth into the night to give all his friends the good news. He afterwards said that this had done him more good than all the doctors in the world could have done for him.

Speaking of my father, reminds me that he was always enthusiastic where cricket was concerned. As a youth he was apprenticed to a chemist, and had to work in the shop until a late hour each day, which prevented him getting any cricket practice in the evenings. So he, along with two companions who were similarly fixed as to spare time, arranged to have their cricket early in the morning, before commencing the day's work. They therefore came to terms with the night watchman to awaken them about 5-30 a.m. For this purpose my father tied one end of a length of twine to his great toe, putting the other end through the bedroom window, and letting it hang down in front of the house. This the watchman would pull at the hour named, which always had the desired effect of arousing the sleeper at the other end of the line.

CARRYING COALS TO NEWCASTLE.

On the occasion of my benefit match at Old Trafford, Manchester, in 1886, a number of boys were offering for sale copies of a booklet giving particulars of my career. My mother, who came over from her home at Ramsbottom to witness the last day's play, kept being accosted by these boys on her way to the cricket ground, who called out " Life of Barlow, 3d. each," and pressed her to buy a copy. At length she said to one of the boys, who was more persistent than the rest, " My lad, I can tell thee about the life of R. G. Barlow ; I have known him for some years. I am his mother. Here's a penny for thee." We had a good laugh over tea that evening as she related this little experience.

AN INTERLUDE.

While at Bradford a few years ago, umpiring in the Yorkshire v. Gloucestershire match, I ran over to Saltaire after the day's play to visit the scene of my five years' engagement in the early Seventies. As I was strolling to the cricket ground in Saltaire Park, I came across a number of boys playing cricket, and seeing that they were neither batting nor bowling in the correct way, I offered them a few hints, which were not well received, for I heard one boy say to his companions, " What does that old chap know abaat cricket ? He can't play." I thereupon asked them to send me a few balls, and offered to give sixpence to the boy who could bowl or catch me out. This just suited the lads, and for a time there was a very heated argument as to which of them should bowl first, which was only settled by my suggesting that they should go on bowling in turns, six balls each. After a few balls I hit one into the river which runs near the park. It was amusing to see the boys' faces, and to hear them remark to each other that they believed I had played before, after all. We recovered the ball from the river, and after each boy had had a turn with it, I put on my coat, and they gathered round and asked me if I hadn't played cricket before. I told them " Yes, many times " and had played in that park before they were born. A boy then remarked " Oh, he's an old professional." I said " Yes, and I am umpiring at the big match at Bradford these three days. Another boy then said, " I think you are Barlow, I've heard my father talk about." Telling him he had guessed correctly, I gave him the sixpence, and smaller sums to his six companions, and left them all smiling. Though only a trifling adventure, I think I never enjoyed half-an-hour's sport better than I did this.

A DISAPPOINTING LUNCH.

The professionals of 20 to 30 years ago were inveterate practical jokers, as the following anecdote will show: It was at a Gentlemen v. Players of the North of England match, at Old Trafford, Manchester, about the year 1880. J. Briggs was at that time living with me, and we occasionally had our dinner sent up to the ground from home. On this occasion we left our dinner—which was in a lock-up hand bag—in the dressing-room. One of the players happened to possess a key which fitted the bag, which, during our absence, he opened and removed the luncheon. Some of the Yorkshire players despatched the same, and replaced in the bag two new cut sods wrapped up to imitate the missing packages. At lunch time, Briggs and I rushed into the dressing-room hungry, and ready for dinner. I unlocked the bag and took out the first parcel which I handed to Briggs who soon discovered the contents. I noticed him, and several of the others giving me a look which I could not at first understand, and proceeded to unwrap my parcel, finding the sod in place of my dinner. My feelings can be better imagined than described. I remarked, "There is always something going on when these Yorkshiremen are about," which just suited Tom Emmett, who laughed uproariously.

We, of course, laughed it off, though I told them it was rather too much of a joke. I have never heard to this day who the culprits were ; but I always feel inclined to give the credit to my old friend and colleague, Alec. Watson, and the late George Ulyett (Happy Jack) of Yorkshire.

BATTING FOR SIX WEEKS.

I should like to take this opportunity of contradicting one story bearing the above title, which has been freely circulated for the past twenty years, and has been copied, and re-copied into many books and newspaper articles on cricket ; as there is not one word of truth in it. It is to the effect that before my cricketing career, I was employed at an obscure railway station in Lancashire, as a porter, and that having plenty of time on my hands, it was occupied in playing cricket with the station-master, booking-clerk, and ticket collector. One day a gentleman, who had some time to wait for his train, got talking to the station-master, and asked him what he did with all his leisure time. " Well, sir," said the official, " we go and play cricket in the field yonder, and often get a very good game. Our porter is the best player amongst us, he's been in six weeks

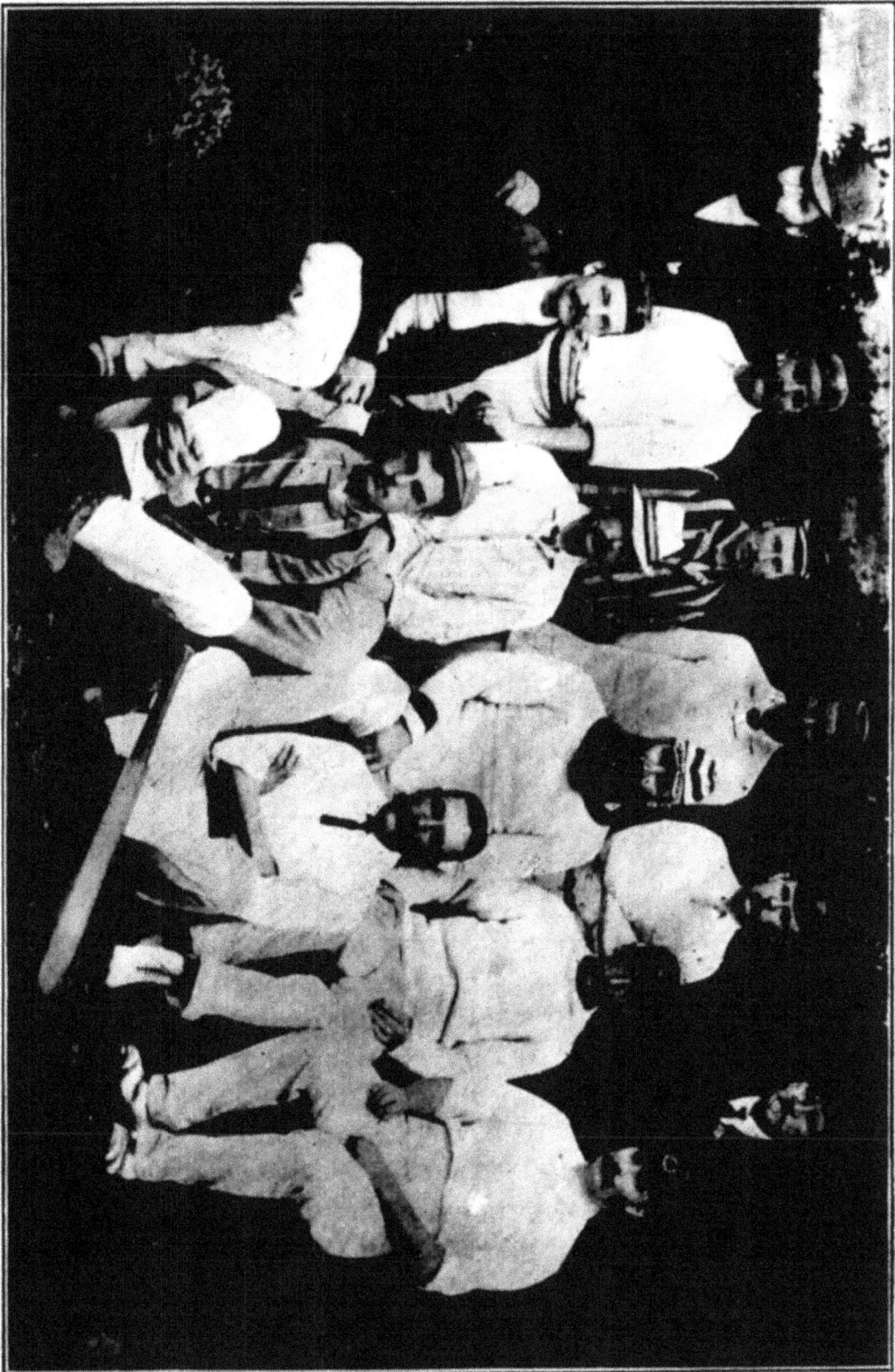

TEST MATCH.—ENGLAND v. AUSTRALIA, 1884.
Played at Lord's, July 21st, 22nd, 23rd.

Pullin (Umpire).   Peate.   A. P. Lucas.   Hon. A. Lyttelton.   Shrewsbury.   Farrands (Umpire).
A. G. Steel.   Lord Harris.   Dr. W. G. Grace.   W. W. Read.   Ulyett.
A. Christopherson.   Barlow.

[Photo. by E. Hawkins & Co., Brighton. Cricket Specialists.]

TEST MATCH.—English Team *v.* Australia, at Nottingham, in May, 1899.   Brockwell was twelfth man.

Barlow (Umpire).   Hayward.   Hirst.   Gunn (W).   Hearne (J. T.)   Storer.   Brockwell.   Titchmarsh (Umpire).
C. B. Fry.   K. S. Ranjitsinhji.   Dr. W. G. Grace.   F. S. Jackson.
Rhodes.   Tyldesley.

The Author (Barlow) is the only cricketer who has been selected both to Play and Umpire for England *v.* Australia, in Test Matches.
Also the only cricketer who has been selected both to bat and bowl first for England *v.* Australia, in Test Matches in England.

[Photo. by A. Shields, Nottingham.]

already and we can't get him out; perhaps you'd like to have a bowl at him." Dr. W. G. Grace has this same anecdote in his book on cricket, but says regarding it that he " doubts its truth, though he considers that Barlow was quite capable of performing the feat named."

THE TWINS.

The following occurred at Kidderminster in 1879, at a match in which I took part, between G. F. Grace's XI. and Eighteen of Kidderminster and District. Two brothers, who were twins, named W. J. Hughes and J. W. Hughes, played in the Kidderminster team, and were as alike as the proverbial two peas. One of the two came in to bat at about the fall of the fifth wicket. He had a good defence, and played very fairly, being out eventually for eight runs. Shortly afterwards the second brother came in to bat, when Mr. Grace immediately went up to him at the wicket, telling him that we didn't play that sort of game—allowing a man to bat twice in the same innings. The batsman protested that he had not been in before, but Mr. Grace was not to be convinced, and he was supported in his opinion by his men. Finally, Mr. Grace, along with most of the players, including myself, went to the pavilion, where we found the other brother, and the mystery was solved, for we positively could not tell one from the other, they were so identical. This affair caused great amusement amongst the players.

A TERRIBLE NIGHT.

A laughable adventure, which might have had a serious termination, once befel the late R. Pilling (the famous wicket-keeper) and myself, during the visit of Shaw's team to Australia in 1881. It occurred at Newcastle, New South Wales, a place which was infested with mosquitos. Pilling and I shared a double-bedded room at the hotel where the English cricketers were staying. The beds, we found, were specially constructed to keep out the mosquitos, being entirely screened on all sides by curtains. On retiring to rest the first night, we noticed a few of the insects flying about the bedroom, but did not attach any importance to them, so climbed into our beds and settled down to sleep, as we thought. We had not been in bed very long, however, before our companions of the night began humming in a most disturbing manner. Some of the pests also managed to penetrate our stronghold, and proceeded to take sundry bites at our exposed faces. Sleeping under these conditions was, of course, impossible, so we arose in order to "settle" our undesirable visitors. Not being accustomed to the mosquito-screens before-mentioned, and it being quite dark, we were unable to find our way out of bed, and, after fumbling for some time, were compelled to tear the curtains and climb through the gap thus made. We lit our candles, there being no gas in the place, and commenced the attack upon our foes. After killing a number of them, Pilling was again preparing to retire, when, on approaching too near the bed with his candle, the curtains caught fire, and there was immediately a big blaze. Our attentions were now withdrawn from the mosquitos, and we began to fight this new enemy. After vigorous efforts, we managed to subdue the flames, but, as can well be imagined, we did not get much sleep that night, our exertions having banished all inclination to slumber. We tendered our apologies to the proprietor and his wife the following morning, and offered to compensate them for the damage done. They, however, good-naturedly refused to accept anything, and joined us and our fellows in a hearty laugh at the account of our nocturnal experience.

A MEMORABLE COACH DRIVE.

I shall never forget a very memorable drive by coach-and-four, which I once had in Australia, along with Shaw's team in 1881-2. We had been playing at a place called Dunolly, and at nightfall of the same day we started off by coach on a journey of sixteen miles through the bush, in order to reach a station on our way to Ballarat, where our next match was to take place. The night was pitch dark, so dark that we could not see many yards ahead, and after covering six or seven miles the old coach-driver missed his way, taking a wrong turn. The coach then began to rock violently, owing to the ruggedness of the track, and several times threatened to turn right over. As it was, three of our party—Tom Emmett, Jack Selby, and Pilling, I think the third was—were thrown from the top of the coach, sustaining a nasty fall; some of our luggage also followed suit. This caused us to have to pull up, which, as it turned out, was extremely fortunate, for we discovered that we were heading straight for a steep embankment, down which we should have been carried but for our timely accident: and probably some of us would never have seen old England again. The coach, of course, had to be turned round, and we had to cover several miles before we struck the right road again. This eventful journey, and the plight of the poor old coach-driver, I shall remember as long as I live.

E

HOW J. BRIGGS, THE LANCASHIRE AND INTERNATIONAL CRICKETER, WAS FIRST DISCOVERED.

Watson and myself were playing in a match at Liverpool, about the year 1878, for the benefit of a professional named Unsworth, who played in several matches for Lancashire in 1871. Briggs, who at that time would only be about fourteen years of age, was playing against us. He made seven runs, and showed very good form. He was also very smart in the field, his favourite place being cover-point.

Briggs also bowled a little, and though he did not take any wickets, we liked his delivery; in short, both Watson and I were very favourably impressed with his good all-round play.

About a week afterwards, Watson and myself were at the county ground at Old Trafford, and saw Messrs. Swire and Rowley (both since deceased) and Mr. A. N. Hornby. We told them what a promising young cricketer had been playing against us at Liverpool, and suggested that if they could see their way to engage him for the ground at Old Trafford, it might be the means of bringing him out.

On meeting Mr. Swire, a few weeks afterwards, he told me that they had engaged Briggs for the following season, and asked me if I could arrange for him to stay with me, so that I could keep an eye on him, as he was only quite a boy. I accordingly arranged to take him in. He came the following April (1879), and remained with me for two seasons, making his *début* for Lancashire in May of the same year. Watson and I took Briggs in hand, and systematically coached him in every department of cricket. We were well repaid for our pains, for, as all the world knows, Johnny Briggs turned out to be one of the finest all-round cricketers for his inches that ever lived.

AN ELDERLY AUSTRALIAN ENTHUSIAST.

When playing at Brisbane, Queensland, in 1882, I was honoured by a visit from an old gentleman who had put himself to great inconvenience to see me. He had travelled over one hundred miles, mostly on foot, along with his son, a youth of sixteen. At one portion of his journey he had had to strip and ford a river, carrying his clothing and his lad across upon his shoulders. He was a Bolton man, and knowing that I came from the same town, he had conceived the idea of coming over for a little chat on kindred topics. We were together about half-an-hour, and he was very reluctant to leave me. His face was a study of conflicting emotions when the moment arrived for us to shake hands and separate.

REMARKABLE INCIDENTS.

When Shaw's team was playing a match at Wellington, New Zealand, in 1881-2, a ball from the late W. Midwinter knocked the leg stump clean out of the ground. After turning one or two somersaults in the air, it descended point down and stuck in the ground again in an upright position. One of the bails also went through the same manœuvre, and came to rest also in a perpendicular position. This caused much comment amongst the players, who all said they had never before seen anything so remarkable.

Another remarkable effect was witnessed at a match at Sandhurst, Australia, during the visit of the Hon. Ivo Bligh's team in 1882-3. A "shooter" was bowled by Barnes which hit the wicket, when both the bails flew backwards, falling almost at the foot of the bowler's wicket. The wickets which were hit remained in a perfectly upright position, and, except for the loss of the bails, it was impossible to tell that they had been touched.

LADIES v. GENTLEMEN.

A match which was in those days much more of a novelty than it is to-day, took place at Ramsbottom in 1886—Ladies v. Gentlemen —the former playing with ordinary bats, and the latter with broomsticks. The gentlemen were also required to field and bowl with the left hand, which caused much laughter. The Barlow family were well represented at this match, my wife and two of my sisters playing on the ladies' side—the first-named being captain—whilst I acted as umpire. One sister bowled well and very straight, taking six wickets, and the other was top scorer with fourteen runs. I must admit that I favoured the ladies, often allowing my sister seven or eight balls to the over, which no doubt helped them to win the match. The full scores were : Ladies, 42 ; Gentlemen, 33.

AN ARMLESS CRICKET SCORER.

It is not often that one sees or hears of a cricket scorer without arms, but when I was connected with the Staveley C. C. in the early Seventies such a rarity used to occasionally score for the Chesterfield and Staveley clubs. He was a young man named Kerwin, who had lost both arms through an accident, having been thrown out of a waggon, the wheels of which had passed over him. He wrote by holding the pencil between his teeth, and, considering his disability, was a very good writer. Kerwin was keen on the game, and watched every ball like a cat watching a mouse. I remember once playing in a match at Staveley when Kerwin and the other scorer had a dispute with regard to my score, the former having got it as 28, and the latter as 27. They made a small bet over it, and appealed to me to decide, as some of our team had told them that I always counted my runs. When I gave my answer as 28 runs, our armless scorer was, of course, highly pleased. This reminds me of a similar incident, which occurred at the North of England *v.* Australians match at Nottingham in 1884, when I made 101. When my score had reached 99, the spectators applauded, thinking I had made the century. Blackham, the wicket-keeper, being of the same opinion, said to me, " Well played, Barlow ; you have got the hundred." I replied, " No, I require another run yet ; my score is 99." We thereupon made a friendly bet of one shilling, which I won. I always made a point of counting my runs when batting.

REPARTEE.

I remember, when playing for Lancashire against Gloucester-shire in the early Eighties, at Cheltenham, I had begun bowling at Dr. E. M. Grace, when he made the remark, " Hold on, Barlow ; I was not quite ready." I replied, " I am sorry, doctor." He hit the next ball I bowled, for a four, saying at the same time, "Ah, Barlow, I was ready *that* time." But the very next ball that I sent down bowled him out. This enabled me to retort, "Ah, doctor, *I* was ready *this* time." J. Street, the umpire, and I often laughed over this little dialogue.

COULDN'T RESIST THE TEMPTATION.

I was on one occasion the subject of an amusing incident when Lancashire was playing against Eighteen of Burnley and district, at Burnley. When batting, I played a ball against my left foot. At the same instant I slipped down on to my knees, and the bat flew out of my hands. The ball was returning on to the wickets, having got within a few inches of them, when I knocked it away with my hand, the temptation proving too strong to be resisted. The fielders laughingly appealed for handling the ball, and I was given " out."

MYSELF AS A RUNNER : A GOOD AFTERNOON'S SPORT.

When engaged as " pro." to the Saltaire C. C.—in the summer of 1875, I think it was—some athletic sports were held, on the occasion of the Feast or Wakes, as they are called. I entered four events, and was succeesful in winning every one, and all from scratch. They were as follow :—100 yards race ; 220 yards race ; 440 yards race, over hurdles ; 80 yards sack race. In speaking of running, I may mention that I won many prizes on the running track in my younger days. For some few years I ran as an amateur, afterwards turning professional for a short time. I then won two handicaps, and once, when running in a £100 handicap at Barnsley, I was just beaten on the post in my heat by the man who won the handicap. His name was Balderson, of Bolton, who at that time was running in the big Sheffield handicaps. After this I was entered for one of the Sheffield events, and several gentlemen wanted me to keep at it and go in for regular training. My parents, however, objected ; so, after the Barnsley experience, I gave up running entirely, and devoted myself exclusively to my favourite game of cricket. My quickest time in running was 122 yards in $12\frac{1}{2}$ seconds, in one of the handicaps which I won.

A PROPHECY THAT WAS REALIZED.

Some years ago, when Lancashire were playing Kent, at Maidstone, Lord Harris came to me when I was looking at the wicket, and said, " Well, Barlow, in which innings are you going to bowl me this time ? You generally do it in one of the innings." " Oh, my lord, it will be in the second innings this time I shall bowl you," I retorted, off-hand. " I am glad you told me," he replied ; " I shall be on the look-out." When I told the players of what had passed between us, the late Dick Pilling and Walter Robinson proposed a friendly bet of two shillings to one shilling that I did not do it. But it came off all right. I bowled Lord Harris for four in the second innings.

FROM A NEWSPAPER CUTTING, 1884.

" In a match at Bolton, in 1863, a certain lad was put on to bowl. He was seen to be far cleverer than any of his companions, and during the match he performed the " hat trick." That lad is now a man ; he is one of the greatest cricketers of the day ; and his name is Richard Gorton Barlow."

ALMOST A FATALITY.

When umpiring at the Crystal Palace some years ago— London County v. Derbyshire—I just escaped within a hair's-breadth of having my face smashed. Braund, of Somerset, was bowling to Mr. Lawton, giving him a very short ball on the leg side. Mr. Lawton (who is one of the hardest hitters we have at the present time) let drive with all his power. The ball seemed to swerve towards where I was standing at short-leg, and came "like lightning," a remark that is often used amongst cricketers. It just shaved the neb of my cap and nose-end, and before I could turn my head the ball was at the boundary, about one hundred yards distant. Dr. W. G. Grace, who saw the incident, said, "My word, Barlow, if that ball had hit you fairly, there would have been an inquest held to-morrow." Several of the other cricketers remarked upon my narrow escape from what might have been certain death.

"BOWLED," BUT "NOT OUT."

An unusual instance of a man being bowled, and yet given "not out," happened during a match at Manchester in 1876— Lancashire v. Notts. Mr. D. Q. Steel was batting against the bowling of the late Alfred Shaw. After a few overs, a ball hit the leg stump slightly, causing the off bail to come off. The batsman, not knowing that he was bowled, remained at the wicket, whereupon Fred Wild (the wicket-keeper) and Shaw appealed to the umpire. The latter gave the batsman "not out" on the ground that he had not seen what had happened. This decision was severe on the bowler, and at the same time a bit of good luck for the batsman, as Mr. Steel afterwards played a very fine innings, scoring 82 runs. I was in batting at the time, and was a witness of the occurrence. Had I been the umpire, I should certainly have given the batsman "out," as I saw the ball hit the stump. As it was, some of the players were arguing the point with the umpire for several minutes. After all, Notts won this match—an exciting one—by one wicket. It was also Mr. Steel's first match for his county.

A DEBATABLE CONTRETEMPS.

A very curious incident occurred on Lord's cricket ground about the year 1889, when Lancashire were playing the M.C.C. Lees Whitehead was bowling to Mr. A. N. Hornby when the ball slipped out of his hand and rolled down the pitch, about half-way between the wickets. On Mr. Hornby seeing this, he came down the wicket to hit the ball, and at the same time, Whitehead, the bowler, followed the ball up, just reaching it before Mr. Hornby made his stroke. Whitehead snatched up the ball and threw it to Carlin, the wicket-keeper, who put the wicket down and appealed to the umpire. The latter hesitated, not knowing what to say just for the moment, when Mr. Hornby called out to him that he (Mr.

Hornby) could not be given "out," as the bowler had obstructed him from hitting the ball. Mr. Hornby was, of course, given "not out." At lunch-time, as well as at the close of the day's play, many of the cricketers and a few of the umpires were arguing the point, and it was a subject of discussion for weeks afterwards. All were agreed in saying that they had never at any time seen such an occurrence either in local or first-class cricket.

A SINGULAR POINT.

" R. G. Barlow, the old Lancashire county man, had a singular point brought before his notice as umpire in a match the other day between the Old Rossallians and the Northern Nomads. E. Roper and A. T. Kemble, two old Lancashire county cricketers, were batting, and Roper returned the ball very hard back to the bowler, Whiston, who made a good attempt to bring off the catch. The ball, however, rebounded off his hand, struck the outstretched bat of Kemble, and went to mid-on, where T. A. Higson 'held.' Roper, of course, was out, but it took nearly half a side to effect his dismissal, and the assistance Kemble gave was unpardonable for a boon companion."—*From a Newspaper Cutting.*

ANOTHER CASE OF " HARD LINES."

At the North *v.* South match at Lord's, in 1878, I was given "out" for infringing Law 27, *i.e.*, hitting the ball twice. I did not hit the ball a second time with any intention to score, which is really what the law in question referred to at that time. I say now, as I said then, that I consider the appeal was a very unsportsman-like one, and was only made by one of the fielders, who doubtless wished to get me out of the way, as I had been batting some time. It was not that I was in ignorance of the law on this point, as I had been quite familiar with it for some years. I merely unthinkingly tapped the ball with my bat a second time, with the above result.

PAST *v.* PRESENT : MY LAST COUNTY CRICKETER'S WICKET.

The very last occasion on which I succeeded in capturing the wicket of a county cricketer was at Coventry, at the Warwickshire *v.* Northamptonshire match, at which I was umpiring—season 1906. Sam Hargreaves, the Warwickshire bowler, was not out, five, on the Friday evening, and on arriving at the ground the following morning he humorously remarked to me that he thought he was improving in his batting, and that he intended to stay in until the required runs were knocked off. I replied that I thought I could bowl him out in a quarter of an hour, although I was out of practice, not having played for some little time. We thereupon made a friendly wager over it. Kinnier also took five shillings to one from Hargreaves that I would bowl him out in twelve balls, and several other small bets were made between the other players, causing some little amusement and excitement all round, amongst both the players and the spectators. One of the players then lent me his cricket boots, and we went on the field. When all was ready, I took the ball and bowled Hargreaves with my very first delivery. He then came to me, and, shaking hands, confessed that the ball had fairly beaten him, and that he would have to give in to the "old Lancashire boy."

A MODEL FIRST-WICKET PAIR.

" It revived memories of old times to see A. N. Hornby and 'Dicky' Barlow strolling off to the luncheon tent together. Evidently 'Dicky' Barlow had forgiven his old chief for all those terrible skurries between the wickets, and some of the incidents that happened. But if those were adventures, they were great triumphs. They were a model first-wicket pair, and Lancashire could do with a combination like them to-day."—"*Manchester Evening Chronicle," July 30th, 1906.*

AN EXPERT WITHOUT A SUPERIOR IN THE WORLD.

" R. G. Barlow was another of the stonewalling brigade, and, like Louis Hall, he was usually put in first. He was an extremely reliable batsman, for although he could make a big score, there was absolutely no hurrying him. When he took his place at the wickets, men regarded him as a fixture. At breaking down the best bowling he was an expert without a superior in the world. He would be content to notch eight or ten runs in the hour. Barlow was invaluable to Lancashire, for he was an all-round player. He was a magnificent bowler, with a grand break, and one who used his head as well as his hands. He is a splendid judge of cricket, an enthusiast of the enthusiasts, a man to extract hints from, and what he does not know about the game is not worth knowing. He retained his form for many years, despite the strenuous work that he was called upon to perform. His age is fifty-four."—*From a Magazine Article on Well-known Umpires, 1904.*

R. G. BARLOW AS A CAMBRIDGE UNDERGRADUATE.

Taken on the suggestion of Mr. A. G. Steel, Mr. O. P. Lancashire, and others, when Lancashire were playing Cambridge in the early Eighties.

Some Cricket Curiosities.

NOW give an account of a few curious and marvellous happenings at cricket, for the truth of which I can vouch, as they occurred at matches in which I was engaged, and before my own eyes.

At a match at Ramsbottom—Barlow's North of England XI. v. Eighteen of Ramsbottom and District—in 1887 or 1888, a fast ball was sent by the old Notts County bowler, J. Shacklock, which went clean through the wickets to the boundary for four byes, without disturbing the bails. Pilling, who was the wicket-keeper, said that the ball opened the wicket in passing through, which then closed again, leaving the bails in their original position. He said that he had never, in his experience, seen anything like it. The ball was brought back to the wicket to be tried, and it was found to be impossible to pass it between the stumps without dislodging the bails.

What was, I think, the most ludicrous episode that I ever saw on a cricket ground, took place at Whitehaven, about the year 1879, in a match between Mr. G. F. Grace's XI. and a local twenty, which included the late J. Platts (Derbyshire) and myself. Platts was batting, when the ball, somehow, stuck in his hands. W. R. Gilbert, who was fielding at point, called out to Pooley, " Get to it, Ted," and as he was trying to get the ball Platts deliberately put it into the top of his trousers, without saying a word. He knew that he had done wrong, however, and Pooley, who was keeping wicket, said, " Jack, what's up ? " Platts then ran away from his wicket, and a most exciting chase began, for he was followed by nearly all the members of the Eleven : they ran him all round the enclosure, and a more comical race was never seen. In running, the ball had slipped down Platts's trousers leg, and he tried frantically to kick it out. Before he could do so, however, one of the fielders—the late J. Selby (Notts), I think it was—caught hold of him, and the other fielders coming up, Platts, still kicking and struggling, was put on the ground and pinned down whilst the ball was removed from his trousers before it could touch the ground. It was a most extraordinary and laughable incident ; but the sequel was, if anything, more so. Platts walked coolly back to his wicket, and prepared to continue his innings. " What's yer game, now ? " said Pooley, " you know you're out ! "

"Ask the umpire," replied Platts. Pooley did so, and he was given "not out," on the ground that the umpires could not see what had happened; yet, in point of fact, Platts was out in three ways—handling the ball, obstructing the field, and caught. Platts told me at the time that he never handled the ball. He used to play in an ordinary grey shirt, and his trousers always came up a few inches above his belt, so there was plenty of room for the ball to lodge. I think, myself, that he played the ball into his shirt, and that when he started to run it was with the intention of jerking the ball out, but it went the wrong way—down the leg of his trousers.

I afterwards heard some of the spectators saying that during many years of cricket they had never before seen the fielders running after a batsman. I do not expect ever to see anything to equal this; and I can now picture to my imagination the spectacle of Platts racing about the ground, and waving his bat about like a club, with all the fielders after him.

When Shaw's team was playing the Australians, at Holbeck, some years ago, I was bowling to T. Horan, and sent a ball which hit the leg stump with great force. Remarkable to relate, the bails were not disturbed, and the ball, glancing off at right angles to the wicket, went near to the boundary for three byes.

I was playing in a local match at Pudsey, near Bradford, in the early Seventies, when a swift ball from the hand of a bowler named West hit the wicket, causing the bails to jump straight up in the air for several inches. In falling back again one bail balanced itself on the top of the leg stump, and the other one returned to its original position.

During another local match at Eckington, Derbyshire, about the year 1869, a ball of mine hit the wicket, causing one of the bails to rest across the top of the middle stump, and the other to lodge between two of the stumps a few inches from the top.

"HANDLED BALL."

In all my long career, I have only seen one batsman given "out," in first-class cricket, for handling the ball. This was the late W. Scotton (Notts), at Melbourne (Australia), in the Smokers v. Non-Smokers' match, 1887. The Non-Smokers made 803 for nine wickets, which was a record up to that time. Scotton, wishing to get the ball to keep as a memento, played the last ball of the match just in front of him, and then, fielding it himself, pocketed the ball before the umpire called "over." The bowler appealed for handling the ball, and Scotton was given "out."

The Author's Opinions on Some Cricketers he has met during the last Forty Years.

OFTEN has it been asked which players, since 1871, have been the best all-round exponents of the game. Of course, this is more or less a matter of opinion, but I should place Dr. W. G. Grace (Gloucestershire), Mr. A. G. Steel (Lancashire), and George Hirst (Yorkshire) at the head of the list, in the order as written, with the Hon. F. S. Jackson (Yorkshire) close up. The first-named has been a most extraordinary all-round cricketer, and I place him the champion of champions.

Amongst the Australian cricketers, I consider Messrs. G. Giffen, M. A. Noble, and W. W. Armstrong to be the best ever produced by that Colony.

For excellence in bowling, the prince of bowlers was the late Alfred Shaw (Nottinghamshire). I have played against or seen all the best bowlers in England and Australia, and I place Shaw, with Spofforth and Turner, the Australians, at the top of the list, taking them on all kinds of wickets. No matter how long you batted against Shaw, he would keep " sticking you up," so that you never felt quite at home. He could bowl on all kinds of wickets, and at the same time preserve a beautiful length. He was a remarkably good "head" bowler, with a wonderful capacity for finding out a batsman's weak points; and could vary his bowling, according to the state of the wicket, as could no other bowler I ever saw. He was, moreover, a fine fielder to his own bowling, and I have seen him effect some marvellous catches. His action was beautiful, and very easy, and I think he could have bowled all day long without turning a hair. I never came across a better-tempered cricketer, and I saw a good deal of him, having played with and against him many times in England, and made two out of my three cricket tours to Australia with him. He was a gentleman, both on and off the field, and I am certain we shall never see his like again on a cricket ground.

The late G. Freeman (Yorkshire) and Tom Richardson (Surrey) would take the next place, with the late George Lohmann and W. H. Lockwood (Surrey) close behind; and with the late E. Peate (Yorkshire) and F. Morley (Nottinghamshire) for left-hand bowling. Lohmann and Peate were both very fine bowlers on all kinds of wickets.

Australia would be represented by Messrs. F. R. Spofforth, C. T. B. Turner, and H. Trumble, with G. E. Palmer and the late H. F. Boyle close up; and the late J. J. Ferris as the best left-hand bowler.

Other representatives of first-class bowling have been the late A. Appleby (Lancashire), the late J. C. Shaw, the late J. Jackson, G. Wootton, W. Attewell, T. Wass, and Hallam (Nottinghamshire), the late G. Tarrant (Cambridge), P. H. Morton (Cambridge University), the late E. Willsher, S. Christopherson, W. M. Bradley, Fielder, W. Hearne, Martin, and Blythe (Kent), the late W. Southerton, the late E. Barrett, W. Lees, and N. A. Knox (Surrey), the late W. McIntyre, A. Watson, A. Mold, and W. Brearley (Lancashire), the late R. Clayton, A. Hill, and S. Haigh (Yorkshire), the late W. Mycroft, the late W. Hickton, W. Bestwick, the late G. G. Walker, G. Hay, and Warren (Derbyshire), S. Barnes (Staffordshire), the late F. Silcock, the late H. Pickett, and W. Mead (Essex), J. T. Hearne, A. E. Trott, and G. Burton (Middlesex), H. Rotherham, H. Pallett, and S. Hargreaves (Warwickshire), F. Roberts, W. Woof, and G. Dennett (Gloucestershire), E. Tyler (Somersetshire), J. Lillywhite and F. Tate (Sussex).

The best "lob" bowlers I ever saw, or played against, were W. Humphreys (Sussex), R. C. Tinley (Notts), and T. Armitage (Yorkshire).

There has been much said of late years with regard to swerve bowling. I have not seen any one yet to compare with Walter Wright, the old Kent left-hand bowler, for this style of bowling. Joe Hulme (Derbyshire) and Hirst (Yorkshire) were also fine swerve bowlers. The first-named would also often make the ball curl in the air.

Yorkshire has always been very fortunate in having excellent first-class left-hand bowlers—as, for instance, the late Tom Emmett, the late E. Peate, R. Peel, G. H. Hirst, and W. Rhodes.

With a wet ball, or against a strong wind, I never saw any one to equal the late W. McIntyre (Lancashire) and A. Hill (Yorkshire).

W. Flowers (Notts) and A. Watson (Lancashire) were also fine bowlers under these conditions.

For all-round cricketers, a few other giants of the past are : Messrs. the late G. F. Grace and C. L. Townsend (Gloucestershire), C. T. Studd and B. J. T. Bosanquet (Middlesex), S. M. J. Woods (Somersetshire), J. R. Mason, G. G. Hearne, A. Hearne, and W. Wright (Kent), the late G. Ulyett, the late W. Bates, and E. Wainwright (Yorkshire), the late W. Barnes and W. Flowers (Nottinghamshire), C. J. Kortright (Essex), and the late W. Midwinter (Gloucestershire).

Other cricketers who have done good all-round work for their county are : W. Rhodes and S. Haigh (Yorkshire), E. Arnold (Worcestershire), W. Brockwell and R. Henderson (Surrey), J. Gunn (Notts), W. Cuttell, J. Sharp, J. Hallows, and G. Baker (Lancashire), J. Rawlin (Middlesex), E. H. Killick, J. Vine, G. Bean, Jesse Hide, A. E. Relf, and G. Cox (Sussex), the late J. Platts, the late G. Davidson, W. Chatterton, and S. Cadman (Derbyshire), D. Pougher, S. Coe, and J. King (Leicestershire), G. Thompson and W. East (Northants), L. C. Braund, E. Robson, and Nichols (Somerset), V. Barton and Llewellyn (Hampshire).

The following have all been champion batsmen in their day :— Lord Harris, F. Penn, W. Yardley, W. H. Patterson, and C. J. Burnup (Kent), A. N. Hornby (Lancashire), W. W. Read (Surrey), E. M. Grace (Gloucestershire), I. D. Walker, A. E. Stoddart, and C. T. Studd (Middlesex), the late R. Daft, the late A. Shrewsbury, W. Gunn, and W. Oscroft (Notts), the late H. Jupp and the late T. Humphrey (Surrey), A. P. Lucas (Essex), the late R. Carpenter and the late T. Heywood (Cambridge), and the Hon. A. Lyttelton (Middlesex).

Other very fine batsmen have been : Sir T. C. O'Brien, A. J. Webbe, E. Lyttelton, C. J. Ottaway, J. Douglas, and C. F. H. Leslie (Middlesex), A. W. Ridley, Captain Wynyard, Major Poore, Captain Greig, E. M. Sprott, A. J. L. Hill, and F. E. Lacey (Hampshire), J. M. Cotterill, W. Newham, and G. Brann (Sussex), J. Shuter, W. E. Roller, K. J. Key, M. Read, and F. Holland (Surrey), (W. Yardley) W. Rashleigh, and E. W. Dillon (Kent), H. K. Foster and F. Bowley (Worcestershire), H. W. Bainbridge), F. S. Fishwick, J. Devey, E. J. Diver, S. P. Kinnier, the Brothers Quaife, and Lilley (Warwickshire), the late H. Charlwood and F. W. Marlow (Sussex), P. Perrin, C. McGahey, F. L. Fane, and H. Carpenter (Essex), F. Townsend, F. H. B. Champain, C. O. H.

Sewell, C. L. Townsend, W. R. Gilbert, W. O. Moberley, W. H. Brain, J. Cranston, H. Wrathall, and J. H. Board (Gloucestershire), J. A. Dixon, A. O. Jones, the late W. Scotton, J. Iremonger, and the late J. Selby (Nottinghamshire), the late J. T. Brown, J. Tunnicliffe, E. Lockwood, the late A. Greenwood, F. Mitchell. D. Denton, C. E. M. Wilson, T. Taylor, L. Hall, and Lord Hawke (Yorkshire), L. G. Wright, S. H. Evershead, R. P. Smith, E. M. Ashcroft, T. Foster, H. Bagshaw, L. C. Docker, A. E. Lawton, and W. Storer (Derbyshire), H. T. Hewitt and R. N. Palairet (Somersetshire), the late J. Ricketts, the late C. Coward, O. P. Lancashire, L. O. S. Poidevin, G. Kemp, J. and A. Eccles, A. H. Hornby, S. M. Crossfield, A. Ward, A. Paul, F. Sugg, E. Roper, D. Q. Steel, R. H. Spooner, and W. Robinson (Lancashire), C. J. B. Wood, A. Knight, and H. Whitehead (Leicestershire).

The best young batsmen at the present day are, in my opinion: G. N. Foster and Pearson (Worcestershire), K. L. Hutchings, Woolley, and Seymour (Kent), Hobbs, Hayes, and J. N. Crawford (Surrey), G. Gunn, Hardstaff, and Payton (Nottinghamshire), R. A. Young (Sussex), Tarrant (Middlesex), Langton (Gloucestershire), and Baker (Warwickshire). Mr. Hutchings (Kent) is a very fine batsman, especially on a fast wicket and against fast bowling. His wrist play, and the power he puts behind his strokes, are marvellous. His style reminds one of Dr. W. G. Grace, Prince Ranjitsinhji, and Mr. A. G. Steel, when they were at their best.

Mr. J. W. H. T. Douglas and Buckenham (Essex), Cuffe (Worcestershire), Santall (Warwickshire), and Dean (Lancashire) have all done some fine work for their county this last season (1907).

Mr. C. I. Thornton (Middlesex) was the biggest and hardest hitter I ever saw, or bowled against.

BATTING.

As the most scientific batsmen, and experts at placing and timing the ball, I would give first place to Dr. W. G. Grace (Gloucestershire), Messrs. A. G. Steel and A. C. Maclaren (Lancashire), Prince K. S. Ranjitsinhji (India and Sussex), and the late A. Shrewsbury (Notts); with the following six close behind—F. S. Jackson (Yorkshire), A. E. Stoddart (Middlesex), C. B. Fry (Sussex), W. Gunn (Nottinghamshire), W. W. Read and Tom Hayward (Surrey).

I have seen all the above-named batsmen play some magnificent innings; and what a wonderful all-round athlete C. B. Fry has been!

The prettiest and most attractive batsman I ever saw was Mr. L. C. H. Palairet (Somersetshire), with the late Richard Daft (Notts) a close second.

Messrs. A. P. Lucas (Surrey and Essex), R. E. Foster (Worcestershire), and K. S. Ranjitsinhji were also very stylish wielders of the willow; the last-named, with his beautiful wrist-play on fast wickets, was worth going miles to see.

I have also seen Mr. A. O. Jones (Notts) play some beautiful innings; and what with his splendid all-round fielding, I call him every inch a cricketer. I must also say the same with regard to Mr. R. H. Spooner (Lancashire).

The most daring and dashing batsman, and, consequently, the most popular, was Mr. A. N. Hornby (Lancashire), who has a unique record for running short runs. Another undaunted batsman is Mr. G. L. Jessop (Gloucestershire). For late cutting behind the wickets, I have never seen any batsman yet to equal E. Lockwood (Yorkshire).

The two finest all-round cricketers, taking into consideration their short stature, were J. Briggs (Lancashire) and R. Peel (Yorkshire); in fact, they were two marvels. I have seen them do some wonderful performances.

Another past hero is R. Abel (Surrey), the finest batsman, I think, for his inches that this country has yet produced. He might aptly be called " The Little Wonder."

Other marvellous players of small physique are J. T. Tyldesley (Lancashire) and W. G. Quaife (Warwickshire). Tyldesley is a fine, dashing, and popular batsman, and one who can play on every kind of wicket. It is wonderful, the power he gets behind the ball.

For excellent play on a soft, sticky wicket, when the ball is breaking about, I would place the late Arthur Shrewsbury (Notts) at the head. He was the safest batsman I ever saw, or bowled against. The reason for this, in my opinion, was that he had a very good and quick eye; he had also plenty of patience, and would play just as carefully after he had made fifty as he did in the first over. Then, again, he was second to none in playing with his legs, and always played at the ball, not at the pitch—as many batsmen do, on this kind of wicket. He never played forward unless he could get well to the ball before the break got on. I have seen him play some wonderful innings on these bad wickets. His untimely death caused a gap in the cricket world which will, probably, never be filled. There are, of course, not many players who can adapt their style to all kinds of wickets, like Shrewsbury could. I would have preferred to bowl against Dr. W. G. Grace, W. W. Read, or any other batsman, rather than against Shrewsbury, on a bad, sticky wicket. I know, and have seen, numerous players who can only play on what I call a good hard wicket, when the ball is coming straight along. As soon as they get on to a soft, difficult wicket, they are all at sea. Messrs. A. G. Steel and Tyldesley (Lancashire), A. Bannerman, M. A. Noble and V. Trumper (Australia), and F. S. Jackson and George Hirst (Yorkshire) have also been seven champions on varying conditions of the wicket.

FIELDING.

The best fielder at short slip, and for fielding his own bowling, was the late George Lohmann (Surrey). A. Hill (Yorkshire), A. Watson (Lancashire), and L. Braund (Somersetshire) were near rivals. J. Tunnicliffe (Yorkshire) has been another fine fielder at short slip, and I have seen him make some wonderful one-hand catches.

I would place the Rev. V. K. Royle (Lancashire) as the best "cover-point" who ever lived. His fielding was even more admired in Australia than in England. I have seen him do some marvellous things. Mr. G. L. Jessop (Gloucestershire) comes second in order of merit. Mr. G. Strachan (Surrey), S. E. Gregory (Australia), J. Briggs (Lancashire), W. Sugg (Derbyshire), F. Hearne (Kent), W. G. Quaife (Warwickshire), G. B. Studd (Cambridge and Middlesex), and W. Rhodes (Yorkshire) have all been champion fielders at cover-point.

By far the best "point" I ever saw, and one who stands alone, was Dr. E. M. Grace (Gloucestershire), and he always fielded close to the batsman. I have seen him make some extraordinary catches. One that I shall never forget was when he caught Mr. W. L. Murdoch, at the Orleans ground, in the match Mr. C. I. Thornton's team against the Australians, in the early Eighties.

In my opinion, A. O. Jones (Notts) is the best all-round fielder this world has ever seen; and he is equally at home in any part of the field. Mr. A. E. Lawton (Derbyshire) is another magnificent all-round fielder.

The best nine long-fielders I ever saw were C. Ullathorne (Yorkshire), the late Mr. G. F. Grace (Gloucestershire), Mr. L. D. Brownlee (Gloucestershire), W. Gunn (Notts), Maurice Read (Surrey), F. Sugg (Lancashire), D. Denton (Yorkshire), J. T. Tyldesley (Lancashire), and Mr. J. Douglas (Middlesex). They were all first-class for judging a catch, quick running, and throwing-in straight to the wicket.

WICKET-KEEPING.

The prince of English wicket-keepers was the late Richard Pilling (Lancashire), who was really a marvel behind the stumps. The smartest bit of work I ever saw—and I have seen a great deal—was when he stumped the Hon. Alfred Lyttelton (late Colonial Secretary), at Lord's, in the match Lancashire *v.* Middlesex. Crossland, the fast bowler, sent up one of his lightning deliveries rather wide on the leg-side ; the batsman got his foot on the crease, when, quick as thought, the ball had flown to the ready hands of Pilling and the bails were off. The Hon. Alfred immediately turned round and patted the intrepid stumper on the back, saying that he had never witnessed such a smart bit of stumping. He afterwards presented Pilling with a half-sovereign, as a small acknowledgment of his prowess.

In taking fast balls from both the off and leg side, the late George Pinder (Yorkshire) was a wonder ; and I have seen him do some surprising things behind the wicket. Two other very fine wicket-keepers have been the Hon. A. Lyttelton (Cambridge and Middlesex) and A. A. Lilley (Warwickshire). I consider J. Humphries (Derbyshire) to be the coming champion wicket-keeper. I saw him perform some very smart work last season (1907).

Other first-class wicket-keepers whom I have seen, or played against, during the last forty years, are: Messrs. G. Macgregor (Middlesex), H. Martyn, A. E. Newton, and Rev. A. Wickham (Somerset), E. Jackson, A. T. Kemble, W. Findlay, Smith, and Worsley (Lancashire), M. C. Kemp, E. F. S. Tylecote, the late E. Henty, and F. Huish (Kent), C. Robson (Hampshire), the late E. Stevenson, the late J. Hunter, and D. Hunter (Yorkshire), the late E. Pooley, A. Steadman, H. Wood, and H. Strudwick (Surrey), H. Phillips and H. Butt (Sussex), T. Plumb and W. Smith (Northants), W. Storer, and A. Smith (Derbyshire), the late S. Biddulph, the late F. Wild, M. Sherwin, and W. Oates (Notts), W. Bush and J. H. Board (Gloucestershire), and T. Russell (Essex).

AUSTRALIAN CRICKETERS.

And now a few words with regard to the Australian cricketers. Having made three cricket trips to Australia (in 1881-82-86), and having either played against every team which has visited

England since 1878 or umpired in their matches, I can speak with some knowledge and authority regarding them.

The best batsmen, to my mind, and using the greatest variety of strokes, were Messrs. W. L. Murdoch, V. Trumper, and C. Bannerman; with H. Moses and C. Hill as the best left-handed batsmen; and with J. Darling and W. Bruce in close attendance. I have seen W. L. Murdoch play some magnificent innings, and shall never forget his 211 for Australia v. England, in 1884, at the Oval; his placing, timing, and late cutting were really grand. V. Trumper has been a wonderful batsman, without a doubt. It was a great loss to Australian cricket when C. Bannerman's health gave way; I always thought what a good judge of the game he was, and what a fine captain he would have made. Messrs. F. A. Iredale and R. A. Duff were also good and stylish batsmen, using a variety of strokes all round the wicket.

The best fielders, in my opinion, were: H. G. S. Trott, at "point," whom I have seen make some magnificent catches, especially one-handed; at his best, he was a fine all-round cricketer. S. E. Gregory, at "cover-point," was a little wonder; he was also an excellent bat—indeed, for his height, a champion. A. Bannerman, at "mid-off," was really first-class, and, with his wonderful defensive batting, was a very fine cricketer. The late H. F. Boyle, at "mid-on," was the best I ever saw, and he fielded close in. As a daring fielder, he ranked with Dr. E. M. Grace (Gloucestershire).

The prince of Australian wicket-keepers was J. M. Blackham. who is considered to be on a "par" with the late Richard Pilling. Two others who have excelled in this line are A. H. Jarvis and J. J. Kelly. In passing, I might also mention Messrs. E. A. Halliwell and P. W. Sherwell (of the South African teams of 1904 and 1907 respectively) as wicket-keepers. I have seen them do some very fine things behind the wicket, and the latter has a beautiful style when taking the ball.

Regarding the Australian bowling of to-day and of twenty-five years ago, the finest bowling sides that ever came to these shores were those of 1882 and 1884, which included Messrs. F. R. Spofforth, the late H. F. Boyle, G. E. Palmer, G. Giffen, T. W. Garrett, and W. Midwinter, who were at that time all at their best.

The team which came to England on the last occasion fell far below the standard of those just named, in the matter of bowling. A champion pair of bowlers, who invariably went on the field together, were Messrs. C. T. B. Turner and the late J. J. Ferris.

They have not their equals in Australia at the present day. Messrs. E. Evans, F. E. Allen, E. Jones, H. Trumble, T. Garrett, and W. Howell were all fine bowlers.

The following five bowlers had more devilment from the pitch than any others I ever saw: Messrs. F. R. Spofforth and C. T. B. Turner (Australia), the late G. Freeman (Yorkshire), and T. Richardson and W. H. Lockwood (Surrey). The first-named could make the ball whip back and do more at his pace than any bowler I ever played against.

BOWLING.

My personal opinion, as regards the bowlers of the present day, is that many of them bowl too much on the off-side, and too wide of the wicket. In a match at which I was umpiring last season one batsman only played at three balls in the first two overs; thus, nine balls out of the twelve sent up were quite useless. Now, I consider this to be a great mistake on the bowler's part for two reasons: In the first place, the batsman is "getting his eye in"; and, secondly, the bowler is uselessly exerting himself and exhausting his strength, without much probability of capturing many wickets. I have seen some overs bowled where not one ball was played at by the batsman, and many others where only two and three of the six balls were played at. I feel certain that if these same bowlers were to bowl more on the wicket, with an occasional ball in each over about six or eight inches outside the off-stump, and one now and again a little wider still—say a foot or two—they would by these means get more wickets, and thus be able to show much better averages.

I do not believe in so much of this "off-theory bowling." My opinion as regards this was confirmed by the bowling of Hallam (Notts), in a match at Dewsbury the season before last (1906), Notts v. Yorkshire. His bowling in the second innings was on the lines of what I have just been advising. Hallam took six wickets for 30 runs, and Notts won the match by 23 runs. Although the wicket was not of the best, Yorkshire certainly ought to have made more runs than they did. There is no doubt, however, that the victory of Notts was due to Hallam's very fine bowling. I complimented him upon this, after the match, telling him that his bowling reminded me of the old school of bowlers of twenty-five years ago. He told me only last season (1907) that he was now bowling more on the wicket.

ILLUMINATED ADDRESS

Presented to the Author in March, 1882, along with a Gold Medal, by Lancashire Residents of Sydney, Australia, in recognition of his services in upholding the reputation of his County on the cricket field.

Hirst and Haigh (Yorkshire) are also bowlers who bowl more for the wicket, with an occasional ball a little outside the off-stump; as also do J. T. Hearne (Middlesex), Mead (Essex), Wass (Notts), Blythe (Kent), Dennett (Gloucestershire), Thompson (Northants), and Trott (Middlesex).

Before leaving the subject of bowlers, it will, doubtless, be of interest to my readers to learn that the fastest bowler I ever saw, or played against, was George Hibbard, who came from a country village in Derbyshire named Barlbro. He was very inconsistent in his length; otherwise, there was the making of a champion bowler in him, as he had a splendid action. However, having a good business, and not being dependent upon cricket, he soon lost interest in the game, and gave it up.

I had the pleasure, in 1871, of playing against the old All-England XI. (the late George Parr's team), which came to play at Staveley, in Derbyshire, in that year, the before-mentioned George Hibbard being one of our Eighteen. I was put on to bowl when the late T. Haywood and the late R. Carpenter, two of the finest batsmen of the day, were batting. To my gratification, I captured Carpenter's wicket in the second over I bowled. The late Richard Daft was playing on the All-England side, and he remarked that he had seen Tarrant, Jackson, and many other fast bowlers, but none of them could come up to Hibbard for speed. I have often seen two long stops on in local cricket when he was bowling, which will give some idea of the speed of his balls. On one occasion, at a match at Bramall Lane ground, Sheffield—in 1870, I think it was—I remember that one of Hibbard's deliveries struck the late George Pinder (Yorkshire), who was batting, on the pads, causing him to go down like a ninepin; in fact, I have seen this happen more than once.

At the same match, at Staveley, Richard Daft expressed his satisfaction with my bowling, and promised to use his influence in getting me an engagement, which promise he faithfully kept.

PAST v. PRESENT-DAY CRICKET.

With respect to the batting, bowling, and fielding of to-day, and of thirty years ago, there is, with one or two exceptions, not much difference in the batting, though batsmen had not such good wickets to play on then as now. The bowling, I am sure, is not so good at the present day. Certainly, we have a few bowlers who are about equal to the giants of the past; but, taking the county bowlers all round, they are not in it with the old school. The wickets are much better now, but when they are a little queer, owing to changes in the weather, many of the bowlers seem quite unable to take the same advantage of them as the old bowlers used to do. This was proved last season.

Never, in the last forty years, have I seen so many bad, soft, and sticky wickets as I did in the wet season of 1907. Although these are eminently in the bowlers' favour, many of the latter did not take advantage of the opportunity thus afforded. The bowling averages should have been much better than they were; and, just to show the difference between the Lancashire County bowlers' averages of last season (1907) and those of the bowlers of 1881, I give them below :—

1907 LANCASHIRE COUNTY BOWLING AVERAGES.

	Balls.	Overs.	Maidens.	Runs.	Wickets.	Average.
Huddleston.	1409.	401·3	102	941	71	13·25
Harry	3401.	566·5	200	1165	75	15·53
Dean	5178	863	252	2080	98	21·22
Cook (L.)	1923	320·3	71	1008	47	21·24

26 matches played.

1881 LANCASHIRE COUNTY BOWLING AVERAGES.

	No. of balls.	Maidens.	Runs.	Wickets.	Average.
Barlow	1969	254	581	63	9·14
Nash	1825	223	528	51	10·18
A. G. Steel	1309	151	453	42	10·33
Watson	3504	512	815	69	11·56

Only 15 matches played.

I also give the batting averages of the two top batsmen for the two seasons named above; and it will be seen what a wonderful year Mr. Hornby had, and what a fine performance it was to make his 1,000 runs, having played in only 20 innings; whereas Tyldesley had 44 innings in making his 1,597 runs :—

1907. J. Tyldesley's batting average for Lancashire :—Innings, 44; total runs, 1,597; most in an innings, 207. Average, 38·02.

1881. Mr. A. N. Hornby's batting average for Lancashire :— Innings, 20; total runs, 1,002; most in an innings, 188. Average, 50·2.

I have frequently made the remark, during the past ten years or so, that many more of the present-day batsmen and bowlers ought to get their 1,000 runs and take 100 wickets in a season, considering that they have to play in so many more matches than formerly.

Taking the fielding as a whole, the catching, ground-fielding, and return of the ball straight to the wicket in order to run the batsman out, is not nearly so good as it was some years ago. Catches are more frequently dropped in county cricket, the reason for which I cannot explain, unless it is that the players do not go in for sufficient practice. Another cause may be found in the fact that there are more pavilions, grand-stands, &c., erected around the grounds, which obstruct the light, rendering it more difficult to see the ball than formerly.

THE FINEST INNINGS I EVER SAW.

The finest innings that I have ever seen played was that of the late Arthur Shrewsbury (Notts), who made 164, at Lord's, in 1886, in the test match England v. Australia. The innings was played on three different kinds of wicket. When Shrewsbury commenced batting, the wicket was hard and fast, and rather fiery ; but, after a time, there was a fall of rain, which changed the wicket into a slow one ; while, later still, the sun came out, again changing the same wicket, making it very difficult. But Shrewsbury kept steadily at it, against some very fine bowling and fielding—Messrs. Spofforth, Palmer, Giffen, Evans, and Garrett being some of his opponents. None of the other batsmen could do much with the bowling, with the exception of Barnes. When the Australians went in to bat they could not make a stand, so difficult was the wicket, and were all put out for a total of 121 runs. Referring to this match, a London daily gave the following pithy report :—

" *A Tribute to the Three.*—England beat Australia, at Lord's, on Wednesday, July 21st, 1886, by an innings and 106 runs, mainly owing to the splendid batting of Arthur Shrewsbury, who made 164 runs, and the excellent bowling of Barlow and Briggs.

> Thanks to you, we're dancing jigs,
> Shrewsbury, Barlow, and Briggs.
> Who'll call England's cricket star low,
> Briggs, and Shrewsbury, and Barlow.
> Here's your health, ye glorious three !
> Barlow, Briggs, and Shrewsbury."

Another extraordinary performance was that of P. S. McDonnell (Australia), who, in the match North of England v. Australians, at Manchester, in 1888, made a very rapid score of 82, out of 101 runs for five wickets. To the excellent play of McDonnell was due the victory of his side. He played on a very bad, sticky wicket, against the bowling of such men as Attewell, Briggs, Barnes, Flowers, and Barlow. A. Bannerman, who was batting at the other end throughout this innings, only made four runs.

TOM HAYWARD'S FINE BATTING.

In the Surrey v. Notts match, at Nottingham, June 4th, 5th, and 6th, 1906, Hayward played two wonderful innings; especially so was the first, when he carried his bat through for 144, out of a total of 225. There were six Surrey wickets down for only 36 runs, when Walter Lees and Strudwick, two of the later batsmen, kept their ends up while Hayward got the runs. The judgment which he used in " getting " most of the bowling was really fine, and was worth going miles to see. In the second innings he had just made the hundred, when I had to give him out leg before wicket. Taking both these innings together, I must say it was the best batting performance I have seen for some years. I heard that Hayward himself considered this to be his best batting feat. He had the full score printed on satin, and gave the members of the Surrey team one each. The Surrey captain, Lord Dalmeny, made Hayward a present, for his two splendid innings in this match, of a fine silver cigarette-case, with all his three-figure innings engraved upon it.

MY OWN BEST ALL-ROUND FEAT.

I have been asked many times which I consider to be my own best all-round performance; so, perhaps, I cannot do better than give it here, for the information of my readers.

The best, in my own opinion, was at Nottingham, in 1884, in the match North of England v. Australians. In the first innings I was 10 not out, and in the second innings I made 101 on a very bad wicket, and against some first-class bowling. I have often remarked since, that I did not know how I managed to remain in so long on such a difficult wicket, and with such bowlers as Messrs. Spofforth, Palmer, Boyle, Giffen, and Midwinter arrayed against me. I also took ten wickets for 48 runs. The London papers gave the following complimentary report of my play :—

" For North of England against the Australian Team, at Nottingham [1884], on a sticky wicket, Barlow was batting four hours and a half for his score of 101, and never gave the semblance of a chance; in the first innings he was 10 not out, and his bowling average was ten wickets for 48 runs. Such a performance in a match of this importance, has never been recorded, and a subscription was made and presented to him, along with a few other presents

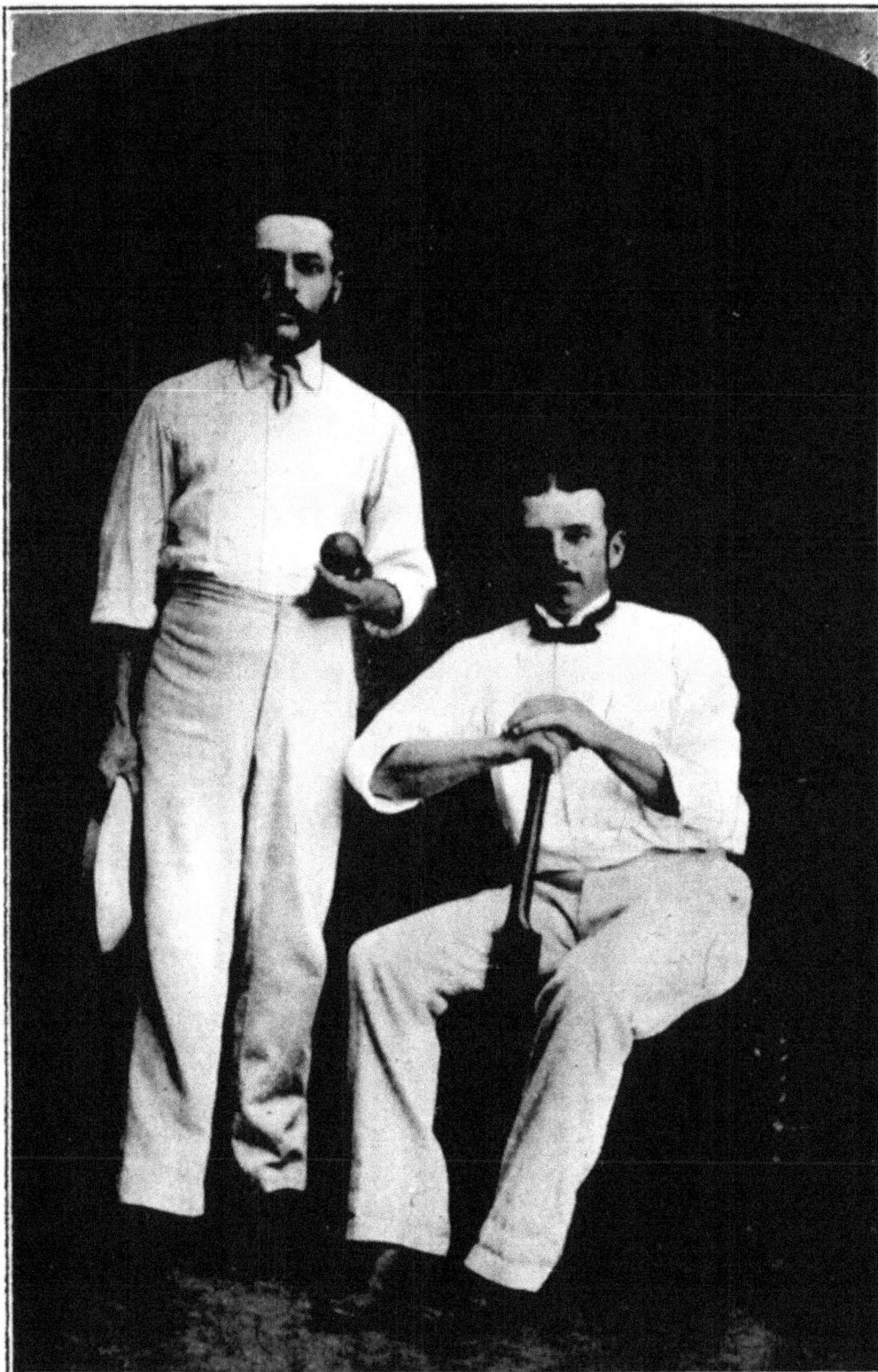

R. G. BARLOW AND A. N. HORNBY, ESQ., 1880.

[*Photo. by C. Voss Bark, Clifton.*]

A. N. HORNBY, ESQ., AND R. G. BARLOW, 1890.

[*Photo. by E. Hawkins & Co , Brighton. Cricket Specialists.*]

(including a silver claret-jug and a diamond breast-pin), whilst he was enthusiastically cheered."

The Australian player, Mr. T. Horan ("Felix"), writing in *The Australasian*, said:—" Throughout the tour we have not seen a finer performance than that of Barlow's, on such a difficult wicket, against splendid bowling, and without giving the slightest chance. His bowling, also, was first-class, and required a good deal of watching."

"VICE VERSA."

The following will serve to show the uncertainty of cricket, and is a remarkable contrast to my innings just given.

At Lord's, in 1887, I was playing for an England Eleven against the M.C.C. Mr. A. E. Stoddart and Shrewsbury commenced batting, and I had to go in at the fall of the first wicket. I put on my pads about 12 o'clock noon, and sat watching the two batsmen named until close on five o'clock in the afternoon, when Mr. Stoddart was out, the total standing at about 300. I then went in to bat. The first ball from Rawlin almost bowled me ; the second ball hit me on the leg, when the bowler appealed for leg before wicket; and the very next ball I was given out leg before wicket. Perhaps the fact that I was accustomed to going in first, or the tension caused by such a long wait, disturbed my equilibrium. But I shall always remember this match. I was waiting close upon five hours, with my pads on, for my innings, and then only had three balls, not one of which I touched.

THE BEST ALL-ROUND COMBINATION

that ever left England was, in my opinion, the Hon. Ivo Bligh's (now Lord Darnley) team, 1881-2. Every man in this team was in his prime, and at his very best ; and eleven out of the twelve who made the journey were each likely to make his hundred at any time, and against any bowling. The team was also really good in fielding, and possessed one of the very best of wicket-keepers in Mr. Tylecote. Then, again, all the bowlers were good batsmen, with the exception of Morley. The following were the players :—

> Hon. Ivo Bligh (captain), Kent.
> E. F. S. Tylecote, Kent.
> A. G. Steel, Lancashire.
> W. W. Read, Surrey.
> C. T. Studd, Middlesex.
> G. B. Studd, Middlesex.

G. F. Vernon, Middlesex.
C. F. H. Leslie, Middlesex.
W. Barnes, Nottinghamshire.
F. Morley, Nottinghamshire.
W. Bates, Yorkshire.
R. G. Barlow, Lancashire.

This team won the rubber in Australia, and " brought back the ashes " to England.

The following is from the *Sportsman*, November, 1903:—
" With regard to the M.C.C. team in Australia, with a couple of celebrated batsmen added, the combination might have been regarded as a representative one, and a famous cricketer with Australian experience told me recently that he considered it inferior only to one previous combination—that under the captaincy of the Hon. Ivo Bligh (now Lord Darnley) in 1882-3. It beat Murdoch's team in two out of the three matches."

Miscellaneous Opinions and Incidents.

TEST MATCH: ENGLAND *v.* AUSTRALIA.

IN answer to the question as to which was my best bowling performance on a good hard wicket, I give the following as being the best. I was bowling for most of the time at one end, the bowlers at the other end being frequently changed. It will be seen that I took seven wickets during the time that the other bowlers only took three wickets amongst them, and this against a very good batting side. The match was played at Old Trafford, Manchester, July 5th, 6th, and 7th, 1886. In the second innings the bowling averages for England were :—

Peate, 46 overs, 25 maidens, 45 runs, 1 wicket.
Lohmann, 5 overs, 3 maidens, 14 runs, 0 wicket.
Steel, 8 overs, 3 maidens, 9 runs, 1 wicket.
Barlow, 52 overs, 34 maidens, 44 runs, 7 wickets.
Ulyett, 6 overs, 5 maidens, 7 runs, 1 wicket.
Grace, 1 over, 0 maiden, 1 run, 0 wicket.

A FEW WORDS FOR AUSTRALIA.

The scoring boards on the Sydney and Melbourne cricket grounds are really first-class. We have nothing in England to compare with them. They have also splendid shower-baths on all the principal Australian cricket grounds. These are most refreshing after a hard day's cricket. I must also say that in all the three cricket trips I made to Australia the behaviour of the crowds was very good, and they gave us some really flattering receptions as we went on the field. We were all well treated and entertained wherever we went, and had many invitations ; in fact, so numerous were they that we had frequently to decline them. We had also free passes to all the theatres and places of amusement, and sometimes boxes were engaged for our team. I am sorry, however, to have to complain about the umpiring in Australia. At some of the matches we played, the decisions were very bad indeed, both for and against us. I have written much more on the subject of umpiring elsewhere.

A CHALLENGE TO AUSTRALIA.

The interest in those early matches in Australia was remarkably keen, and it extended to the players themselves. During the 1881-2 visit a few of the Australian men were in one of the Sydney hotels one night, where a heated discussion on the respective merits of English and Australian cricket took place. Finally, Lillywhite and Selby said that to clinch matters they would find two of their men who would play any couple in Australia, and asked Barlow and Ulyett to back up the challenge, but it was not accepted. Both the players named were then at their best, and it would probably have gone hard with the representatives of the Cornstalks.

CRICKETERS WHO HAVE BOWLED DR. W. G. GRACE.

Following are the names of the bowlers by whom Dr. W. G. Grace (Gloucestershire) has been bowled, 1865-96.

A. Shaw (Nottinghamshire)	21	times.
R. G. Barlow (Lancashire)	14	,,
F. Morley (Nottinghamshire) ...	11	,,
T. Emmett (Yorkshire)	10	,,
A. Hill (Yorkshire)	10	,,
W. Flowers (Nottinghamshire) ...	9	,,
J. Southerton (Surrey)	8	,,
J. C. Shaw (Nottinghamshire) ...	9	,,
E. Peate (Yorkshire)	9	,,
G. A. Lohmann (Surrey)	7	,,
F. R. Spofforth (Australia)	7	,,
C. T. B. Turner (Australia)	7	,,
J. Briggs (Lancashire)	7	,,
J. T. Hearne (Middlesex)	6	,,
A. G. Steel (Lancashire)	6	,,
W. Bates (Yorkshire)...	6	,,
G. E. Palmer (Australia)	6	,,
R. Peel (Yorkshire)	6	,,
G. Wootton (Nottinghamshire) ...	6	,,

A WORD OF ADVICE ABOUT BOOTS.

Many of the present-day bowlers are not so particular as they ought to be with regard to their cricketing boots. I have often noticed this when umpiring. A bowler should wear a good strong pair of boots, having rather thick soles and with suitable spikes, for hard and soft grounds. I may say that I was very careful on this point, and possessed two pairs of cricketing boots—one pair for the hard grounds, with short spikes, and the other pair for soft grounds, with the spikes rather long. Before leaving home for each match, I always saw that my boots were all right for bowling, and also took a few loose spikes with me. Only last season, when umpiring, I overheard some of the players complain about slipping when bowling, owing to their spikes not being right. I am certain no bowler will keep the same good length if he cannot get a good foothold.

"BARLOW'S MATCH."

"In reviewing the games played between the North of England and past Australian teams, two at least call for special mention. That in 1884 took place at Nottingham, and will go down to posterity as Barlow's match. The famous Lancashire 'stone-waller,' then in his prime, scored 10 not out and 101, and took 10 wickets for 48 runs. The second is that famous display in 1888, at Old Trafford, Manchester, when Percy MacDonnell, on a soft wicket, won a grand victory for the Colonists ten minutes before time by hitting 82 out of 86."—*Vide Press.*

A WORD ON "L.B.W."

It is frequently a subject of remark as to how often batsmen at the present day are given out "leg before wicket." When umpiring in the match Leicestershire *v.* Nottinghamshire, 1906, at Leicester, no fewer than six batsmen were given out "lbw." in the Notts first innings—three from each end—which I think is a record of its kind. And last season (1907), at Cheltenham, in the Kent *v.* Gloucestershire match, Moss and I had to give seven of the former team out "lbw." I have frequently seen three or four out from this cause in an innings during the last few years. The only reason I can give for this is, that the batsmen move their feet about much more than formerly, and unconsciously get in front of their wickets.

"NO-BALLS."

Then, as regards the "no-balls," there are far too many bowled at the present time, and many more than formerly. If certain well-known county bowlers whom I could name would take more pains, marking the spot from which to start the run, taking the same length and number of strides each time, they would never bowl "no-balls." A bowler should always bear in mind that "no-balls" might be the means of losing a match for his side. It would, in fact, be even possible for a county to lose the championship owing to the bowlers sending so many "no-balls." In connection with this

I might state that in 1880 and 1881 the Lancashire bowlers did not have a single " no-ball " recorded against them. This achievement has, I believe, never before been alluded to, though it constitutes a unique record in the annals of bowling. The bowlers who did most of the work the two seasons named were Mr. A. G. Steel, A. Watson, G. Nash, and R. G. Barlow. Many of the counties at the present day award marks to their players during the season for good batting and bowling, such marks representing so much talent-money. If marks were also deducted from the bowlers for " no-balls," there would be fewer bowled, I feel sure. I may say I have no sympathy with players who bowl " no-balls," as they can always be avoided by careful bowling.

When umpiring in the Northamptonshire v. South Africans match, at Northampton, last season (1907), I had to " no-ball " Geo. Thompson no fewer than nineteen times, which I should imagine is almost a record. Again, in the Somersetshire v. Worcestershire match, at Worcester, I had to " no-ball " Lewis, the Somerset bowler, seventeen times. Curiously enough, Arnold was twice caught off " no-balls " bowled by Lewis. This is the first occasion in all my experience on which I have seen a batsman caught twice in the same innings from " no-balls."

I ought to add that Thompson never once questioned my decisions in " no-balling " him, and if all cricketers were like him the umpire's lot would be a much easier and happier one. For I regret to say that many cricketers of the present day generally receive the umpires' decisions with a bad grace, frequently disputing and criticising them, thus ignoring the well-known rule that " the decision of the umpire shall be final." I feel sure that many of the county umpires will support me in making this statement, as I speak from a long experience.

EXCITING MATCHES.

Of all the many matches in which I have played, the most exciting, without exception, was the test match England v. Australia, in 1882, at the Oval, when the Australians won by seven runs. I shall never forget this match while I live. The excitement was indescribable, and the scene after the match something to remember for all time.

" Felix," in a recent number of the *Australasian* newspaper of Melbourne, recalls the closing incidents of the memorable test match at the Oval, in 1882, when Australia won by seven runs. As

G

"Felix" is no other than Mr. T. Horan, who represented Australia in that historic match, his recollections will be interesting reading :

"We talk together of exciting matches," writes 'Felix,' "and I mention one in England in 1882, in which the strain, even for the spectators, was so severe, that one onlooker dropped down dead, and another with his teeth gnawed pieces out of the top of his umbrella. That was the match in which for the final half-hour you could have heard a pin drop, while the celebrated batsmen, A. P. Lucas and Alfred Lyttelton, were together, and Spofforth and Boyle bowling at them as they had never bowled before. That was the match in which the last English batsman had to screw his courage to the sticking place by aid of champagne, when one man's lips were ashen grey and his throat so parched that he could hardly speak as he strode by me to the crease ; when the scorer's hand shook so that he wrote Peate's name exactly like 'Geese,' and when, in the wild tumult at the fall of the last wicket, the crowd in one tremendous roar cried 'Bravo, Australia !' with a special cheer for Spofforth, who in that grand final bit of bowling took four wickets for two runs off forty-four balls against the cream of English batsmen. That was a match worth playing in, and I doubt whether there will ever be such another game for prolonged and terribly trying tension. Lest we forget—Australia won that test match by seven runs."

Another very exciting match was the Gentlemen v. Players match, at Lord's, in 1877. When Mr. W. S. Patterson, the last man, joined the late Mr. G. F. Grace, they wanted 46 runs to win. They both played very fine cricket, against some first-class bowling and fielding, and got the required runs, amidst great excitement. Mr. A. J. Webbe made some fine catches in the Players' second innings, and caught six men out.

In my opinion, the Gentlemen's team in this match was the best that was ever got together in Gentlemen v. Players fixtures. The following are the names :—Lord Harris, Dr. W. G. Grace, A. N. Hornby, I. D. Walker, A. P. Lucas, G. F. Grace, Hon. A. Lyttelton, A. J. Webbe, J. M. Cotterill, A. W. Ridley, and W. S. Patterson. A very warm lot, indeed, to bowl at. I can just imagine how they would be on the present-day wickets.

Four other matches in which I played, and which finished amidst great excitement, were :—

1. Gentlemen v. Players, in 1883, at the Oval, when the late E. Peate bowled Mr. H. Rotherham, and the match ended in a tie.

2. Gentlemen v. Players, at Brighton, in 1886, for J. Lillywhite's benefit. At the close of the first innings, the score stood at 204 for each side, and at the finish the Players won the match by the extremely narrow margin of one run, the scores for the second

A VIEW OF THE FAMOUS CRICKET GROUND AT SYDNEY, AUSTRALIA,
Which, in the Author's opinion, is the finest and best appointed in the world. [Photo. by Kerry, Sydney.]

innings being—Players, 112; Gentlemen, 111. The last batsman, Mr. A. Appleby, was caught and bowled by A. Shaw; and a brilliant catch it was—one-handed, the bowler having to jump out to reach the ball.

3. Another exciting match, and one which I shall always remember, was Lancashire v. Yorkshire, at Manchester, in 1875. Lancashire required 146 to win in the last innings, and Mr. A. N. Hornby and myself got the runs without the loss of a wicket. The crowd signified their approval by collecting and presenting me with about £10, and several other presents.

4. The last exciting match which I shall mention was played at Sydney, Australia, in 1883—the Hon. Ivo Bligh's (now Lord Darnley) English Team v. Murdoch's Australian Team. This was a Test match, and the one which decided the rubber. On the fourth and last day of the match the Australians required 152 runs to win. They only made 83, so the English team won by 69 runs. My bowling average in this last innings was as follows : 34 overs, 20 maidens, 40 runs, and seven wickets. Some of the spectators carried me shoulder-high, and were so demonstrative that they almost pulled me limb from limb. A collection of over £20 was made for and presented to me, along with a beautiful silver cup and several other articles, for this bowling performance.

SOME CLEVER CATCHES.

I must also place on record a few remarkable catches which it has been my good fortune to witness. The finest and most marvellous of all, and one which will never be forgotten by those who saw it, was made by the late George Ulyett (Yorkshire), in the match England v. Australia, at Lord's, in 1884, when he caught and bowled Mr. G. J. Bonnor, the big hitter. The ball came from the batsman, with the speed of a shot from a gun, straight into the hands of the bowler, which were forced backward over his shoulder with the impetus of the ball. Had the ball struck a vital part, it must have meant certain death, and it would have shattered any bone which had happened to get in its way. Ulyett afterwards remarked to me that this catch was as much due to good luck as to skill ; he had just time to see the ball coming, and threw up his hands, with the result named.

A second wonderful catch was made at Leicester, some years ago, when Leicestershire was playing Hampshire. The catch was made by one of the Hampshire gentlemen, Mr. Raikes, who ran a considerable distance at top speed, and caught the ball low down, close to the ground, at long-off and near the boundary. The on-lookers and the batsman (Mr. De Trafford) quite thought that this was a boundary hit for four. For this feat Mr. Raikes received an ovation lasting several minutes.

Yet another sensational catch was made by Mr. J. Douglas, of the Middlesex team, in a match on the Leeds ground, Yorkshire v. Middlesex. He will, doubtless, remember to this day the outburst of applause which greeted this feat. The ball was a big drive, made by Mr. F. S. Jackson, towards long-on, and it was necessary for Mr. Douglas, who was fielding at long-off, to run at full speed for a distance of some 40 or 50 yards, along by the boundary. He made the catch while running, and then tumbled head-over-heels on to the asphalte outside the boundary, still holding on to the ball.

BRILLIANT FIELDING AND CATCHING BY MR. C. C. PAGE.

At the Middlesex v. Essex match, at Lord's, last season (1907), at which I was umpiring, Mr. Page made three remarkable and extraordinary catches in different positions of the field, and all within a short time of each other. In fact, throughout this innings Mr. Page's fielding and catching were most brilliant. The *Sportsman* of June 6th, 1907, gave the following report of this feat :—" The outstanding feature of yesterday's play was some remarkably fine catching by the old Malvernian, C. C. Page. It appeared as if fate —or, shall we say, the home captain's intelligent anticipation—had willed it that this brilliant fieldsman should be always in the right place ; for, by a peculiar combination of circumstances, he made his four catches from three positions—two at 'short-leg," one at 'long-off,' and another at 'deep-square-leg.' The first was tolerably easy, but the last three were brilliant in the extreme, the remarkable run that he made from 'short-leg' to secure the ball which disposed of Freeman causing much surprise. When he started it appeared impossible, yet, to the surprise of all, he just got beneath the ball— about 25 yards from his original position—and made the catch. Those in the 'long-field' and at 'deep-square-leg' were made when the ball was travelling very fast, the leather on both occasions being taken when it had almost reached the ground."

I might add that my fellow umpire and myself measured the distance covered by Mr. Page when making the catch above referred to, which we found to be about 40 yards.

MY "RIVER CATCH."

My own best catch was at Saltaire, in 1874 or 1875. Saltaire was playing a club called, I think, Bradford Albion. I was fielding at "long-on," and the batsman, a great hitter, made a very big drive. I ran at my utmost speed for thirty or forty yards, and caught the ball, at full stretch, just inside the boundary. I was unable to stop myself for some yards, and ran on to the asphalte outside the boundary, almost falling over into the River Irwell, which runs by one side of the cricket ground in Saltaire Park. For some years afterwards they called this " Barlow's river catch."

EXCITING MATCHES WHEN UMPIRING.

I have umpired at some very exciting matches in my time, the following four, I think, being especially worthy of mention. The first was at Huddersfield, some few years back, when Yorkshire was playing Essex. I had to give the last Yorkshire batsman out leg before wicket, and Essex won by the exceedingly narrow margin of one run.

A second exciting match was at Leyton—Essex v. Sussex—in 1899, when the former county won by one wicket. I remember the Sussex bowler, Cox, appealing against Young, the last batsman, for leg before wicket. The bowler happened to get in my way, preventing me from seeing the ball-pitch, so, of course, I was bound to give the batsman " not out."

Another very fine and exciting match was at Dewsbury, in 1906—Yorkshire v. Notts. Yorkshire only wanted 94 to win, but Hallam and Wass bowled splendidly, and Notts won by about 20 runs. Mr. A. O. Jones played a magnificent innings of 88 on a queer pitch, which had been spoiled by the rain overnight. It was rather singular that Haigh, who commenced the bowling to Mr. Jones, should bowl him the very first ball sent down, but I had to " no ball" him, which was " hard lines," as it was a beautiful ball and, to my mind, seemed to beat Mr. Jones " all the way." Such is the game of cricket.

There was another very exciting match, which took place at Blackpool in 1905, between Lancashire and An England Eleven, The latter declared their innings closed with four wickets in hand. leaving the County 169 to win. In the last over of the day the scores were level, but as Cook was caught in endeavouring to make the winning hit, the game ended in a draw, Lancashire, with three wickets in hand, requiring one run to win. The fielding of Mr. Lawton (Derbyshire) in this match was very fine indeed.

A BATSMAN v. BOWLER INCIDENT.

I was bowling in a Lancashire v. Oxford University match, at Oxford, some years ago, when I noticed the batsman going out of his ground before the ball had left my hand. Pilling was keeping wicket, and I called his attention to this, and told him that I should put the wicket down if the batsman repeated the proceeding in the next over. Sure enough, it all "came off," and the batsman was given "out." Some people would consider the above to have been rather sharp practice on my part, but I fail to see it in this light; it is in strict accordance with the rules of the game, and no batsman should try to gain an unfair advantage by leaving his crease before the ball is bowled. I afterwards told the batsman in question that I regretted having to put him out in this way; but he took it in good part, saying that I was quite right, and that the experience had taught him a lesson for the future.

COUNTY CRICKET GROUNDS : PAST AND PRESENT.

A few words about the county cricket grounds of to-day and thirty years ago. My opinion is the same as that of many other old cricketers, viz., that they are much better at the present day than formerly; still, I played on a few of these grounds in the early Eighties which were almost as good then as they are now. I always did prefer a good sporting wicket, and I think that cricket on this class of wicket is a much better game, and creates more interest and excitement for both players and spectators. Moreover, it brings out all the batsman's good qualities, as the ball requires more careful watching and timing. Then, again, there would not be so many drawn matches.

On the present-day first-class wickets I think that the batsman has too great an advantage over the bowler, whereas on the kind of wicket I have just referred to, bowler and batsman would be more on an equal footing, as was the case some years ago. I never believed in artificial wickets, and I know they are not popular. If there is an element of risk in playing on a wicket not thoroughly prepared, that is the bowler's opportunity, and it is part of the game for him to take advantage of it.

FAST AND SLOW RUN-GETTERS.

Much has been said and written of late about brightening cricket, and there is no one who likes to see a fine free batsman better than myself. Every batsman, however, cannot be a free hitter; there always were, and always will be, three different kinds of batsmen—fast, moderately fast, and slow run-getters—just as there are fast, medium, and slow bowlers; and I think it is better that there should be a little variety in our national game.

To illustrate my meaning, I may recount that some years ago, when Lancashire was playing Notts, at Nottingham, Mr. Hornby didn't "come off" in either innings, through "having a go" at the ball a little too soon, as cricketers term it. We lost this match, and Mr. Hornby afterwards said to me: "Oh, Barlow, I wish I had some of your patience!" I replied: "Yes, Mr. Hornby, and I also wish I had some of your hitting powers." I remember, too, that on one occasion Dr. W. G. Grace, in speaking of Mr. Hornby, said that if he only had a little more patience, when batting, he would get more runs in a season than any batsman who ever played.

NIMBLENESS.

For nimbleness, and jumping out to the ball when batting, I have never seen any batsmen to equal Messrs. A. N. Hornby and A. G. Steel (Lancashire). It was a real treat to watch them playing to medium or slow bowling. I can just imagine what runs they would get on these present-day plumb wickets, and how they would "go for" that off-side bowling. Mr. V. Trumper (Australia) is another batsman of this kind.

HARD-HITTING FIRM-FOOTED MEN.

The hardest hitters amongst what are called firm-footed batsmen, or batsmen who stand firmly in one position, whom I ever saw were Messrs. H. H. Massie, the late P. S. McDonnell, G. J. Bonner, and J. J. Lyons (Australia), and Messrs. G. L. Jessop (Gloucestershire), J. F. Leese (Lancashire), and E. Hayes (Surrey).

A FEAT IN COUNTY CRICKET.

In the Lancashire v. Notts match, at Nottingham, July 6th, 7th, and 8th, 1882, I carried my bat right through the second innings for five runs. Again, in the return match, at Aigburth, near Liverpool, a few days later—July 21st, 22nd, and 23rd—I carried my bat through the first innings, this time for 44 runs out of a total of 93. When we were four wickets down in the last-named innings, Selby, one of the Notts players, came to me and said, "Barlow, I'll take twenty shillings to one that you'll go through the innings again." I replied, "All right, I'll lay you twenty to one that this time I don't."

I added that I hoped to lose the bet, as I should like to repeat the feat. I lost the bet to my satisfaction. In the second innings of this match Selby again came to me when we had lost four wickets and offered me the same bet, which I took. This time, however, I only managed to carry my bat past the seventh wicket, being then unfortunately run out by Flowers, who threw the wicket down from cover-point after I had made 49 runs. But for this, I should most probably have carried my bat out in three consecutive innings, which would have been an extraordinary performance, as I had to face the bowling of such experts as Shaw, Morley, Flowers, Barnes, and Mills. I might state, in connection with the afore-named matches, that the wickets both at Nottingham and Liverpool were greatly in the bowlers' favour, as is proved by the low scores for each side in both matches.

ON "STONE-WALL" BATTING.

As it is at times the fashion amongst certain would-be critics of the game to depreciate what is commonly known as "stone-wall" batting, I should, as an old "stone-waller," like to make a few remarks with respect to this kind of play. Though I don't like to see too much slow play, especially on the plumb wicket of the present day, yet there are occasions on which it cannot be avoided ; as, for instance, when the wicket is playing queerly, and at the same time the bowlers are keeping a good length, and are bowling on the wicket. Then, again, it is not the lot of every batsman to be a free bat. My opinion now is the same as it was thirty years ago, viz., that there should be at least one steady, defensive batsman, or "stone-waller," in every team.

The following, which is an extract from the chapter on R. G. Barlow in "Old Ebor's" book on "Old English Cricketers," expresses my sentiments in a very concise manner :—

"Richard Barlow on the ethics of 'stone-walling' might form a chapter to itself, but what the famous 'stone-waller' has to say on the matter may appropriately come in here. Asked first to explain how he received the title of 'stone-waller,' Barlow replies :—

"'I think it may be traced to the late W. Barnes, of Nottingham. It was in the match with Notts, in 1882, when I kept at the wicket about two hours for five runs. This innings was played on a very sticky wicket. After our innings was over, Barnes came up and remarked that bowling at me was like bowling at a stone wall. From that time I was always named a "stone-waller."

" ' But, you ask, what was the reason of that extraordinary cricket ? Simply this : the wicket was in the bowler's favour, and Mr. Hornby told me to " stick." So I stuck. I tried to keep Alf. Shaw from mischief, whilst our other fellows got the runs. This ability to " stick " has, I may venture to say, been repeatedly beneficial to our side. Louis Hall, Scotton, and I were often run down by press and public for " stone-walling "; but those who criticised did not seem to understand that we were playing for our side, and that the " stone-walling " they did not like, helped to win our sides many matches. Further, they did not know that—in my case, at least—I was very often acting strictly on my captain's orders.

" ' There is one match which I remember very well to which this remark applies. It was Murdoch's Australian team v. Lancashire, played at Old Trafford on June 1st, 2nd, and 3rd, 1882. We had to follow on, 141 runs behind, and Mr. Hornby, on going in a second time, said to me, " Barlow, I should like to make this a good match. You play the ' old man's game.' " I replied, " All right, sir ; I'll bat Spofforth as much as I possibly can ; you get the runs at the other end." Well, unfortunately Mr. Hornby was a victim to Mr. Spofforth at six, but by the aid of the " old man's game " I batted through the innings, and carried out my bat for a score of 66 in a total of 269. For that performance £15 was collected and presented to me, and I also had a bat given to me by an admirer of the innings. We lost the game by four wickets, but Mr. Hornby had his wish in that we made it into a good match.

" ' Then take another match. On September 1st, 1884, the North of England played the Australians at Nottingham, and the North were out for 91 in the first innings, and the Australians scored 100. When I went in a second time, the " old man's game " enabled me to score 101, and Flowers (who made 90) and I put on 150 for the sixth wicket. Result : the North won by 170. So much for the utility of the " old man's game." I always consider that match contained the best performance of my career, for not only did I get the century on a sticky wicket, but I captured 10 wickets for 48 runs. The score was presented to me on satin, £16 was collected and given to me, and I had several other presents. Among these was a diamond breast-pin from a stranger who had come over 100 miles to see the match, and who was so delighted with it that he insisted upon me accompanying him to a jeweller's shop that he might make me a present.

"'Singular to state, two years afterwards—June 21st, 22nd, and 23rd, 1886—playing again at Trent Bridge, Nottingham, for the Players of England against the Australians, Flowers and I added 172 for the ninth wicket, I making 113, and Flowers this time missed the century by 7. In each instance I had worn the bowling down with the "old man's game," and Flowers reaped the benefit as well as myself. It will be seen, therefore, that "stone-walling" has its uses.

"'I will give two more instances of the value of the so-called "stone-wall" tactics. I think they also show that "stone-walling" and nerve are not unassociated. In the England v. Australia match at Lord's, in 1884, Lord Harris came to the players' tent and said to me, "Barlow, play your old defensive game; keep your end up; I should like to win this match." "All right, my lord," was my rejoinder. I went in when Mr. A. G. Steel, who was playing brilliant cricket (he made 148), needed a steady partner. Before I left, the score had been increased by over 100 runs, the greater portion of which were from the brilliant Lancashire amateur's bat.

"'The other occasion was England v. Australia, at Old Trafford, on July 7th, 1886. The wicket was difficult in the last innings, and England needed 106 to win, and lost Dr. W. G. Grace, Shrewsbury, and Mr. W. W. Read for 24 runs. Mr. Steel, our captain, came to me and wanted me to go in earlier than he had arranged, saying, "For goodness' sake, Barlow, stop this rot; go in next!" I went in, made 30, and Mr. Steel, coming in afterwards, finished off the work, and we won by four wickets. These cases show that the "old man's game" pays your side, that it requires some nerve, and that the public are not generous when they growl at the so-called slow play.

"'But I was not such a dreadfully slow scorer after all, even if I did make something like a record in scoring five runs at Nottingham in about two hours. I can produce many instances in which I scored as fast as the recognized hitters of the day. But a few will suffice. Take Lancashire v. Surrey, in 1873, 40 out of 95 from the bat; 56 out of 114 against Kent, in 1877; 35 out of 99, and through the innings against Shaw, Morley, Mycroft, and G. G. Hearne, in 1878; 52 not out, out of 105, at Old Trafford, in 1886—do these figures show slow play? Then the first time I met Shaw and Morley, at Nottingham, in May, 1876, I played through the innings for 34. That is a feat that required some doing against those bowlers, and they, at least, would not call it either slow play or "stone-walling."'

" From all of which the reader will be justified in opining that Barlow is anxious it should be made known " the devil is not as black as he is painted."

" When not called upon to play the 'old man's game,' Barlow could hit. Strange though it may seem, there is a record of his once having hit three fours in one over at Lord's. That was in the course of an innings of 117 in 1884, which he made in three hours, a rate of scoring that no one could cavil at. In the same year, against Cheshire, at Stockport, he hit the ball out of the cricket enclosure and into a potato field, where it was lost! Even fieldsmen have found he could hit so hard that they were compelled to retire to a respectful distance for safety."

AN ENGLAND ELEVEN v. DERBYSHIRE.

A NEWSPAPER CORRESPONDENT'S PROTEST.

" Sir,—In your report of this match, R. G. Barlow at Derby comes in for some detracting remarks from your reporter. He is described as dismissed after having played in 'tedious' style for 63. Now a score made up of one 5, four 4's, seven 3's, three 2's, etc., against the crack bowling of Derbyshire, such as W. Mycroft, G. Hay, J. Platts, and J. Richardson, must have been, to my mind, very smart cricket indeed, and on a wicket which was not one of the best. The report seems at variance with that given by the *Sportsman* (an authority, I presume), wherein his innings is described as made up of brilliant cricket, and he also bowled 5 overs, 2 maidens, 3 runs, 3 wickets. The remarks alluded to would scarcely call for comment, but it is not fair criticism. There appears to be an aversion to Barlow in some quarters (probably because he does not play for Derbyshire). No doubt his batting on some occasions is too patient for those who do not understand cricket, but in this innings he appears to have scored about twice as fast as anyone else. Many of our best bowlers do not like his stubbornness at times, though *Lillywhite's Cricket Guide* says, in commending his play, 'Give us more Barlows instead of second-rate sloggers,' or what may be termed hitting without aim or object.—Yours truly,

"*July 4th, 1878.*"   "Y. X.

In 1904, at the dinner given by the Lancashire County C. C. in honour of winning the county championship, Mr. A. G. Steel, speaking of giants of the past, said, "He might mention old Richard Barlow, who was ever ready to run when called upon. A courageous and grand cricketer he was. He always knew that

The above Timepiece was presented to the Author by a few Manchester friends for first batting and bowling averages for Lancashire in 1882.

BATTING AVERAGE: Matches, 20; innings, 36; runs, 856; most in an innings, 68; times not out, 8. Average, 30.16.

BOWLING AVERAGE: Overs, 670; Maidens, 368; runs, 729; wickets, 73. Average, 9.68.

he could bowl any batsman out, and was also convinced that no bowler could get him out.   He was a giant of the past."

The late Mr. C. W. Alcock, in his well-known book, " Famous Cricketers and Cricket Grounds," says :—"An all-round cricketer, with few superiors, at his best Barlow was one of the mainstays of the Lancashire Eleven, both in batting and bowling, for over fifteen years.   Going in first with Mr. A. N. Hornby, his defensive style was a complete contrast to the dashing and vigorous cricket of the amateur. No eleven of Players for some years would have been complete without him, and at his best he would have been eligible for a representative side of England.   He also did good service for more than one English team in Australia.   With a stubborn defence, he was at all times a difficult batsman to get out.   Besides being an excellent field at point, he was also a left-handed bowler (rather over medium pace) of great merit, quite one of the best of his time."

My first two matches for the Players against the Gentlemen were—first, in 1876, at the Oval, June 29th and 30th and July 1st, when I made 27 and 33 ; and second, at the Prince's Ground, London, July 6th, 7th, and 8th, when my scores were 6 and not out 45, out of a total of 134.   In this last innings I went in at the fall of the first wicket and carried my bat out.   I did not bowl in these two matches.

It is very surprising to me to find what a large number of batsmen there are at the present day who show bad judgment in calling for and timing their runs.   The early Australian teams had this same fault, but the later teams show a decided improvement in this respect.   The South Africans were very much better in judging their runs, etc., this last season than in 1904.

A HORNBY AND BARLOW COMPARISON.

Mr. E. H. D. Sewell, in the St. James's Gazette, says :—" It would be difficult to name two professionals of the day more likely and more able to avail themselves of every single run obtainable than Knight and Braund.   Both are splendid between wickets, and together might bear comparison favourably with Hornby and Barlow, S. M. J. Woods and Gregor McGregor, in their prime, to say nothing of Trumper and Duff."

MY FAVOURITE GROUNDS.

I have sometimes been asked which grounds I liked best to play on.   Every cricketer has his favourites.   In my opinion, the best-appointed cricket ground in the world is the Sydney ground, Australia, and this and the grounds at Old Trafford (Manchester), and Trent Bridge (Nottingham), were always my favourite grounds for playing on.

ENGLAND *v.* AUSTRALIA.

In his cricket reminiscences of past conflicts, George Giffen, the Australian cricketer, says : " The strongest side which, in my humble judgment, has ever represented England was the following magnificent eleven, 1884 :—Lord Harris, the Hon. Alfred Lyttelton, Dr. W. G. Grace, A. G. Steel, W. W. Read, Barlow, Barnes, Shrewsbury, Peate, Ulyett, and Scotton."

I have often been asked this last few years which I considered the best Australian team that ever came to England. I must say, without a doubt, the best all-round teams were those of 1882 and 1884, viz., 1882 : Messrs. W. L. Murdoch (captain), G. Giffen, P. S. M'Donnell, G. E. Palmer, T. Horan, H. F. Boyle, F. R. Spofforth, H. H. Massie, A. C. Bannerman, G. J. Bonnor, J. M. Blackham, S. P. Jones, and T. W. Garrett. 1884 : Messrs. W. L. Murdoch (captain), G. Giffen, P. S. M'Donnell, G. E. Palmer, H. F. Boyle, F. R. Spofforth, H. J. H. Scott, A. C. Bannerman, W. Midwinter, G. J. Bonnor, J. M. Blackham, W. H. Cooper, and G. Alexander. I think Australia will be a long time before she can send another team to equal either of them.

HANDSOMEST CRICKETERS.

The two handsomest cricketers whom I ever saw were Messrs. C. F. Buller (Middlesex), and G. Freeman (Yorkshire). R. Daft (Notts) was another fine, lithe, healthy-looking man.

THE ADVENTURE OF A STUMP.

I was umpiring at Scarborough last September (1907), in the match Mr. C. I. Thornton's England Eleven *v.* South Africans, when Mr. Faulkner bowled Haigh, the ball breaking the middle stump clean in two. Strange to say, there was no other stump available on the ground, and as it was nearing the tea interval, play was suspended for tea a little earlier than usual. Meanwhile, Mr. R. W. Frank and I procured a few yards of twine and repaired the stump as well as we could, and a messenger was despatched to the town to buy a new set of stumps. The break in the play thus caused—including the tea interval—was of nearly half-an-hour's duration. In all my experience I have never seen or heard of an accident like this in first-class cricket. I am also reminded of a similar incident which occurred at a school match in Bolton Park in 1864. We lost the ball after we had been playing only a short time, and as it was the only ball we had with us, the game had to be abandoned.

STRUDWICK AND PILLING.

The best wicket-keeping that I saw last season (1907) was that of Strudwick, of Surrey, in the match at the Oval—Surrey v. Leicestershire. It was a treat to see him stand behind the wicket, and I remarked to his captain, Lord Dalmeny, that Strudwick was a marvel for his inches. He reminded me of the late R. Pilling, who, in my opinion, was the prince of wicket-keepers.

A FINE BATTING DISPLAY.

When umpiring in the Surrey v. Middlesex match at the Oval last season (1907), Hayes, of Surrey, played a really fine and dashing innings of 202. His hitting all around the wicket was magnificent, against some first-class bowling and fielding. I greatly enjoyed seeing this batting display, which was worth going miles to witness. This innings made me think of the brilliant batting of Mr. A. N. Hornby in his best days.

A TRIBUTE TO A. ECCLES.

It will be interesting to my readers to learn that I have been the recipient of many presents for coaching. One especially that I have always valued highly and still wear is a fine diamond ring which was given me by Mr. J. Eccles, of Myerscough Hall, Brock, near Preston, for coaching his son, Mr. A. Eccles, who has since played many fine innings for Lancashire. He made 109 in the Oxford v. Cambridge match in 1898, and here is a tribute to Eccles' batting from the London Press. The *Daily Telegraph* says:—
" Judging from the splendid innings he played on Saturday, we should take it that the best has not yet been seen of Mr. A. Eccles in the Lancashire Eleven. In facing Albert Trott, Mead, Young, and Alec Hearne, on a wicket that was beginning to recover from Thursday's drenching rain, he was put to a very severe test, out of which he came triumphantly. Going in first wicket down, he scored 51 not out, in a hundred minutes. As regards both hitting and defence, his innings was quite a model of how to deal with first-class bowling on a slow wicket. Up to Saturday, the best innings Eccles has ever played in London, or probably anywhere

else, was his memorable 109 in the Oxford and Cambridge match of 1898. During his early days at Oxford, Eccles had the advantage of being coached by Barlow, and that famous professional—a first-rate judge of the game, as well as a great player—confidently predicted that he would be a successful batsman."

THE BEST 1907 INNINGS.

The best innings I saw played last season (1907) was that of Mr. P. F. Warner, in the Middlesex v. Notts match, at Nottingham. He went in first, and carried his bat through the innings for 65 runs out of a total of 120 runs from the bat. This was on a bad wicket —worse still after lunch—which greatly favoured the bowling of Wass, Hallam, and J. Gunn.

Mr. Warner played a perfect defensive game against some really first-class bowling on a sticky wicket, and reminded me very forcibly of the late Arthur Shrewsbury, whom I always considered to be the finest batsman who ever lived, on bowlers' wickets of this class.

After the close of Mr. Warner's innings, I was one of those who went to him and complimented him upon his very fine performance on a really difficult wicket.

JESSOP THE MARVELLOUS.

For hitting any kind of bowling, and for rapid scoring, I have never seen any batsman to equal Mr. G. L. Jessop (Gloucestershire). I remember when umpiring at Harrogate—Yorkshire v. Gloucestershire match—last season (1907), I saw Mr. Jessop make 89 in a very short time against some really first-class bowling. In one over he made 20 off Hirst's bowling. When the over was finished, Hirst turned to me with the remark: " Well, he is a regular d——l; the better I bowl, the better he hits 'em !" and he asked me how I should have bowled at him in my best days. I replied that " I would give it up."

This reminds me of a similar remark which the late Tom Emmett, the famous Yorkshire bowler, once made to me in a Gentlemen v. Players match, in the early Eighties. Tom was bowling to Dr. W. G. Grace, who looked like making a big score; in one over he hit Tom for several 4's from good-length balls. The latter came to me at mid-off, and said: " I wish that 'long-shanks' was out; he's a regular d——l! the better I place 'em, the better he paces 'em."

H

Another wonderful innings by Mr. Jessop was at Nottingham, in 1904, when I was umpiring there in the Notts v. Gloucestershire match. He made 206 in 110 minutes, which so delighted the spectators that they went almost wild. It was a treat to see.

There is only one "Jessop" for his style of batting, the nearest approach to him, in my opinion, being Dr. E. M. Grace, in the old days.

I consider that the most extraordinary innings for quick scoring that was ever played against first-class bowling was at Hastings, at the Gentlemen of the South v. Players of the South match, on September 2nd, 3rd, and 4th of last year (1907), when Mr. Jessop made 191 runs out of 234 in 90 minutes. He hit five 6's and thirty 4's, giving only one chance—a difficult one—when his score was 159.

ADVICE TO BOWLERS.

As I travel about from place to place during the cricketing season, I find that many county cricketers—especially bowlers—think they are much better informed on the game than the old school of players. I found that Attewell, the old Notts bowler, had also noticed this, when we were chatting together at one of the matches at which we were umpiring last season (1907). Some there are, however, among them who will take a little good advice when it is offered. A case in point occurred last season, when I was umpiring in one of the county matches. As the bowler had been bowling for some time without taking a wicket, I ventured to remark to him that he was bowling a little too fast, as the wicket was rather soft, and that if he would bowl a trifle slower he would get more spin on the ball, which would accordingly turn more. He took my advice, with the result that, after a few more overs, the wickets began to fall in regular succession. Since then he has thanked me on several occasions for my timely advice.

Many bowlers do not adapt their bowling to the state of the pitch or wicket, though this should be their first consideration. A. Shaw (Notts) and Watson (the old Lancashire bowler) were two of the best I ever saw or knew for quickly finding out the pace of the wicket. A few of the present-day bowlers who, when bowling, use their heads as much as their arms are: Rhodes and Haigh, Yorkshire; Dennett, Gloucestershire; Hallam, Notts; Blythe, Kent; Trott, Hearne, and Tarrant, Middlesex; Mead, Essex; Hargreaves,

Warwickshire; Thompson, Northamptonshire; Arnold, Worcestershire; J. N. Crawford, Surrey; and C. M. Wells, Middlesex. Alec Hearne, of Kent, was a fine head bowler; also W. Attewell, of Notts.

A FIELDER'S GOOD SHOT.

A very curious, if not an unique, incident occurred during the Surrey *v.* Middlesex match at which I was umpiring last season. Mr. J. N. Crawford and Hayes were batting, when the ball was hit to long-on. Mr. C. C. Page smartly fielded it, and threw it back with such force that the middle stump of the bowler's wicket was knocked out of the ground. The ball then travelled across to the batsman's wicket and knocked the leg stump down. Each batsman had, however, just got home in his crease at each end. Brown, my fellow-umpire, and some of the Middlesex team, like myself, said that they had never before seen such a case, and, in my opinion, they never will again.

WAS HE OUT?—A DIVERSITY OF OPINION.

It was very remarkable—when J. Iremonger left the wicket, in the Notts *v.* Surrey match at Nottingham last Whit-Monday (1907), when I was umpiring there—to hear the many different opinions expressed as to how he was out. Mr. Knox was bowling to Iremonger when the off-bail fell to the ground at the exact moment that the ball passed the stumps. Iremonger lifted his bat, but did not play at the ball, and, seeing the bail drop, he walked away to the pavilion without saying a word. Mr. Knox, the bowler, could not tell what had happened; neither could Mr. Jones, who was batting at the other end. Strudwick, the wicket-keeper, who was standing back, thought the ball might have just grazed the off-stump, but could not be certain about it. Hayes, at short-slip, was of the opinion that the ball hit the off-stump. Holland, fielding at second-slip, said the ball was near the wicket but did not touch it. Lees, at mid-off, said the ball was several inches from the wicket. Lord Dalmeny, fielding at point, believed that Iremonger hit his wicket, though my opinion, from short-leg, was that he did not do so. In short, it seemed a perfect mystery to us all. A possible explanation was, however, forthcoming shortly afterwards, when John Gunn and I were discussing the case at the wicket whilst waiting for a fresh man to come in. Happening to glance down at the wicket, we both saw, to our great surprise, the same bail drop off again, though no one was near the wicket, neither was there any wind blowing at the time. My own opinion is that the stumps were rather too close together at the top, and were compressing the bail too tightly, which had thus been jerked off. Had Iremonger only had the presence of mind to appeal, there is no doubt that he would have been given " not out."

A CAUTION TO BATSMEN.

I consider it to be a great mistake for a batsman, when he has returned from the wicket, to pass remarks to the other players who have still to bat, such as, that the wicket is playing badly, that the bowlers are making the ball turn, etc., as in many instances it disheartens them, especially in the case of young players.

I remember umpiring in one of the county matches a few years ago at which one of the first batsmen was "caught" early in his innings. Just after lunch I overheard him telling the other players who had to follow that the wicket was playing badly, and that it was impossible to make many runs. I was much surprised to hear this, as the wicket was not half so bad as he was making it out to be. In fact, in my batting days, I should have called it a fairly good wicket ; and yet I never saw a worse exhibition of batting from a county team as in this match.

GOOD ALL-ROUND CRICKET.

The all-round performance of George Hirst (Yorkshire) in 1906 was extraordinary, when he created a record of 2,385 runs and 208 wickets. A more plucky and hard-working cricketer never went on the field. The same might also be said of Wilfred Rhodes, of the same county. I have at the present time a high opinion of F. A. Tarrant, the Australian and Middlesex player. His all-round cricket for last year (1907) was very fine indeed, when he made 1,552 runs and took 183 wickets. He is also a smart fielder at slip, and from his own bowling. It is rather remarkable that Hirst never did anything very great with the ball in the test matches.

THE SOUTH AFRICAN CRICKETERS OF 1907.

I had the pleasure of umpiring in three of the matches of the South African team of last season, and can speak of them as an eye-witness. Being at the wickets, I could note their action and what the bowlers were making the ball do. It is remarkable how much they have improved since their visit here in 1904, and England will have to look to her laurels to win the rubber the next time they visit us, which I hope will be in 1910. They are gentlemen and

SOUTH AFRICAN AND NORTHAMPTONSHIRE TEAMS, 1907.

TOP ROW: *J. J. Kotze, L. Bullimer (Scorer), *S. D. Snooke, G. A. T. Vials, *Rev. D. C. Robinson, C. J. T. Pool, and *C. Allsop (Manager).
CENTRE: Attewell (Umpire), *W. A. Shalders, Buswell, *G. A. Faulkner, Wells, *J. H. Sinclair, East, *A. D. Nourse, Thompson, Cox,
Percy W. Dale (Hon. Organising Secretary), and Barlow (Umpire).
BOTTOM ROW: *L. J. Tancred, S. G. Smith, *G. C. White, W. H. Kingston, *P. W. Sherwell (Captain), E. M. Crosse (Captain), *R. O. Schwarz,
T. E. Manning, *H. E. Smith, L. T. Driffield. (or John Seymour)

*South Africans.   [Reproduced from a Photo. by S. H. Greenway, Northampton, the recognised Sports Photographer for the County.]

good sportsmen. I never heard an objectionable expression from any of them either in 1904 or 1907, and they played together in perfect harmony and good fellowship. I only wish I could make the same remark with regard to a few other teams whose names I could mention. The South Africans have a capable captain and a good judge of the game in Mr. P. W. Sherwell, who is also one of the best of wicket-keepers. They are a good all-round team, with no tail-end, and their bowling was an eye-opener. Mr. R. O. Schwarz is a first-class bowler, and one who uses his head very much. His action at the wicket suggests that the ball will break from leg to the off, but it comes in the contrary direction, which is very puzzling to the batsman, and often beats him. Those who saw how Mr. Schwarz "stuck up" the Yorkshire team at Bradford last July (1907) will bear me out in this. Some of the Tykes might never have held a bat before.

On the slow wickets which we had last season (1907) the bowling of the South Africans was really magnificent. Messrs. Schwarz, Vogler, White, and Faulkner all bowl with a leg-break action, and make the ball come in from the off at a very good pace from the pitch; at the same time keeping a fine length.

In my opinion, Messrs. Schwarz and Vogler were the best pair of bowlers in England last season; Hallam and Wass, of Notts, following close behind.

Should the South African cricketers improve in their batting in the near future, which I have no doubt they will, both England and Australia will have a most difficult task before them to retain their present position.

STRATEGIC BOWLING.

An English bowler who also used to put much strategy into his bowling was to be found in Mr. B. J. T. Bosanquet, of Middlesex. I saw him when umpiring at the Middlesex v. Notts match at Nottingham in 1903. I have stood behind some first-class bowling in my time, but never saw such puzzling balls sent down as those bowled by Messrs. Schwarz and Bosanquet in the two matches named. They each kept a beautiful length, and made the ball almost talk. Their bowling would have dismissed the finest batting team ever got together, for very few runs.

The following is from *Wisden's Cricket Almanack*, with regard to Mr. Bosanquet's bowling in the match referred to above :—" Notts, going in 59 behind, failed in extraordinary fashion against the slow leg-break bowling of Bosanquet, and were all out in ninety-five minutes."

A. SHAW'S ALL ENGLAND ELEVEN, WHICH VISITED AMERICA, AUSTRALIA, AND NEW ZEALAND, 1881-2.

G. Ulyett.   R. Pilling.   J. Lillywhite (Umpire).   J. Conway (Manager).   W. Midwinter.   W. Bates.
A. Shrewsbury.   A. Shaw.   T. Emmett.   E. Peate.
R. G. Barlow.   W. Scotton.   J. Selby.

Barlow is the sole survivor of the above illustrious eleven.

[*Photo. by Bardwell, Melbourne.*]

My Three Australian Cricket Tours.

THE following is an account of my three tours with English cricket teams. My first was in 1881-2 along with Alfred Shaw's team of English professional cricketers, composed as follows :—

Alfred Shaw (Captain), Notts.
A. Shrewsbury, Notts.
W. Scotton, Notts.
J. Selby, Notts.
R. G. Barlow, Lancashire.
R. Pilling, Lancashire.
T. Emmett, Yorkshire.
George Ulyett, Yorkshire.
W. Bates, Yorkshire.
E. Peate, Yorkshire.
W. Midwinter, Gloucester.
J. Lillywhite (Umpire).

This particular tour took us round the world, as we went first to America, thence to Australia and New Zealand, and back home *via* the Suez Canal, making various calls *en route*.

I believe this to be the only team which ever left England for Australia with exactly eleven players, and it was very fortunate that we all kept fit, and required no reserve men, except in one or two up-country matches. Shrewsbury was too ill to make the journey with us through America, and left England a few weeks later, travelling to Australia *via* the Suez Canal where he joined us. I may remark in passing that of this team I am the sole survivor, for fuller information on this matter the reader is referred to another part of the book.

After playing two matches at Holbeck and Nottingham respectively, we left the latter place to join our boat at Queenstown, Ireland, on the 17th September, 1881. Our train was due to depart at 5-40 p.m. and the station was packed, a crowd numbering several thousands having foregathered to give us a hearty send-off.

We boarded our vessel, the " Algeria," of the Cunard line, on the following day, and set sail for America at 4-0 o'clock in the afternoon. Our passage across was an exceedingly rough one, and it left an indelible impression upon my memory. Bates, Emmett, Lillywhite, Pilling, and myself suffered severely from "mal-de-mer," and with the exception of a little fruit, could not touch food for several days. The other members of our party were all more or less ill. How we longed to be back in old Manchester again with some good solid earth beneath our feet. Pilling caused a laugh by remarking that if he ever got back to England and anyone asked him to undertake another sea journey he should shoot them on the spot. Not one of us was able to get any sleep for several nights owing to the excessive rolling of the vessel, and upwards of 400 articles of crockery were broken through the same cause. A gentleman passenger who had made 18 trips across the herring pond told me that he had never known it to be so rough before. Our voyage occupied 14 days and we arrived at New York 3½ days behind time. One of the stewards was heard to remark that there had been more sea sickness on this voyage than for 21 years. Needless to say we were overjoyed to find ourselves once again on *terra firma* and heartily congratulated ourselves and each other.

The Customs officials made an exhaustive search through all our luggage, and coming across our cricket bats charged us a dollar each on them, old and new. We, of course, had to pay up, but did not omit to state our opinions to them on the subject in unmistakeable English. New York impressed me as being a magnificent city, and I was especially struck by the large dimensions of the hotels and other buildings.

The first match of the tour took place at Philadelphia on October 1st, 1881, against the Philadelphians; it ended in an easy win for our side. I was very well pleased with this place, there is an excellent cricket ground with really good wickets. The weather here was very close—the thermometer registering over 100° F. in the shade—and we were compelled to don the lightest clothing in our kit. The people of Philadelphia were very cordial and gave us a hearty welcome.

Our second match was against eighteen of Hoboken and district, at Hoboken, and was drawn in our favour. There was a very remarkable difference in the temperature at this place, it being no less than fifty degrees colder than at Philadelphia, and we played in our overcoats, an unique experience.

The third match again took place at Philadelphia against eighteen of the United States, and we won by more than 100 runs.

We went on to St. Louis to play our next match, which was against eighteen of St. Louis and district, and was drawn.

We tried our hands at the great American game of baseball at St. Louis just by way of a little recreation; but did not care much for the game. The ball travels with great speed and some brilliant catches are made by the regular players.

We left St. Louis for San Francisco on October 14th, travelling by the Pacific Railway, and arriving at our destination on the 19th. This was a wearisome journey and proved to be a very unlucky one for us, as Ulyett lost a diamond ring; Shaw, a large rug; Bates, his leather bag and contents; Selby, an umbrella; and I lost my black hat. The last day's railway journey to San Francisco was however really grand and took us along the sea coast. At one portion of the route our train was run on to a large steamboat which carried its heavy burden across many miles of water. We found San Francisco (since destroyed by earthquake and fire) to be a magnificent place, containing some splendid hotels. The one at which we stayed, "The Baldwin," was the finest I. had ever seen and one of the most elegantly appointed in the world. At San Francisco we played a two days' match against twenty-two of San Francisco and district, which was drawn in our favour. This team included a base-ball pitcher who pitched most of us out in the first innings, our total being only 98. In the second innings, however, we profited by our experience, and Ulyett and myself put on 166 before we were separated.

We left San Francisco for Australia on October 22nd by "The Australia," a very fine steamship, calling at Honolulu after a very rough voyage which lasted seven days. King Kalakana, the black monarch of Honolulu, was on board our vessel, returning home from a tour round the world. In spite of his colour and nationality he was a thorough gentleman and of splendid physique. He spoke English well and often sent for us cricketers to come into his cabin where we chatted to him and entertained him with songs. He was especially suited with a song of Bates's, entitled "My bonnie Yorkshire lass," which went with a good swing, and quite took his fancy. The king received an enthusiastic welcome from his black subjects on landing. The ship stayed at Honolulu for about twelve hours which gave us an opportunity of going ashore and taking a look round. We then resumed our voyage, making a second call at Auckland, New Zealand, remaining six hours. We had just time to admire the harbour here, which is a very fine one, before proceeding. When the weather was favourable we had cricket matches on board and athletic sports, at other times we amused ourselves with dominoes, cards, and quoits, and also held a few impromptu concerts. We landed at Sydney, Australia, on November 16th, after an enjoyable voyage of about twenty-four days. Sydney Harbour is one of the finest in the world and is surrounded by magnificent scenery. The committee of the Sydney Cricket Association gave us a very cordial reception on landing, and our first evening in Australia was one long to be remembered for the good fellowship extended towards us. We played a few local matches to begin with, just to get our hands in. The first was at Maitland against eighteen of Maitland and district on November 24th and 25th, and was drawn in our favour. The second match took place at Newcastle, versus twenty-two of Newcastle and district, and was also drawn in our favour. Newcastle was the scene of our encounter with the mosquitoes, named elsewhere.

For our next match we travelled about 190 miles from Sydney to a place called Orange. This journey took us through some of the grandest scenery it is possible to imagine, by way of the Zig-zag Railway over the Blue Mountains; I shall never forget it, and should strongly recommend everyone whose lot it is to visit Australia, on no account to miss this trip. On arrival at Orange station we found almost the whole of the inhabitants awaiting us, to give us a welcome; they had secured the services of a brass band and a number of torch bearers; these headed a procession, behind which we were driven in a carriage and four in great state to our hotel, amid scenes of great excitement and enthusiasm. Here we played against twenty-two of Orange and district, and won the match in one innings; the wicket was without grass, but, nevertheless, played fairly well. My score on this occasion was 62 not out, and I carried my bat through the innings. Our next match was at Bathurst on December 2nd and 3rd, against twenty-two of Bathurst and district, and was a win for our side. We then played twenty-two of Parramatta and district at Parramatta, which ended in a draw. Speaking of this match reminds me of our opponents' umpire, who was A1 for his own side, and never failed to give them "the benefit of the doubt."

I now come to our first big match on December 9th, 10th, 12th, and 13th. It was against New South Wales at Sydney, and as will be seen lasted four days. It was a good match, and we came out the victors by 68 runs. My contribution was 75, for which I was batting most of the first day. Being the first big match of our tour there was much excitement, and on the second day (Saturday) we had over 20,000 spectators.

The Sydney cricket ground is, taking it all round, the finest in the world; the accommodation and appointments are excellent.

After a minor match against eighteen of Cootamundra, which we won, we next played Victoria at Melbourne. We beat the Victorians by only 18 runs after a most exciting match. Shrewsbury played a fine second innings for 80 not out, and Peate was in excellent form for bowling in this same innings as the wicket just suited him after the rain. Melbourne cricket ground is a very fine one, I also like the city, well laid out streets and imposing buildings meet the eye on every side.

We then had a journey of 600 miles by water to Adelaide, a fine, clean-looking town, with an ideal climate. We experienced a rough passage, and many of us were ill. At Adelaide we received a hearty welcome. They have an excellent cricket ground, with perfect wickets. Here we played fifteen of South Australia on December 23rd, 24th, and 26th, the match ending in a draw in our favour. Bates played a good innings of 71, and I made 62. The umpiring at this match was defective, and some bad decisions were given.

We returned to Melbourne to play our next match, which was against the combined teams of Australia, on December 31st and January 2nd, 3rd, and 4th, 1882. Ulyett played a very fine innings of 87, and I had the misfortune to come out without scoring, the only occasion during the whole tour, in a first-class match. For Australia, T. Horan played a capital innings of 124. After four days' play the match was drawn.

On the last day of this match (January 4th) we had to leave Melbourne for New Zealand, and were so short of time that it was necessary to rush off the cricket ground and take a bee-line for the steamer, which sailed at 6-30.

The boat made a call of a few hours at Hobart Town, Tasmania, which is another fine, healthy place, possessing mountainous scenery.

We reached Dunedin, New Zealand, after a very pleasant voyage of seven days, and were entertained on board by a troupe of genuine negro minstrels, who, with their songs and music, made the time pass very pleasantly. Dunedin is a bright, healthy spot, situated among some fine scenery. The people received us very heartily. We won our first match, which was against an eighteen, on January 12th, 13th, and 14th, by ten wickets.

We then travelled by rail to Oamaru. For many miles this railway is laid on the side of the mountain, and in some places passes within very few yards of the edge of the rocks which descend to the sea thousands of feet below. The knowledge of this gave us a creepy feeling, and we felt much easier in mind when we had arrived safely at our destination. We played twenty-two of Oamaru, and won the match in one innings. We then went forward by rail along the sea coast to Timaru, where we again played a twenty-two side, winning by six wickets.

Christchurch was our next calling-place, where we played eighteen on January 20th, 21st, and 22nd, the match being drawn decidedly in our favour. Ulyett made 59 and myself 77. Emmett bowled in fine form. The Christchurch cricketers are the best in New Zealand. I was very favourably impressed with the place, which has a lovely climate.

After Christchurch, we journeyed by water (sixteen hours) to Wellington, and played another drawn match against twenty-two of Wellington and district. The scenery here is very imposing, the cricket ground being surrounded by lofty mountains.

A four-days' sea trip next took us to Auckland. This was very enjoyable, as the sea was quite calm throughout the voyage. Having a day to spare, a match was arranged at Waikato, in the Maori district. This place was reached by an eighty-mile railway journey and a fifteen-mile coach run from Auckland. Here we played a twenty-two, which included a number of Maoris; and curious-looking men they were, with tattooed skins, and wearing heavy earrings. The wicket was like a ploughed field, but we won the match. Bates played a very good innings of 47 on this vile wicket. The Maoris were highly charmed with Pilling's wicket-keeping, and gave free vent to their admiration.

We then returned to Auckland, where we played a twenty-two on February 2nd, 3rd, and 4th, winning the match by ten wickets. Shrewsbury batted well for 77 runs. Auckland is another fine, healthy place. Many of the houses are built entirely of wood. This concluded our tour in New Zealand. We were all highly delighted with the country, and brought away with us some very pleasing recollections. The climate is simply ideal, and this, combined with the grand scenery, makes it one of the finest residential parts of the world.

We left Auckland for Sydney on February 7th, arriving back after a five-days' voyage. On February 14th and 15th we played an eighteen at Stanmore Park, a few miles out of Sydney. The wicket here was of cocoa-nut matting, and played fairly well. The match was drawn in our favour.

Our next match was at Sydney, on February 17th, 18th, 20th, and 21st, against a combined team of Australia. After four days of good all-round cricket, we lost the match by five wickets. Ulyett, in the second innings, batted excellently for 67. I made 62. Our fielding was rather faulty. The Australians played very fine all-round cricket, and well deserved their victory.

We next played at Windsor, and won the match. Peate and Midwinter bowled very well. I made 50 not out.

We reappeared at Melbourne on February 24th, 25th, 26th, and 27th, when we played the return match against Victoria, which we won by eight wickets. Bates played a dashing innings for 84 ; Shrewsbury, 72 not out. Bates bowled splendidly.

When at Melbourne we always stayed at the "Old White Hart" hotel, which was a capital hostelry, clean and homely. It was just like being at home in England. We returned to Sydney from Melbourne—a dreary railway ride of five hundred miles, through prosaic scenery made up of woods, bush, and a few worked-out gold mines.

At Sydney we played the Australian team which was to visit England in 1882. The match lasted four days, viz., March 3rd, 4th, 6th, and 7th, and we lost by six wickets. Shrewsbury played very fine cricket for 82 and 47. This was our last match of the tour at Sydney.

The Lancashire residents of Sydney presented Pilling and myself with an illuminated address and a gold medal each before we left. We also had a good send-off from the people at the "Oxford" hotel, where we always stayed when at Sydney.

After leaving Sydney we proceeded to Melbourne to play the return match against the Australian team which was going to England. This match took place on March 10th, 11th, 13th, and 14th, and ended in a draw. The full scores were : Shaw's team, 309, and 234 for only two wickets down ; Australians, exactly 300. Ulyett played two fine dashing innings for 149 and 66, though it is only fair to add that he had a little luck in the early part of his first innings. I made 16, and 56 run out.

On the following two days—March 15th and 16th—we played a twenty-two side at Dunolly, on a cocoa-nut matting wicket, and won the match in one innings. After we had finished here, we travelled by coach and four to the railway station, a distance of about sixteen miles through the bush. The startling adventures that befel us on this ride are recorded on a previous page.

At Ballarat, on March 17th and 18th, we played the last match of our tour, which was drawn in our favour. We played against a very good team of twenty. They have a nice cricket ground at Ballarat, and some good players. The place is noted for its gold mines, and we had the good fortune to be taken down one of them, and were shown round by the manager. Amongst other things, we saw a nugget of gold weighing 280 ounces, and I brought away with me two pieces of quartz with particles of gold embedded in the crystal, which are still in my possession. The people of Ballarat accorded us a hearty reception and send-off. We arrived back at Melbourne on March 22nd, and sailed for England the same day by the Orient liner "Chimborago." Many friends and spectators gathered together to see us start off on our long journey, and wished us a hearty farewell and safe journey.

The voyage was uneventful except for two deaths—those of a young boy and an old lady of sixty, whose remains were buried at sea. This at any time is a sad and solemn spectacle, and casts a temporary gloom over everything.

We whiled away the time by playing cricket and various other games, and by holding concerts and entertainments. We also joined in sweepstakes for the run of the ship.

Our boat touched Naples on May 2nd, after a pleasant but slow passage of six weeks, and as I felt rather wearied of sailing, I left the vessel at Naples, and travelled overland for the remainder of the journey, along with Lillywhite, Midwinter, Bates, and Peate. We had a good look around Naples, which is a beautiful place, but could not, of course, understand their language, and should have been in a quandary had we not engaged the services of an interpreter.

We passed through some glorious scenery on our way home from Naples, and enjoyed this portion of our outing immensely. After spending a few hours sight-seeing in Paris, we left for Dover, arriving there at 3-40 a.m. on May 5th, and reached London about three hours later. I took train for Manchester, reaching home at about four o'clock in the afternoon, thus completing my long journey round the world. I had been absent over eight months, and had travelled about 40,000 miles. It had all been most enjoyable, but nevertheless I was glad to get back again to old England. The only fault I had to find with the cricket on the other side of the globe was in respect to the umpiring, which was at times bad, and gave rise to a little unpleasantness occasionally.

On arriving back in Manchester, I received a hearty welcome home from a large crowd which had gathered for the purpose. This quite took me by surprise.

Shaw, Shrewsbury, and Lillywhite, the promoters of the tour, made each of the members of the team a present of a gold medal to keep as a memento. This I wear on my watch-chain at the present time.

HON. IVO. BLIGH'S ENGLISH ELEVEN WHICH VISITED AUSTRALIA, QUEENSLAND, AND TASMANIA, 1882-3.

Barnes.   Morley.   C. T. Studd.   G. F. Vernon.   C. F. H. Leslie.

G. B. Studd.   E. F. S. Tylecote.   Hon. Ivo. Bligh.   A. G. Steel.   W. W. Read.

Barlow.   Bates.

[*Photo. by Tuttle & Co., Melbourne.*]

J

Second Tour.

I MADE my second trip to Australia—which also included Tasmania—in 1882-3, as a member of the Hon. Ivo Bligh's team of English cricketers. The composition of this team was as follows:—

Hon. Ivo Bligh (Captain).
Mr. A. G. Steel, Lancashire.
Mr. C. T. Studd, Middlesex.
Mr. G. B. Studd, Middlesex.
Mr. E. F. S. Tylecote, Kent.
Mr. C. F. H. Leslie, Middlesex
Mr. G. F. Vernon, Middlesex.
Mr. W. W. Read, Surrey.
W. Barnes, Notts.
F. Morley, Notts.
W. Bates, Yorkshire.
R. G. Barlow, Lancashire.

Five of this band have already passed over to the " great majority," namely, the seventh, eighth, ninth, tenth, and eleventh on the list.

Seven of the team secured berths in the fine P. and O. liner " Peshawur," which sailed from Gravesend on September 14th, 1882. The remaining five, including myself, left England on the 21st, and travelled overland to Brindisi, passing through some fine scenery *en route*, especially in Italy. Here we boarded the " Poonah," a vessel of some 3,000 tons, and left Brindisi at six a.m. on September 25th, touching Alexandria three days later. Ours was the very first boat to call here after the war and the now historic bombardment of Alexandria. A few of our party went ashore for a few hours to see the effects of the bombardment. The havoc wrought by the shells and projectiles which were fired into the town from the guns of the " Alexandra," " Monarch," " Invincible," " Penelope," " Condor," and other British vessels, baffles description. The buildings were completely wrecked, and the place a heap of ruins. At the request of the British soldiers in charge of the place, we signed our names in a visitors' book. Anchored outside in the harbour were several " men-of-war " keeping a look-out. The whole

scene was most impressive, and one which I shall never forget.
We called at Port Said for a few hours the next day, and were
allowed to land and view the place, and soon afterwards our boat
entered the Suez Canal.

On October 1st we arrived at Suez, where we found the
" Peshawur," and went aboard her to join the other portion of our
team which had sailed from England.

We set sail at 10-30 p.m. of the same day, and the following
day found us passing through the Red Sea. The weather was
terribly hot at about this time, and remained so for several days.
We passed Aden on the 6th, and on the 9th were in the Indian
Ocean, having on this day made 328 miles, the best run of the
voyage so far. On the 10th the stewards of the ship gave a very
creditable " nigger-minstrel " performance for the entertainment of
the passengers.

On October 13th we reached Colombo, where our vessel
remained for two days, so we improved the occasion by arranging a
cricket match with the Colombo C.C., playing against an eighteen.
The match was drawn in our favour. I was bowled with a " no-
ball " when my score had reached 10. This is the first and only
occasion on which I ever remember being bowled with a "no-ball."
The natives of Colombo are almost all blacks. The team we played
against included several hardy fellows, who batted in their bare feet
and wore neither pads nor other protection.

Our two days at Colombo were most enjoyable, and we were
sorry to leave. We sailed again on the 15th, and at 9-15 p.m. of
the same day had a most alarming experience, for the " Peshawur "
came into violent collision with a large sailing vessel named the
" Glenroy." We were then about 350 miles out from Colombo.
Our ship was cut down almost to the water-line, while the
"Glenroy" had her bows smashed in to within half a yard of the
water's edge. The excitement which followed the collision was
indescribable, and all—including myself—thought we were about to
meet with a watery grave. Very fortunately, the damage to the
two vessels was all above the water; it was also most fortunate
that the sea was calm. We turned about, and put back into
Colombo again for repairs, where we were detained for nearly a
week. The accident was the beginning of the end with one of our
team—poor Fred Morley. He sustained several broken ribs, and
did not live long after his return to England. Our systems received
a very severe shock, and it was some days before we felt quite

ourselves again. This collision is also referred to elsewhere in this book.

We left Colombo for the second time on October 24th. On the 28th, and for several days, the sea was very rough, preventing many of the passengers from going below for meals. We held some athletic sports on deck on November 2nd, and on the 10th landed at Adelaide twelve days overdue, after a protracted voyage of nearly seven weeks. Owing to the delay, caused by the collision, we had to begin play on the same day we landed. We were opposed by a fifteen of Adelaide, and the match was drawn.

On November 14th we arrived at Melbourne, and met with a very cordial reception, including a few hearty English cheers for Bates and myself, who were the only two cricketers of the team who had been out to Australia previously. The first evening, we were entertained at a supper, held in the Melbourne Cricket Club pavilion. There were also present the Mayor of Melbourne, and many of the leading citizens and colonists. Needless to say, we spent a very jolly evening.

We played our first match here against Victoria, on November 17th, 18th, and 20th, and won by ten wickets. Mr. C. T. Studd played a fine innings of 56, Mr. Leslie made a good 51 not out, Bates contributed 48, and myself 44. Our next match was at Sandhurst, against a twenty-two of Bendigo, on November 22nd and 23rd, which was drawn in our favour. Mr. Steel bowled very well in both innings, Mr. Leslie played another good innings of 48 not out, and Mr. C. T. Studd performed the hat trick. Sandhurst is where the three Australian cricketers, Messrs. Murdoch, Boyle and Midwinter were brought out. There are a few gold-mines at this place, and we had the pleasure of a visit through the workings of one of them, named the " Garden Gully United Mine."

Castlemaine was the scene of our next match, against a team of twenty-two of this district, on November 24th and 25th ; and the match was drawn in our favour. The people here received us very well, and invited us to the theatre in the evening. The performance was advertised as " under the patronage of the English cricketers."

On Monday, November 27th, the whole of our team was invited to a banquet, held in the Melbourne Town Hall, to welcome the return of the Australian cricketers from England. It was a very fine affair, as well as an enjoyable one, and when we left, at the close, the company gave us three hearty British cheers.

On December 1st, 2nd, 4th, and 5th we played New South Wales, at Sydney, winning the match in one innings. Mr. Leslie was in very good form, and made 144. His hitting was a treat to witness. My score was 80, the pair of us putting on over 220 runs for the second wicket. We then went on to Maitland, by water most of the way, and played against Eighteen of Maitland and District, which match we won by one innings. Mr. Steel and Bates did most of the bowling on this occasion.

We next played at Newcastle, against an Eighteen. They have a good cricket ground here, with a fairly good wicket. This match was drawn greatly in our favour. Mr. Read played a capital innings for 64. Messrs. Steel and Studd bowled well, the former doing the hat trick—three wickets in three balls. Our wicket-keeper had a hand in all three, catching one and stumping two. Our umpire (George Coulthard) had a sunstroke during the match, and had to retire. Mr. G. B. Studd and Morley did not play, owing to illness.

Our next match was at Tamworth, a journey of over 200 miles from Newcastle; it was a weary ride, and occupied nine hours. This was the first occasion on which a good cricket team had visited the place, and the people received us very heartily This is supposed to be the hottest part of Australia, and we found the mosquitoes and flies to be very troublesome. Play should have commenced on December 11th, but a severe thunderstorm came on, with heavy rain which flooded the cricket ground, making play quite impossible. This was a great disappointment, especially to those who had come long distances to see the match. As at Newcastle, a grand dramatic performance was held under our patronage: a banquet was also spread in our honour. There are a few good-sized mountains at Tamworth, and we made the ascent of one of them. The view from the top was glorious, beautiful scenery meeting the eye in every direction. Tamworth is also a good place for game, and some fine shooting and hunting may be had. A few of us accompanied four local gentlemen, one morning, on a kangaroo hunt. We arose as early as 4-30; each mounted a good steed, and we started off. We enjoyed some excellent sport in our chase after the kangaroos, which can travel at great speed. We soon had a kill of a fine specimen of this animal. How I managed to keep my seat astride the horse has always been a mystery to me, as I was quite unaccustomed to horsemanship. I remember that I was very stiff all the next day, and had great difficulty in walking and sitting.

The Tamworth people gave us a good send-off when we left them to proceed to Melbourne, another long journey of between 800 and 900 miles, accomplished partly by rail and partly by boat. We arrived on December 18th, and had a nice little interval of one week to ourselves for recreation. Some of the team went into the country for shooting, while the others spent the time in sight-seeing. Our next match was at Ballarat, against an eighteen, on December 26th, 27th, and 28th, which was drawn, after three days' very good cricket. Mr. Read was top scorer, with a well-played 55, and Mr. Bligh made a good 44. Mr. Steel was the most successful bowler.

The atmosphere at this place is very clear and healthy, and there are some gold mines, which I mention in the account of my first visit with Shaw's team.

A banquet was held in our honour at Melbourne, on December 29th, which we all enjoyed. The next match was played here on December 30th, and January 1st and 2nd, 1883, against the Australian team. We lost by nine wickets. Mr. Tylecote was our top scorer, with two excellent innings of 33 and 38. G. Palmer bowled splendidly for the Australians. J. Bonner made 85, his hitting being magnificent; while A. Bannerman (my brother "stone-waller," as they called him out there) played two very steady innings for 30 and 25 not out. We missed several catches in this match; but English teams never field so well out in Australia as they do at home. I think this is due to the light, which is, at times, intensely bright and dazzling. We also felt the need of Morley's bowling. He had never been right since the collision at sea, and was only able to play occasionally after his arrival in Australia.

On the 4th of January we were entertained at a dinner, along with the Australian team, by Sir W. J. Clarke, Bart. It was held at Scott's Hotel, Melbourne, and was a big success. The tables were beautifully laid out. I think it was the best occasion of the kind I have ever attended, and we all spent a most enjoyable time.

Our next match was at Launceston, Tasmania, on January 8th and 9th. We had a rough passage, and nearly all on board were bad, including most of the team. A large number of people were assembled on the wharf to welcome our arrival. Launceston is noted for its gold and tin mines. I like it very well.

We played against an eighteen and won the match in one innings. Mr. C. T. Studd played a splendid innings for 99, when he was unlucky enough to be run out. Barnes bowled well in the first and Mr. Steel in the second innings. The cricket ground here is surrounded by magnificent scenery. From Launceston we proceeded through beautiful scenery to Hobart for our next match. We were met at the station by a brass band and a large number of people, who loudly cheered us as we stepped on to the platform. A four-in-hand brake conveyed us from the station to the Town Hall, where we were received by the mayor and many leading citizens of Hobart. We played an eighteen here on January 12th and 13th, and won by seven wickets. The cricket ground is situated in a lovely spot at the foot of Mount Wellington (5,000 feet), amid some of the most charming scenery I ever saw. The Hobart harbour is a very fine one and the climate ideal.

We arrived back in Melbourne on January 16th after a good passage. This day was extremely hot, being about 108° in the shade. We played our next match against the Australian team at Melbourne on January 19th and following days. Our captain—Mr. Bligh—won the toss for a wonder; he had previously lost it twelve times running. We won the match by an innings and 27 runs. Mr. Read batted well for 75, and Bates played a dashing innings of 55. His bowling also was really excellent, and included a performance of the hat trick. Messrs. Palmer and Giffen bowled well for the Australians. Mr. F. R. Spofforth, the demon bowler, did not take a wicket this time.

The next match took place at Sydney, on the 26th, 27th, 29th, and 30th of January, 1883, against the Australians, and as we had each won a match, there was great excitement over this, especially as it would decide who should win the rubber, or take the ashes, as it was termed. On the second day there were upwards of twenty thousand spectators on the field. Our captain won the toss, and, of course, sent his side in to bat. We put together the respectable total of 248 in the first innings. Messrs. Read and Tylecote each made 66 and played very good cricket. My contribution was 28. Mr. Spofforth bowled well in this innings.

The Australians responded with 218 runs, including a very fine innings by Bannerman of 94.

Our second innings only produced 123. Mr. C. T. Studd was top scorer this time, with 25. I was batting a long time for 24. This left the Australians 153 to get to win, and most people thought they would get them without much difficulty. Morley and I, however, felt in good bowling form, and got them all out for 83 runs, leaving us the victors by 69 runs. We thus won the rubber and brought back the ashes to old England. In the second innings

I took seven wickets for 40 runs. I shall never forget the excitement at the close of this match; it reminded me of the occasion when Australia beat England by seven runs at the Oval in 1882.

Our team was vociferously cheered by the great crowd, and most of the gentlemen and myself were called out of the pavilion. When I was coming away for lunch, some of the spectators caught me and carried me shoulder high. I received several presents, including a silver cup; also about £25, which was collected for me on the ground.

Between 60,000 and 70,000 people witnessed this match, and the gate amounted to about £3,500.

From Sydney we travelled by water 500 miles to Brisbane, in Queensland, and had a very pleasant voyage. The people here turned out in thousands to see us arrive. For the last few miles of our voyage up the river each bank was lined with spectators, including many children, who cheered us and waved their hands and handkerchiefs. This was the heartiest and most touching reception we had so far had in Australia, and our captain, Mr. Bligh, said he felt quite overcome with emotion.

This was the first visit of an English cricketing team, consequently it was a red-letter day in the annals of Queensland. Brisbane is a beautiful place, but very hot. We played a two-days' match, commencing on February 2nd, and won it in one innings. Mr. Read played an excellent innings for 84, and Bates played a hard-hitting game for 41. His batting highly pleased the spectators. Bates and I received a good offer to come out here for a few years, to coach and play for the Brisbane C. C., but we could not see our way to accept. We found the mosquitoes to be very troublesome at this place. Before leaving Brisbane a grand ball was held in honour of our visit. We departed on February 6th by steamer for Maryborough, distant about 170 miles, and again received a hearty welcome on landing. We played against eighteen on February 8th and 9th, and won the match in one innings. The weather here was frightfully hot; several of our team were quite overcome by the heat, and had to leave the ground for a time, substitutes being found to take their places until their return. I may remark here that I stood the Australian climate very well at all times, as is proved by the fact that I never missed one match in any of the three tours.

Whilst at Maryborough, a dramatic performance was given under our patronage, and on the second night a grand ball was held in our honour at the Town Hall, which was tastefully decorated for the occasion. One evening during our visit to Maryborough the blacks and real natives in this district gave a special entertainment for our benefit, which they called an "Aboriginal Corrobborree." A huge fire was kindled, and the blacks, painted and decorated in the most extravagant style, danced and sang around it, striking fantastic attitudes and going through various evolutions. The king of the Aboriginals was introduced to our captain. We were all highly amused at this performance, which was the first of its kind we had ever seen. This closed our outing to Queensland, which had been most enjoyable. We left for Sydney on February 11th, and arrived back on the 14th, after a pleasant passage.

We commenced our next match, against a combined team of Australia, on February 17th, on the Sydney ground. Over fifteen thousand people witnessed the first day's play. It was arranged that a fresh wicket for each innings could be had if required by either team, so that winning the toss was not so much in one's favour as usual. We lost the match by six wickets. Mr. Steel played a very fine innings for 135 not out: his late cutting was splendid. Mr. C. T. Studd also batted very well for 48. He was quite a favourite in Australia with his fine style of batting. G. Bonner, the big hitter, made 81 for the Australians; he was very lucky indeed, being missed five times. Mr. J. M. Blackham played two useful innings for 57, and 58 not out; he was carried by the crowd into the pavilion, and well deserved his reception. I never saw him bat so well before. A. Bannerman also played a very good game for 63. Our captain and Mr. G. B. Studd were the only two on our side who fielded up to their usual form in this match. We were playing four days, before an aggregate of about 60,000 spectators.

The last match of this tour took place at Melbourne on March 9th and following days. We lost by an innings and 75 runs. Rain spoiled the wicket for our batting, and the bowling of Messrs. G. Palmer and Cooper was too good for us on this sticky wicket. The Melbourne Club gave us a farewell banquet in the pavilion on March 13th, at which we were each presented with a gold locket, and the four professionals also received £10 each. We spent a very jolly evening together.

The four professionals—Barnes, Bates, Morley, and myself—left Melbourne for England on the 15th of March, the gentlemen following a fortnight later.

We sailed in the P. and O. liner "Niyani." The time was passed away on deck with the usual games and sports. These included cricket, quoits, and athletic events. In these latter I was successful in winning the 100 yards race, the hurdle race, and the egg-and-spoon race. I also came second in the high jump. Several first-rate amateur concerts were also held during the voyage.

We arrived at Colombo on April 2nd, and as we remained here for nearly two days, we had plenty of time to take another good look around the place. There was the usual large number of black boys here, on the look-out for coins thrown to them by the passengers. These boys are excellent swimmers and divers, being quite at home in the water. For a few coppers they will dive under the keels of the large steamships anchored in the harbour, and think nothing of it. We were most interested in watching them going through their aquatic performances. Our ship left Colombo on April 4th. The sea was smooth, and the weather exceedingly hot. On April 11th we did 315 miles, one of the best runs of the voyage.

Arrived at Aden on the 12th. This day we entered the Red Sea, commonly known as passing through the "Gates of Hell." We passed six large outward-bound steamships on this day, and eight others on the 14th, including a "man-o'-war." We reached Suez at nine o'clock on the evening of April 14th, at which place we four left the ship and proceeded to Alexandria by rail. After a rest and a tour of inspection, we went forward by steamer to Brindisi, which place was reached on April 21st. After Brindisi, Venice was our next stopping-place, where we spent a most enjoyable time. Most of the streets here are of water, as is generally known, and instead of carriages, boat-like conveyances called gondolas are used to convey people to different parts of the city. The buildings are very fine, but, strange to say, the place is dirty; which proves that abundance of water does not necessarily imply cleanliness. Glass-making is one of the chief industries of Venice, and we were greatly entertained by being shown over some of the many glass works. We left Venice by rail for Paris, which city was reached on April 25th. The scenery en route was magnificent, and we also had the experience of passing through the lengthy Mont Cenis tunnel.

We saw as much of "Gay Paree" as we could in the short space of time at our disposal, and then left for London, via Calais and Dover, reaching the great Metropolis in the evening of the 25th.

We remained in London overnight, and proceeded home the next day, April 26th, 1883.

I was again accorded a hearty welcome home by a large assemblage of my townspeople at the Manchester Central Station, who had got wind of my return and time of arrival.

The Melbourne Cricket Club were the promoters of this second tour. They presented me at the close with a gold locket and £10, and also sent £15 towards my benefit match in 1886.

SHAW, SHREWSBURY, AND LILLYWHITE'S TEAM OF ENGLISH CRICKETERS WHICH VISITED AUSTRALIA, 1886-7.

Flowers.   Shrewsbury.   Lohmann.   Gunn (W.)   Barnes.   Read (M).
Bates.   Shaw.   Lillywhite (Umpire).   Sherwin.   Scotton.   Barlow.
Briggs.

[Photo. by Tuttle & Co., Melbourne.]

Third Tour.

MY third and last journey to Australia was in 1886-7, when I formed one of Shaw and Shrewsbury's team of English cricketers. This was a very fine combination, second only to the Hon. Ivo Bligh's team of 1881-2, which in my opinion was the finest which has ever left England. The following are the names of the cricketers composing the team of 1886-7 :—

*A. Shaw (Captain), Notts.
*A. Shrewsbury, Notts.
*W. Barnes, Notts.
 W. Gunn, Notts.
*W. Scotton, Notts.
 M. Sherwin, Notts.
 W. Flowers, Notts.
 R. G. Barlow, Lancashire.
*J. Briggs, Lancashire.
*W. Bates, Yorkshire.
*G. Lohmann, Surrey.
 M. Read, Surrey.
 J. Lillywhite (Umpire), Sussex.

Death has again been busy in our ranks, no less than seven of this team (marked with an asterisk) having since passed **away**.

We left Plymouth in the Orient liner "Cuzco" at noon on the 18th of September, 1886. The sea was rather rough in the Bay of Biscay, causing Gunn, Briggs, Bates, Lillywhite, and myself to be placed on the (sea)sick list. We, however, found our sea-legs in a few days, and settled down in our quarters. We reached Naples on September 25th, and remained for nine hours. This gave us time to go ashore and see the sights. The town itself is only ordinary, but the scenery around is magnificent, including as it does that fiery mount, Vesuvius. Port Said was reached on the 29th, but passengers were not allowed to land, as cholera was prevalent. Here we again saw the blacks diving for money, and heard their monkey-like chattering ; we also noticed many "ships-of-the-desert," as well as the more familiar kind. We then entered the Suez Canal, through which vessels are only allowed to steam at the rate of five knots an hour, as the canal is very narrow in parts. Suez was touched on October 2nd.

We were now having our usual sports each day. When playing cricket we had five balls and run, *i.e.*, if no run was scored in five balls, the batsman had to retire. This was a source of great amusement to the passengers. In the evenings we held concerts, and as our team included several good singers, these were very successful. Gunn, Scotton, Sherwin, and myself contributed to the programme.

On the 6th, a death occurred on board—that of a child a year old, and a few days later an old lady of seventy died. Both were buried at sea—always a most pathetic and solemn spectacle.

On October 8th we arrived at Aden. A few of us took a walk ashore late in the evening, when we witnessed a unique sight. Most of the natives were asleep in the streets, lying here and there in all positions, like so many sheep.

On the 10th we sighted several large whales, which caused some excitement amongst the passengers, many of whom had never seen a whale before. We also frequently passed schools of porpoises at about this date. The second-class passengers gave a concert on the 12th, which was much enjoyed. We were now in the Indian Ocean, and crossed the "line" on this day.

On the 13th the crew entertained us by having fire practice. The fire-bell rang, and immediately the crew were running about in all directions, each to his particular duty which would devolve upon him if fire were to break out on board. We also enjoyed good fun each morning by having a sweep for the run of the ship. Small bets were made on the result, to add a little excitement to the fun. Whist tournaments were also held at intervals.

The weather was rather rough on the 16th, and the sea choppy, which again caused several of us to have qualms in the region of the stomach, and prevented us from filling our usual places at the saloon table. We witnessed some glorious sunsets about this time.

On October 21st, more athletic sports were held, and were greatly enjoyed. The potato race was won by Briggs, Read second. The hopping race was won by myself, Briggs second. Trial of strength was won by Sherwin, Gunn second. Tug-of-war, the first-class passengers beat the second-class. There were twelve a side. Most of the cricketers were in the winning team. Hop, stride, and jump : Gunn won this, a gentleman named Bruce being second.

The walking race was won by myself, Mr. Bruce being again second. The winner of the hurdle race was Gunn, Mr. Bruce second. I won the five minutes' "go-as-you-please," a Mr. Galbraith coming in second. Bates and myself won the three-legged race, Briggs and Scotton second. The long jump was won by Gunn. I consider that I did fairly well to win five first prizes. Gunn also was very successful. The prizes were of considerable value, and well worth winning.

On October 26th a fancy-dress ball was held in the evening. It was a splendid affair, and surprised us all. On the following night, October 27th, a nigger-minstrel performance was presented. The troupe were Messrs. Shaw, Gunn, Sherwin, Scotton, Flowers, Bates, Briggs, and myself from among the cricketers, and Messrs. McKenzie, Bruce, and Christian of the other passengers, with Mr. Wallett as accompanist. We were a comical sight with our black faces. The entertainment went off in fine style, and delighted all the passengers, who passed a very favourable verdict upon our singing. Gunn was the "tambourine," and Sherwin the "bones," and they took their parts so well that some of the passengers remarked that they might have been professional minstrels.

On October 29th our long voyage came to an end, and we landed at Adelaide, Australia. We got to business the following day, and played a match against fifteen of South Australia, which was drawn in our favour. Shrewsbury just made his 100, though it was not one of his best innings. Barnes made 82, and batted very well. I was again most favourably impressed with Adelaide, which is a nice, clean, healthy town.

We left on the 3rd of November for Melbourne by the overland route, which had at that time only been open a few months. On our arrival we put up, as usual, at the "Old White Hart." We played our second match, which was against Victoria, on November 6th, 8th, 9th, and 10th. After four days of very good cricket, this match was also drawn. Mr. T. Horan, Victoria, played a remarkably good innings of 117 not out. He is a fine sportsman—one of the best in Australia—and also a clever writer on cricket. Barnes batted very well for 109, and his placing of the ball on the off-side was a treat to see. I made 86, and Flowers played a good innings for 53. Lohmann was in fine form with the ball, and in the second innings took eight wickets.

I have spoken about Melbourne and its cricket ground in the accounts of my earlier tours; but since my last visit, four years ago, they had made many improvements. The new grand stand on the ground is one of the finest I have seen.

Our next match was at Parramatta, against an eighteen, on November 12th and 13th. After a good match, we won by 23 runs. The wicket was bad, consequently the scoring was low on both sides. The bowling and fielding of our opponents were, however, really first-class, and came as a surprise to us all.

We next played New South Wales at Sydney on the 19th of November. This match was over in two days, and we lost, to the astonishment of everyone, as the Sydney team was rather weak. Their bowling and fielding, however, were excellent.

We now had an interval of three days, and several of us occupied our time in an inspection of Sydney's fine harbour. I have elsewhere spoken of this as being one of the finest in the world. The same remark also applies to the cricket ground here. Since I was last over they had carried out many alterations and improvements. I like Sydney very well; it is more homelike than any other place in Australia.

We played our next match at Goulburn, on the 24th, against eighteen, and won in one innings. The wicket was of cocoa-nut matting, and played fairly well. The welcome we received here was very practical. A brass band met us at the station, and in the evening a dramatic performance was held "under the patronage of the English cricketers." We found flies and mosquitoes to be very troublesome at this place.

Our next match was at Cootamundra, against twenty-two, on November 29th and 30th. This time we won by ten wickets. Flowers performed the hat trick, taking three wickets with as many balls. At 3-0 a.m., on the morning of the 30th, there was a slight earthquake, lasting several seconds. It was felt all over the town, and awakened most of the inhabitants. It caused the walls and windows to shake and rattle, and the glasses and ornaments to dance upon the sideboards. This was our first experience of an earthquake, and most of us were afraid. We spoke of it for long afterwards, and shall not easily forget it.

Cootamundra was the place where the amusing umpire episode took place, which has been quoted in many books on cricket. The local mayor was umpire, and Briggs, having "run out" a batsman very easily, appealed. Instead of the expected decision—"out"—being given, the pseudo-umpire replied, "D——d good bit of fielding that, wasn't it?" As a second appeal only brought forth the same remark, Shaw, our captain, said, " Oh ! let him go on batting," and the batsman was allowed to have another innings. The umpire's reply provoked much laughter at the time, and has proved a source of merriment whenever related. The last-named match was played on a concrete wicket.

We next played Eighteen Juniors of Sydney and District, on December 3rd, 4th, and 6th, and won by an innings and 31 runs. This was followed by a match at Lithgow, against a twenty-two, which we also won—by 77 runs. Briggs performed the "hat trick" in this match.

The journey to this place is by the Zig-Zag Railway over the Blue Mountains, and passes through some magnificent scenery. I have referred to this previously. Visitors to Australia should not miss this trip.

We next played a return match against New South Wales, at Sydney, on December 11th, 12th, and 13th, which we won by nine wickets. Shrewsbury played a very fine innings for 62, and Lohmann made a good 40 " not out." The two umpires gave some very bad decsions against us in this match, although we won easily.

We had to cover a long journey of over 500 miles to Melbourne to play our next match, which was against the Australian Team, on December 17th, 18th, 20th, and 21st. We won this match by 57 runs, after four days of very good all-round cricket. The umpiring here was again defective, and several bad decisions were given.

Geelong was the next on the list, where we played an eighteen on December 23rd and 24th, which ended in a draw in our favour. I made my first century in Australia on this occasion, my score being 104. Shrewsbury played a capital innings for 70.

Geelong is a fine, healthy place. The people gave us a hearty reception.

We next proceeded to Ballarat, where the gold mines are (mentioned in one of my previous tours). We found many people at the station, awaiting our arrival, and they received us with a few good English cheers. The match here lasted three days (December 27th, 28th, and 29th), against Twenty of Ballarat, which included some good players. We won in one innings. Read played a dashing innings of 121, Gunn made 48, and myself 45. I spent an enjoyable time at this place on each occasion that I visited it.

We played our return match against the Australian Team at Melbourne, on January 1st, 3rd, 4th, and 5th, 1887; it was drawn in

K

our favour. Barnes played very fine cricket for 93. Gunn also batted well in both innings, making 48 and (not out) 62 ; his style of batting was very much admired out there.

The long journey to Sydney was again undertaken, to play our third match against the Australian Team on January 7th, 8th, 10th, and 11th. We spent nineteen hours in the train. We won by nine wickets. Briggs was in good form with the bat, and made 69 runs; Read's score was 53, and mine 23. Barnes bowled splendidly in both innings.

We next went on to Bathurst, to play on January 14th and 15th. The match was drawn in our favour. This place will always be remembered by us on account of the heartiness and hospitality of the people. The population is about 12,000. We were warmly received at the station ; and, on the Saturday, they gave a complimentary dinner in our honour. We had a day to ourselves here, which we occupied, some of us in kangaroo and 'possum hunting, and others in driving. Altogether, we spent a most enjoyable time at Bathurst.

We played our next match at Orange, against a twenty-two, on January 17th and 18th. The wicket was of cocoa-nut matting, and played rather badly. The match was drawn in our favour.

We should have played at Yess on January 21st and 22nd; but, much to the people's disappointment, it rained heavily on both days, and prevented play. A concert was held in the evening, at which Gunn, Sherwin, Scotton, Briggs, and myself took part. The audience were very pleased with our singing, and we were each presented with a silver medal.

Our next match was at Bowral, on January 24th and 25th, against a twenty-two. It was a draw, as the rain stopped the play early in the game. The match following was also drawn—at Camden, on January 26th and 27th—rain again putting a stop to the play in good time.

The combined Australian Eleven were our next opponents, at Sydney, on January 28th, 29th, and 31st. It was a most exciting match, and we won by the narrow margin of 13 runs. Barnes and Lohmann both bowled well for us, and Turner and Ferris for the Australians. The wicket was rather queer, so that the bowlers had it their own way a little.

A journey of six hours by water and ten hours by rail conveyed us to Narrabri, where we next played, on February 4th and 5th, against a twenty-two side, the match ending in a draw in our favour. Flowers batted well for 63, Shrewsbury scored 53, and myself 44. A gentleman named Mr. Moseley was very kind and hospitable to us at this place. One treat he had arranged for our entertainment was in engaging a native to throw the boomerang—that curved weapon which always returns to the feet of the thrower after having accomplished his object. We were greatly astonished by this exhibition. We found the weather exceedingly hot at Narrabri, and the flies and mosquitoes very troublesome. Many of the houses are built of wood, and grapes grow in great profusion. The names given to the railway stations on the local line are most extraordinary, the following being a few of them :—Werris Creek, Boggabri, Turrawan, Baan Baa, Gunnedah, Breeza, Curlewis, Waratah, Lochinvar, Quirinde, Quipolly, Currabuanla, and Murrurundi. The porters here must have a lively time in calling out the names of the stations.

Our next match took place at Armidale—or, as it is called here, New England. We played a twenty-two on February 7th and 8th, and again made a draw in our favour. Flowers was the top scorer, with 54 well-played; I made 38. The climate here is very agreeable. The people received us most heartily. During our visit an amateur entertainment was held, in aid of the Cricket Pavilion building fund. The committee asked us English cricketers if we would take part in it, and we willingly consented. Gunn, Sherwin, Scotton, Read, Briggs, and myself gave the anthem, "How beautiful upon the mountains," also several songs and a trio, "Tell me, Shepherds." I contributed "When other lips," and, receiving an *encore*, replied with my cricket song. The effort produced close upon £100, and the committee were so pleased with the result that they presented us each with a gold medal. It is scarcely necessary to add that we all enjoyed our visit to Armidale. We played our next match at Newcastle, on February 10th, 11th, and 12th, against an eighteen, which resulted in a draw in our favour. Read was in capital form with the bat, and knocked up 72. I made 42, run out. They have some very good cricketers here, and a fine ground. Newcastle is noted for its coal mines; one pit, named the "Wallsend," yields more coal than any other in the world, the average daily output for the last few years having been 2,000 tons.

We next played Eighteen of Singleton and District, at Singleton, on February 14th and 15th; this was also drawn in our favour. The wicket here was of cocoa-nut matting, which did not play so well as some others we had tried. There are some splendid vineries at Singleton, and grapes are very plentiful. The people made us most welcome, and were very hospitable towards us.

We then returned to Sydney, the journey including six hours by water and several hours by rail. We played there, against New South Wales, on February 18th, 19th, and 21st, and lost by 122 runs. Read was top scorer, and played two dashing innings of 48 and 40. Shrewsbury got a "pair of spectacles," something most unusual for him. These were the first pair he had ever "made," from what he told me. Turner bowled in first-class style.

The following match was also played at Sydney, against the combined Australian Team, on February 25th, 26th, 28th, and March 1st. We came out the victors by 71 runs. Lohmann bowled well, taking ten wickets. I was top scorer with 34, and 42 not out.

We went on to Melbourne for our next match, against Victoria, and having a day's interval to ourselves we attended the races, and saw the Australian Cup run for; it was one of the finest sights I ever saw. We began play on March 4th, and the match lasted into the fifth day—March 8th. We won by nine wickets. Shrewsbury played one of his very best innings for 144. Bates, in the second innings, played a dashing game for 86, which pleased the spectators immensely. I made 43, and 4 not out. Our next match was also played at Melbourne, against Fifteen of East Melbourne Club, on their own ground, on March 11th, 12th, and 14th. This was drawn in our favour. Lohmann played a fine, free game for exactly 100; Scotton played a useful innings of 71; myself, 24.

We then proceeded to Sandhurst, to play against an eighteen on March 15th and 16th. This match also ended in a draw. Read was in good form with the bat, and played a fine hitting innings for 140. Briggs made 43, and myself 46.

We again played on the East Melbourne Club ground, at Melbourne, on March 17th, 18th, 19th, and 21st, in the Smokers v. Non-Smokers match, and I cannot do better than adopt the words of "Felix," of the Melbourne *Australasian*, regarding this match. He wrote:—"I must congratulate my fellow 'Non-Smokers' on our magnificent achievement against our friends the 'Smokers.' Our score of 803 for nine wickets stands alone, unprecedented in aggregate and brilliance. This score will be for ever memorable in the annals of cricket, for it beats the record of the world in first-class cricket, and against some of the very best bowling we have."

There were only three byes recorded in this long score. Shrewsbury's innings of 236 was very fine indeed ; his cutting, leg-hitting, and driving were faultless and finished ; he only gave two chances—one to the wicket-keeper, and the other to Boyle at " cover-point." Gunn's innings of 150 was a perfect one in every way, and his hitting on the " off-side " was a treat to witness. Bruce played very fine cricket for his score of 131. I made 29. I was lame in the foot, and had to have a runner, and could not bowl in this match.

The " Smokers' " scores were 356 and 135 for five wickets ; thus the match was drawn, after four days' play, in our favour—the " Non-Smokers." Palmer was in good batting form, and put together 113. Our little friend Briggs made two good scores of 86 and 54 ; his hitting pleased all present.

We left Melbourne for Adelaide by train, on March 22nd. There were many Victorian cricketers and others on the platform, who had gathered to bid us farewell.

We played our last match at Adelaide, on March 24th, 25th, and 26th, 1887, against Fifteen of Adelaide and District, ending in a draw in our favour. Briggs and I each made 53, and Read 44. Jarvis, of Adelaide, played well for 77.

We sailed for old England on March 27th, by the fine P. & O. liner " Massilia." The captain's name was Shallard—a very nice fellow. The first few days of the voyage were calm ; consequently, we were all good sailors for the time-being. We touched King George's Sound, or Albany, for about nine hours on the 30th, when most of us took a walk on shore. Our ship left again at midnight of the same day, the weather having changed for the worse in the meantime, and the sea being very rough. Many of us were again seized with the " dread complaint," and were compelled to go upon starvation diet until things became quieter. The vessel rolled a great deal, so that we could neither eat nor sleep, and we were all thankful when, in a few days, we got away from the rough weather.

On April 5th the run was 332 miles, which took us into the tropics, where it is quite fine and bright one hour, and the next it is raining in torrents. We were now amusing ourselves during the daytime with cricket and other games, and in the evenings by holding concerts. On the 8th a concert was held in the saloon, at which I sung " When other lips." On April 9th we witnessed the finest sunset that it had ever been our good fortune to see ; it was simply too magnificent to put into words.

In the evening a Christy minstrel performance was held for the benefit of the Seamen's Orphan Fund. The cricketers who took part in it were Gunn, Sherwin, Scotton, Bates, Briggs, and myself. Mr. Clarke, a professional banjoist, also took part, and was quite a host in himself. Sherwin and Gunn manipulated the tambourines in a very creditable manner, and I contributed two songs. Church service was held on board each Sunday, Gunn, Scotton, Read, and myself being in the choir.

Colombo was reached on Easter Monday, April 11th, where we stayed two days. We, of course, landed and took another good look around the place, and had some fine fun with the darkies. Several large "men-o'-war" were anchored at this port, and I had the interesting experience of being shown over one of them named " The Bacchante." This was the ship in which the two young princes—George and Leopold—made a tour round the world. We left Colombo on the following day, the weather being very calm and the sea like a mill-pond for several days. A whist tournament was held on the 13th, which was won by Messrs. Graves and Shrewsbury; also a Calcutta sweep on the 14th, the first prize being close on £20. This was won by a gentleman named Cook. We kept our hands in at cricket by playing on deck almost every afternoon.

On April 16th our vessel made 315 miles, and on the 17th 312 miles, the weather being very hot and the sea smooth as glass. The coast of Africa came in sight on the 18th, and we reached Aden on the 19th, where I and a few others landed for a short time.

Another Calcutta sweep was held on the 21st, the lucky winner on this occasion being our friend Bates, who cleared about £21.

Our final athletic sports were held on April 22nd; they were discontinued owing to many of the cricketers declining to take part in them. The most successful competitors on this last occasion were Messrs. Crossland and Gunn.

On April 23rd the second-class passengers gave a concert which was, without doubt, the best entertainment I have ever attended on board ship. The artistes included two professionals—a Mr. and Mrs. Clarke—who were really first-class.

We reached Suez on April 24th, but passed on through the canal without landing, the latter being illuminated at night by the electric light.

At 5-30 the following morning we arrived at Port Said, and as we had to wait nearly two days for the Bombay passengers, we went on shore and amused ourselves amongst the negroes and donkeys. Our vessel weighed anchor again on the 27th, and soon afterwards we entered the Mediterranean.

Another whist tournament was held this week, which was won by Messrs. Graves and Scotton. Three hundred and six miles were covered on April 29th, and the next day we had got as far as Malta, where we remained for seven hours. This allowed us to land and inspect the various places of interest on the island, which include the Governor's palace, the church of St. John's, the garrison library, the public library of the knights, the beautiful gardens, and many other. Malta struck me as being a beautiful place, and it possesses a magnificent harbour. We sailed again under very favourable weather conditions, and touched " The key to the Mediterranean " on the 3rd of May. The few hours our vessel remained here just allowed us time to hire a cab and take a drive round. The rocky scenery at Gibraltar is very grand, standing as it does 1,400 feet above sea level, and the fortifications appear to be impregnable.

On May 5th a complimentary concert was held by the passengers for the benefit of Mr. and Mrs. Clarke, the professionals before referred to. They had been very good on several occasions in giving their services for the entertainment of the other passengers.

Our ship reached the notorious Bay of Biscay on May 6th, which this time belied its reputation and was quite serene.

Plymouth was gained on the 7th, after a passage of forty-one days from Adelaide, and Briggs and I arrived at Manchester at 1-20 a.m. of May 8th, 1887, and were soon at " Home, sweet home." Thus ended my third and last tour to Australia. I think I can say that it was the most enjoyable of the three. The umpiring and other matters incidental to cricket were also much more satisfactory.

R. G. BARLOW, AS UMPIRE
(Present day—1908).

[*Photo. by E. Hawkins & Co., Brighton.*]

Hints to Umpires.

SOME remarks on "Umpiring" will not, I think, be out of place. I speak as a present-day county cricket umpire, and one with an experience of many years. Umpiring at the present day is much better than it used to be. One reason is that all umpires are now strictly neutral, and never umpire at matches in which their own county is engaged, as was formerly the case. A second reason is that they have more matches, which gives them (unlimited) practice and confidence.

Umpiring, like cricket coaching, is a profession to itself, requiring plenty of practice and experience, as will be readily understood by all followers of the game.

The position of umpire is a thankless one, and at all times very trying, as it is impossible to please both sides; the umpire has not yet been born who can always do this. The only safe rule to follow is to give your decisions according to the dictates of your conscience, without fear or favour. A cool head and an even temper are also very necessary qualities in an umpire. He should have a thorough knowledge of the laws of the game, and should have been a county player himself, or have played some years in good club cricket, and have had practical experience.

It is well to remember that an umpire will find it safer to have the rules at his finger-ends. I know several umpires who never got out to officiate before first reading the rules; and, in fact, I often read them over myself, although I know almost all the cricket laws off by heart.

When umpiring, you should stand perfectly still, because if you move about you may attract the attention of the batsman, and lead him to make a mis-hit. You must watch that the bowler does not go over the bowling crease, and he must deliver the ball with one foot on the ground behind the bowling crease, and within the return crease. If you see any breach of either of these rules you must call " No ball," though you should wait until the ball has left the bowler's hand.

On giving a decision, the umpire should make sure that the batsman understands what the decision is.

I must say one thing especially is necessary, and that is for umpires to learn to fix their attention immediately upon the game in hand, for unless they give their whole attention to it, their opinions will not be worth very much. But, besides the possibility of becoming a fine judge of the game by looking on, there are difficult points that will arise which can only be thought out by those who have had the opportunity of playing in first-class cricket.

Much may be learned by going to watch a first-class cricket match ; and if any of my readers are thinking of umpiring, I would advise them to go to a first-class match and concentrate their attention upon the umpires. There are many who go to pick up hints as to fielding, batting, or bowling ; but many who umpire or captain local teams might learn a good deal by watching how trained umpires go about their work.

The most difficult thing is to give a man out "leg before wicket." Many first-class umpires find it a hard matter. This I can speak of from my own experience—it is the one particular decision about which the batsman and bowler will rarely both be satisfied. I have found batsmen who would calmly tell you that the ball did not pitch straight, or else that it would not have hit the wicket had it not broke or twisted.

I will just give one case in point, where cricketers alter their opinions with regard to umpires. I was umpiring some few years ago in a county match, and when I arrived at the ground, on the Thursday morning, a few of the cricketers asked me who the other umpire was. When I told them, they all seemed pleased, and said: "A very good one, too ; we have had him standing in two of our matches this season, and he did very well ;" and made other favourable remarks to his credit. When this very match was over, which they had lost, I remember going into their dressing-room on the Saturday night and overhearing the same cricketers, who had spoken so well in this umpire's favour only a few days before, calling him all kinds of names, such as "a bad umpire," and saying that he "had given some very wrong decisions, and that they hoped they would not have him again ;" and so on. Of course, this is all in the game ; and—speaking again from a long experience—there is not much in it at the end of each season, with regard to the umpires' decisions. Sometimes a batsman will be given "out" when he is "not out," and sometimes he is given "not out" when he is "out." As the late Arthur Shrewsbury, of Notts, once said to me : "It cuts both ways for all cricketers, and one never ought to grumble so very much." I often think of his words now that I am umpiring. An umpire has his good and bad days, like the batsman and the bowler. He should have a good eye and a quick ear.

I remember, in 1884, playing for Lancashire against Cheshire, at Stockport, when I was caught at the wicket off my glove, from Sam Brown's bowling. Several made the appeal, but I was given " not out " by their own umpire. This was before I had scored; in fact, it was the third ball I received. I went on batting after this, and made my hundred runs.

All umpires make mistakes at times, which cannot be avoided; but, of course, the best are those who make the fewest.

It should be a rule never to argue with the batsman whom you have given " out," as this is certain to create an unfavourable impression, and no good can possibly result. County cricket umpires belong to a profession, and an honourable one. Great interests are at stake, and they have to devote much time and trouble in making themselves proficient.

The following cutting contains a few remarks made by Captain McCanlis, of Kent, an old county cricketer, on the subject of umpires, and I endorse every word :—

" Captain McCanlis is strongly of opinion that umpires are often blamed without sufficient reason. ' People do not realise how difficult it is to act as umpire,' he said, ' and I think it would be a good thing if some of those who are perpetually finding fault would have a try to see what they could do themselves. I'll be bound that they would afterwards be much more moderate in their opinions. In connection with the misjudging of umpires, I was told a little anecdote by Jim Lillywhite about Jupp. Now Jupp, in his day, used to be very free in expressing his dissatisfaction with decisions that did not accord with his desires. When he left off playing he acted as umpire, and one day, after his duties were ended, he said to Jim Lillywhite: ' Do you know, Jim, I should like to have all the umpires, who used to stand when I played, before me and apologize to 'em.' "

To illustrate how an umpire can be blamed after giving a good decision, two instances occurred in my own experience, when I was umpiring at Brighton, in 1902, in a Sussex v. Notts match. The first instance was when Mr. G. Brann was batting against Wass, the Notts bowler, Oates being the wicket-keeper. The latter, as well as several fielders, appealed for a catch at the wicket, when I at once replied " Not out." Later, when Harry Butt (another Sussex batsman) was batting, Hallam, the bowler, along with some of the fielders, made a precisely similar appeal, to which I again responded "Not out." I afterwards learned that a few of the Notts team had been taking me severely to task among themselves for giving what they considered to be two incorrect decisions. Arthur Shrewsbury, with whom I was at all times on the best of terms, also told me, after the close of the day's play, that he considered both of these decisions were wrong, and that, in his opinion, both men were caught at the wicket. I replied that I could not agree with him, as the ball had, in Mr. Brann's case, hit his shirt-sleeve, and in Butt's case the ball just grazed his pad at the knee. This was fully confirmed, as the two batsmen named told me, the following morning, that they had neither of them played the ball, but that it had hit each exactly as I had explained to Shrewsbury.

I could multiply cases of this kind, though I admit that we are all liable at times to make mistakes.

As for myself, I can say that I have, throughout my career as an umpire, given my decisions without fear or favour, no matter whether the appeal has been made against a " Prince," " Lord," " Sir," " Mr.," or " pro." Neither have I ever found cause to withdraw a decision. If I have at any time made a mistake, it has been quite unknowingly. I trust that a certain team which came to England in 1899 will please note the few foregoing remarks.

Two new resolutions were passed by the county captains, at a meeting held at Lord's Cricket Ground, on December 9th last (1907), as follow :—

1. " That each umpire selected shall present a certificate, or letter of fitness, as to the satisfactory condition of his eyesight and hearing from a well-known Infirmary doctor, before his appointment is confirmed."

2. " The fact that glasses are worn shall not be a bar to umpiring."

I think the county captains were well advised in passing the foregoing resolutions, as it is very important that the " man in the white coat " should both hear well and see well.

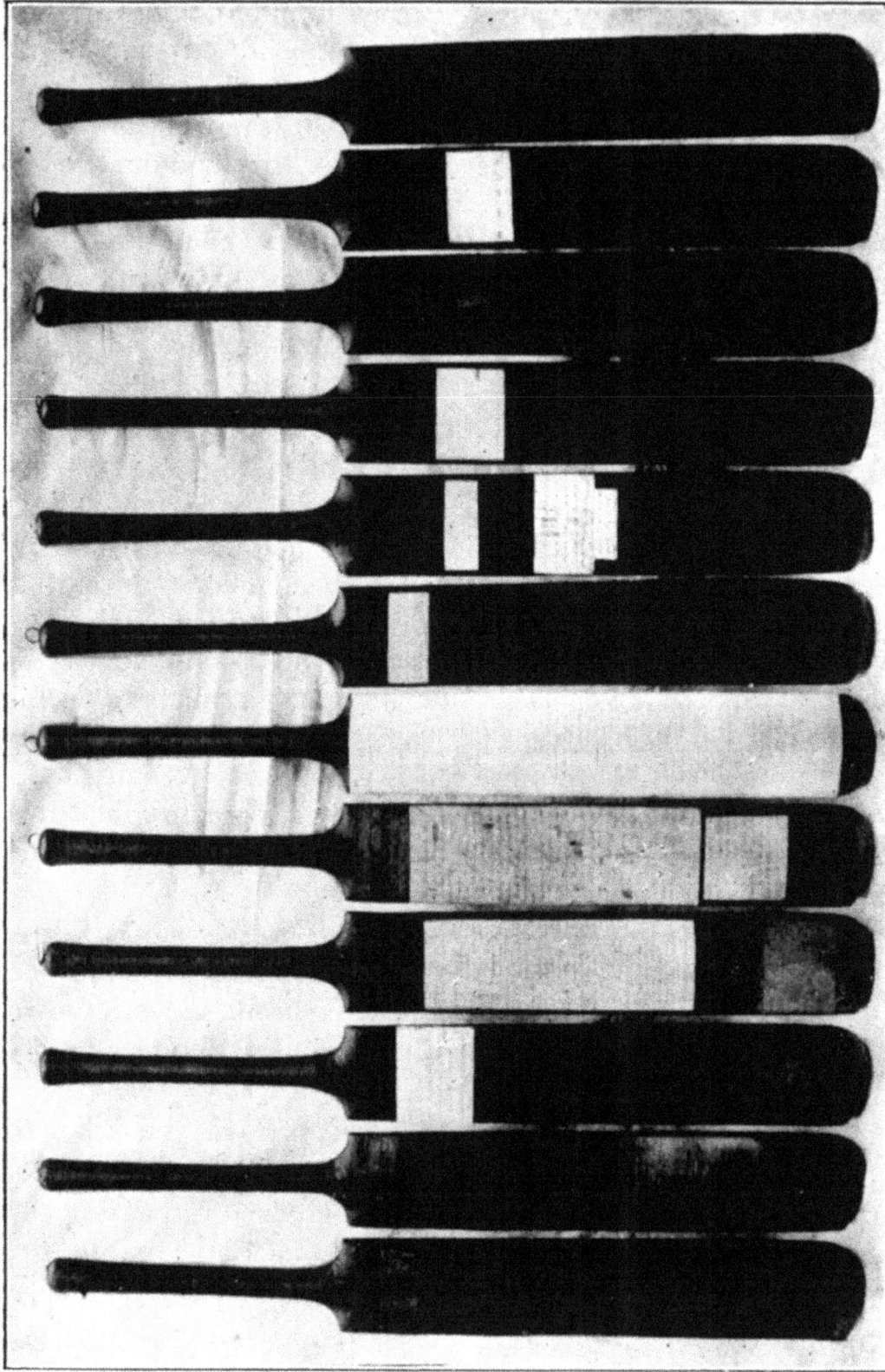

TWELVE OF BARLOW'S FAMOUS BATS,

All of which have done excellent service in the field. The sixth from left travelled round the world with him in 1881-2. With this bat Barlow made over 4,000 runs, and in 1882 he carried it through the innings on six occasions. This was Barlow's favourite bat.

Captainship.

CAPTAIN should be a good judge of the game; he should also possess an even temper, and have a kind word for his men at all times, especially if they miss a catch or make a mistake. I know from experience that no one is more upset than the fielder himself who drops a catch. A captain will get far more out of a bowler by kindness and consideration than by being exacting and overbearing in his manner.

A good captain will, if possible, never have two bowlers on together who are alike in speed and delivery; the greater the contrast and the better. I always advocate a right-hand and a left-hand bowler being on at the same time. The captain should always ask the bowler which end would best suit him. Captain and bowler should try and discover the batsman's weak points, and place their field accordingly.

A captain should, if possible, have one or two left-hand batsmen in his team. I have known them win many matches, as they often upset the field by crossing over, etc., and, again, often put the bowler off his length. Many bowlers cannot bowl quite so well at a left-hand batsman as a right-hand one. In this I am speaking from experience.

There are also times when the captain should consult his men with regard to change of bowling and the conduct of the game.

The discreet captain will always try and save the bowler all unnecessary exertion when bowling, and never let him run very far in fielding the ball, as it takes very much out of a bowler having to run after the ball. Then, again, no bowler should throw any great distance oftener than he can really avoid, as he might injure his bowling arm by wrenching the muscles. I have known this to occur several times in my career, causing the bowler to be off duty for several days at a time. I remember some years ago Allan Hill, the old Yorkshire fast bowler, injuring his arm by throwing the very first ball from long-field, which prevented him from bowling again for some weeks.

There is more in a good captain than many people are aware of. I have frequently seen matches lost through bowlers being put on to bowl on wickets which did not suit their particular delivery and speed, and also through not changing the bowlers and fielders at the right moment for the batsmen's different styles of play. How much a captain can do, and how far he can go towards imbuing his team with the proper spirit necessary for success, can scarcely be estimated. But I do know that captains can do much by force of example. Instances of this have been found in Messrs. I. D. Walker, A. N. Hornby, and J. Shuter; Mr. W. L. Murdoch, the Australian captain, was another of this kind.

In my opinion, it is a mistake for a captain to advise a batsman, as is done at times, to play in this or that style. It is often quite contrary to what the batsman has been accustomed to, and he will, not unfrequently, lose his wicket through it, as I have seen them do many times, and have heard the players afterwards say that they wished the captain had allowed them to play their own game. It is a great mistake to fidget any batsman just before he goes in to bat. Many batsmen cannot alter their style; it takes a first-class player to do this and to play according to the state of the game, and the condition of the wicket.

I have often noticed grave mistakes made by captains, and I feel convinced that captainship has deteriorated since the old days. Of course, there are some good men left yet, but, taking them all round, they do not compare with the old school of captains, of whom I might mention Lord Harris (Kent), Lord Hawke (Yorkshire), Messrs. A. N. Hornby and A. G. Steel (Lancashire), I. D. Walker and A. J. Webbe (Middlesex), J. Shuter (Surrey), S. M. J. Woods (Somersetshire), and the late W. Oscroft (Nottinghamshire). The last-named was the best professional captain I ever saw, and a fine judge of the game. The late R. Daft and Mr. J. A. Dixon (Notts) were also good captains. At the present day, in my opinion, the three best captains are Messrs. A. C. Maclaren (Lancashire), A. O. Jones (Notts), and G. Macgregor (Middlesex); these might be called born captains.

A GOOD POSITION AT THE WICKET.

A. C. Maclaren (Lancashire) batting; the batsman who made the highest individual score on record in a first-class county match, viz: 424 for Lancashire *v*. Somersetshire, at Taunton in July, 1895.

[*Photo. by W. Smith, West Didsbury.*]

Hints to Young Cricketers

ON

Batting, Bowling, Fielding, and Wicket-Keeping.

Batting.

IN penmanship the young pupil has first to be taught how to hold his pen ; so in cricket the learner should first know how to handle his bat ; and while those who know how to do so may smile at this elementary advice, those who do not will be glad to be informed. It is a general opinion amongst the best batsmen, and one which I endorse, that an average-sized man should grip the handle of the bat by the middle, the circumference of which should be in proportion to the size of the hand. From my own experience, I have always found it to my advantage to hold the bat half-way up the handle, and to keep it off the ground poised pendulum fashion, in order to be prepared for either forward or back play. This, in my opinion, gives the greatest scope for freedom of play, without diminishing the powers of defence. The weight of the bat should stand in close relation to the batsman's strength. From 2 lbs. 2 oz. to 2 lbs. 8 oz. will represent a range which will suit all players. When batting, take a firm hold with your right hand, keeping your left hand rather loose, that it may be twisted round or half-round as the case requires ; at the same time always keep the bat handle well forward, as by so doing you will keep the balls down much easier. Although a few hours of good professional coaching is of more value than volumes of book learning, yet written instructions may be studied when practice cannot be had. Now the batsman's motto should be that of the British volunteer, viz., " Defence, not defiance." Let him first take care of his wickets, and the runs will take care of themselves.

It must not be supposed that I am tendering advice to such skilled hands as the Hon. F. S. Jackson, Messrs. C. B. Fry, A. O. Jones, R. E. Foster, P. F. Warner, P. Perrin, and Tom Hayward, G. Hirst, J. T. Tyldesley, J. Iremonger, D. Denton, E. Arnold, F. C. Holland, and many others, who are better able to take care of both wickets and runs than I am to tell them how. This is addressed to those who desire to emulate the cricketers named.

It is a virtue in cricket to consider your side more than yourself, and he is beyond dispute a most desirable partner who has the fortitude, patience, and endurance to go in first and come out last. Though he may not have increased the score to any great extent by his own batting, he has been the means of enabling all his fellows to add to the grand total. I would advise all young batsmen to practise the defence of the wicket as much as possible for the first few years, and learn the various strokes all around the wicket before beginning to do much at hitting. When you do hit, however, hit as hard as you can; but this will come to you with practice and experience and a little good coaching.

There is not so much leg-hitting to-day as formerly, owing to the present-day bowlers bowling so much to the off-side, but whenever you get the opportunity for a leg-hit put your left foot a little to the left side, and hit the ball as squarely as possible in front of your left toe. When the ball is just outside your legs on the leg-side, my advice is to turn it off in the direction of long-leg, or "gliding it down," as many cricketers term it. Always stand as upright as possible, and do not lose half an inch of your height when batting. The more you can look down upon the ball, and the better you will see it; at the same time you will get over the high balls much better in order to keep them down. Remember once more that patience and defence are everything in batting to the young beginner.

I hope that it will not be considered self-laudation if I emphasize the advice already given by mentioning the fact that few batsmen, if any, have gone in first and come out last as frequently as myself. Attitude and position are no small factors in the make-up of a good batsman. First acquire a position which suits you and is at the same time not incorrect; stand with the right leg quite firm, the right foot six or eight inches inside the crease, with the toes in a' line with the leg-stump, which line should always be marked when practising, say from the leg-stump to about three feet outside the popping crease; and when playing forward at all balls on the wicket, the left toe should be up to this line. 'By this means your body and your bat will come straight to the ball. Remember to keep your right foot firm as a rock when playing forward, or you may easily be stumped; make it the pivot on which every movement of the left leg, arms, and body may turn with ease, rapidity, and precision; and be ready to stride well forward, backward, to the on or to the off-side, as the exigencies of the moment may require. The muscles of legs, arms, and wrists should be relaxed, that being the most favourable condition for sudden action. Stand with your bat full face to the bowler, protecting the leg and middle stump, having the handle well forward and down, though not so much so as to hinder your quick recovery in case of making a hit. Bring the left shoulder well round, with your face looking over that shoulder. You are now prepared for the attack, and ready to deal with the ball in whatever manner it may be delivered.

Whilst admitting that cricketers are not like poets—born, not made—I must maintain that many natural qualities may be, and undoubtedly are, of great advantage. Not the least of these is a keen and quick vision, which, if not possessed naturally, must be trained to the highest perfection attainable by practising the eye to follow objects, and especially cricket balls, in rapid motion. In my own experience, I take it as an indication of being in good health and form when a cricket ball is as readily seen as a football. Practice must be against the best and most varied bowling that it is possible to get, and let your practice wicket be as good as your match wicket. You cannot be too particular about this. I am sure you will not make much improvement in batting if you do not have good practice wickets to play on. I would recommend having a matting wicket for practice if you cannot get a good turf wicket. I have often played in matches in Australia on these matting wickets, and some of them played very well. When at practice, play just as keenly as when in a match. In my young days I often put a sixpence on the stumps, telling the bowlers that they could have it if they knocked it off. This caused both bowlers and myself to play very keenly, and made very fine practice.

Young players should never go in to bat either at practice or at matches without first putting on both leg-guards and both batting-gloves. The fewer knocks you receive, and the better you will enjoy the game. Some players say that they cannot hold the bat so well with batting-gloves on, but this is only for want of practice. Personally, I would never bat on either good or bad wickets without wearing leg-guards and batting-gloves. Also be careful to have a bat of the correct weight and size; see that it is well-balanced and not too heavy. I say more on this matter in another place. I also strongly advise having a rubber cover or sleeve over the bat handle, as this gives a better grip and prevents your hands from slipping.

I know that some of the masters and professional coaches at the schools are not so particular as they should be about these little matters. When coaching boys, I think that it is a great mistake to bowl them out too often, as it disheartens them. They should be encouraged as much as possible. Give them a few balls which they can hit, and a cheering word now and then, such as "Well hit," "Well played," etc.

I should now like to say a few words about forward play, which always was with me a hobby. Some may think I have ridden it rather hard, but I consider that this style of play does not receive the attention it deserves. I would therefore, in all cases of doubt as to whether to play a ball forward or backward, adopt the former, and avoid the mistake frequently made by young players of putting the right leg across to an off-ball. This is wrong, as it is the left leg which should be thrown across to the off-side to hit in front of point, and the right leg put across to hit the ball behind point, when making the cut.

In playing forward, get as near to the pitch as possible and take a long stride, by which means you have a much better chance of killing the good length balls before the break gets on. I have found this method valuable to myself in an experience extending over many years.

The batsman putting into practice the foregoing advice must, of course, be careful not to give such wicket-keepers as Lilley, Humphries, Hunter, Oates, Strudwick, Butt, Huish, and Messrs. Martyn and Macgregor a chance of stumping him through over-reaching himself. Do not be tempted to lunge out at every ball, nor to trust more to chance than to judgment. When the pitch or wicket is hard and fast, play oftener forward than backward; but on a soft or sticky wicket, when the ball is turning about, I strongly advise back play more than forward, and play at the ball as much as possible, and not so much at the pitch on this kind of wicket.

When match playing, never overrun your ground, as I have seen many players do, running yards beyond the wickets, instead of planting the bat just within the crease and turning at once in hope of another run. Have your bat well in front and along the ground when nearing the popping crease, and always bear in mind that when you hit the ball in front of your own wicket it is for you to judge the run; but if you strike it behind, it is your partner who must decide; your business is to watch your partner, and not the ball.

It would be equally satisfactory to me as to my reader if I could impart to him the ability to make straight drives for fives, and square-leg hits for fours; but I fear the task is beyond the power of my pen, and I must perforce fall back upon my advice to practise, practise, practise with your bat until you have acquired by habit that which pen cannot write nor tongue explain.

Finally, when match playing always have confidence in yourself. Think that you are going to make some runs when batting; the same when bowling, think you are going to get some wickets, and that you can bowl any of the batsmen out. As my father often told me, to be successful in cricket, and especially in batting, a boy or man needs plenty of patience.

R. G. BARLOW IN THE ACT OF DELIVERY.

[*Photo. by R. Berry, Blackpool.*]

Bowling.

MY advice to all young bowlers is to make it their business first of all to discover the weak points of the batsman, and then to adapt themselves thereto. Patience is a virtue at all times, and especially so in bowling; study and calculation are great helps. Avoid tearing away until you are too fatigued to lift your arm. Be careful, be deliberate; mark the place where you wish to start from, and take the same run and the same strides every time; by so doing, you never ought to bowl any no-balls. When you are bowling, try for place, not for pace. When at practice, only bowl for, say, half an hour at a time. Never tire yourself out, and never bowl beyond your strength; but proceed by easy stages to a high delivery.

Whenever you practise, give all your mind to it, and bowl just the same as you would at a match. Bowl for the wicket as much as possible, with an occasional ball from six to twelve inches outside the off-stump. Try to keep a good length, and vary the pace, the height, the flight, and spin of the ball; but you will learn all this by practice and experience.

Never try to break the ball both ways, or to make it do too much. My advice is to learn to break the ball only one way, just enough to beat the bat; but above all, keep a good length, as I have already advised. The "demon bowler" (Mr. F. R. Spofforth), A. Shaw, A. Watson, J. T. Hearne, W. Attewell, and other first-class bowlers whom I could name, have all taken the same run and the same strides at each delivery, and have only gone in for breaking the ball one way, just sufficient to beat the bat : but they have all been good "length" bowlers, and have, when bowling, used their heads as much as their arms.

To perfect myself, when practising I used to mark out with pieces of paper the correct pitches for a fast and for a medium-pace ball. Remember, the length of the pitch depends on the speed as a rule. Fast bowling requires a shorter pitch—*i.e.*, a shorter length from the wicket—than slow or medium bowling, always, of course, keeping in mind any peculiarities the batsman may possess.

Take every opportunity of studying the style of high-class bowlers, and note the perfection to which practice and concentration can attain. I do not recommend holding the ball in the palm of the hand. The late Alfred Shaw, the late E. Peate, the late J. Briggs, the late G. Lohmann, Messrs. A. G. Steel, F. R. Spofforth, C. T. B. Turner, Willis Cuttell, and other first-class bowlers whom I have met, grasped the ball by the tips of the fingers, and against the seam. By this means, the greatest amount of spin can be given to the ball. The fingers may be said to rule both the delivery and the direction of the ball. Some bowlers also use their wrists a little. All batsmen are puzzled by variety of speed and pitch ; therefore, if possible, let every ball be different— at least, until you have found out the weak spot in your adversary. If he favours forward play, give him a shorter ball with plenty of life ; if back play, let the ball pitch further up. But let all your efforts have the distinct object of taking his wicket, and not of merely gaining a " maiden over." Practice bowling both over and round the wicket. Most right-hand bowlers bowl over, and left-hand bowlers round.

Boys should not try to bowl the 22 yards until they are over fifteen or sixteen years of age. When I am coaching boys younger than this, I never let them bowl over 18 or 19 yards. If the captains and professional bowlers who are engaged at schools and colleges would pay more attention to this matter, there would be more boy bowlers I feel sure. The cricket ball also should be a little under the full size for young boys.

As regards my own bowling, I think it was a natural gift, always coming with my arm more or less. I never tried to make the ball go away, or break back, as it is termed. I always endeavoured to keep a good length, varying the pace and flight of the ball, &c., and studying the batsman's weak points, making him play almost every ball, and giving him a few balls in each over to make him play both forward and back.

The bowler should at all times when bowling be on the alert for a catch, especially when the batsman is playing forward. I have seen many catches missed through neglect of this precaution. I have also seen many batsmen who would have been run out if the bowler had only got back to his wicket in time to receive the ball when thrown in from the field.

THE AUTHOR IN THE FIELD.

This shows the correct attitude to be adopted when in the act of catching any high balls.
The hands should be allowed to give a little at the moment of impact. This minimises the
sting and prevents the ball from rebounding out of the hands.

[*Photo. by R. Berry, Blackpool, 1908.*]

Fielding.

THOUGH usually regarded as a minor essential, fielding is at least of equal importance with the other accomplishments that make the good cricketer, and if conducted in a careless, slovenly manner will end in defeat and disgrace. To be a good fielder requires—like the acquisitions of batting and bowling—steady, constant, persevering practice. Almost perfect examples of fielding are to be found in Messrs. G. L. Jessop (Gloucestershire), A. O. Jones (Notts), L. G. Wright (Derbyshire), R. H. Spooner and A. H. Hornby (Lancashire), Braund (Somerset), Tyldesley (Lancashire), J. Gunn (Notts), Denton (Yorkshire), Quaife (Warwickshire), and Vine (Sussex). These are well worthy of imitation, and of travelling miles to see.

Smart fielding often gets wickets which have defied the best of bowling. Meeting the ball is essential to quick fielding, and requires practice of its own. Run in to meet a straight ball, with your hands ready and well down ; practice jumping, to make a high catch; and keep your eye well on the ball. Let your throwing-in be by a single action of the arm, free from flourish, and straight to the wicket-keeper or bowler, without a long hop. Also practice catching with the left hand, as well as with the right. A fielder must not neglect backing-up, to save overthrows. Bad fielding disheartens both bowler and wicket-keeper, and one bad fielder is a loose screw in any eleven. I may mention a practice I adopt several times a week in my tuition of young cricketers. I place them in the field as though a match were being played, and throw the ball to different players, varying the height, speed, and course of the ball, expecting them to return it to me in the shortest possible space of time. Another method I have also often adopted is to spread the boys about the field, and then to take the bat and hit catches to them, both high and low, also giving them ground fielding. This is really good practice.

Still another plan is to place the boys so as to form a large circle, and then to throw the ball about from one to another, trying to take the boys unaware ; also giving them balls to catch with the left hand, as well as with the right. I have found this to be very good practice, and splendid training for the eye.

Long-stopping without a net is also very good practice in fielding, and will mature the habit of quick return; it should be frequently practiced by all young beginners. Fielders should remember that their duty is to prevent runs being scored; to adapt a well-known proverb, "a run saved is a run gained." In catching, keep your hands well together, yielding a little at the moment of impact so as to neutralize the sting of the ball. Fielding is a science, and as such requires careful study. How can a bowler throw his whole heart and energy into his play if he feels no security in his field? How can a team play well together if some of its members are untrustworthy in picking up, throwing, or catching the ball?

Good coaching in batting, bowling, and fielding, I strongly recommend; but from what I have seen and heard, many of the professionals engaged at the schools and colleges do not take pains with the boys as they should, nor do they know very much about coaching, which, I maintain, is a profession to itself, the same as umpiring. I am afraid there are not so many good coaches now as there were some years ago, some of whom I could name.

Just a little more advice on fielding, before I leave the subject. Always keep your eye on the batsman. By watching him closely, you can tell what he is going to do even before the bat strikes the ball. Whenever possible, get both hands to the ball, except in the case of a chance of running out a batsman, when you are justified in risking the loss of a run or two.

I have always said, "Give me a good fielder and a moderate batsman, before a bad fielder and a good batsman." I know several very fine batsmen who would have been selected to play in more important matches if they had been better in the field. Remember that fielding is, after all, the most important part of the game. Good fielding helps moderate bowling. Boys should learn to love fielding.

R. PILLING (LANCASHIRE), THE PRINCE OF WICKET-KEEPERS.
[*Photo. by E. Hawkins & Co., Brighton.*]

Wicket-keeping.

AS I do not profess to have a thorough knowledge of the art of wicket-keeping—although I kept wicket very often in my early days—it is outside my province to tender much advice on my own account. But the fact that, some years ago, my friend the late Richard Pilling (Lancashire), known as " the prince of wicket-keepers," kindly revised my remarks on the subject, will, I feel sure, make them acceptable to every cricketer who desires to fill this important position ; and important it undoubtedly is.

If there is one department of cricket requiring, more than another, that wonderful sympathy between eye and hand which I attempted to describe in concluding my remarks on batting, that department is wicket-keeping. A wicket-keeper must be firm as a rock, as bold as a lion, quick as thought, cool as a cucumber, and as hard as nails ; he should possess one of the finest tempers in the world ; and must run the risk of having his eyes blackened and his fingers put out of joint. It will thus be admitted that the post is no sinecure. Still, I am glad to know that, in spite of all this, we have such wicket-keepers as Messrs. G. Macgregor (Middlesex), H. Martyn (Somerset), and A. Lilley (Warwickshire) ; Humphries (Derbyshire), Oates (Notts), Strudwick and Stedman (Surrey), Huish (Kent), Hunter (Yorkshire), and Worsley (Lancashire),

Having said so much about the marvellous results of patient, persevering practice, it is perhaps somewhat discouraging to state that no amount of practice will make a brilliant wicket-keeper, unless he has an electric wire laid on between his eye and hand. When he finds this connection to be already laid on, he may practise with some prospect of success.

I notice with regret that few writers on cricket give any advice on wicket-keeping, though I very much doubt, were all the wicket-keepers to combine to tell the cricket world how it is done, if they would add much to the theoretical knowledge of wicket-keeping already possessed. All and every one of the wicket-keepers I have named can *show* you how it is done, but to put it into words is quite another matter. However, here is what my late friend Pilling said on the subject :—

" A wicket-keeper must possess the following qualities, if he wishes to attain perfection in this difficult art, viz., patience, perseverance, and a certain amount of fearlessness. He must also be steady, quick of sight, and, above all, able to control his temper. If he allows his temper to get the better of him, through having missed some chance of a catch or of stumping, depend upon it mistakes will continue until he cools down to his normal temperature.

"I would strongly impress upon all who have any desire to become wicket-keepers to be temperate in all things. In your position behind the wickets you will always require to be in the best of form, with a clear head and an undimmed eye, seeing that upon you will devolve the duty of stopping every ball missed by the batsman. A large amount of patience will have to be exercised by the aspirant for wicket-keeping honours. Be content with small successes at first, and climb the ladder of fame by degrees. Do not be downhearted or nervous, for a nervous man will never make a wicket-keeper, as he occupies the most dangerous position in the field, and, without doubt, gets more knocks and bruises than any other person engaged in the game. But if he wishes to excel he must not allow this to discourage him, but stick to it, resolving to be more careful, and try to escape such accidents another time.

"You cannot make a wicket-keeper of *any* one; to some it comes naturally, as a gift. But to all I would say, it is with wicket-keeping, as with everything else, 'Practice makes perfect'—and the best practice is to be obtained in matches. During practice nights choose, if you may, the best bowlers on the field to practise with, as fewer accidents will happen to you from first-class than from second or third-rate bowling; and remember that success follows perseverance."

Conclusion.

BY way of general advice, and in conclusion, I would remark that he who aspires to be a good all-round cricketer, must not only have command of his bat and ball, but also of himself; and should abstain from every indulgence that would injuriously affect his mental, physical, or nervous system. He should live well, but plainly; avoid intoxicating liquors, excessive smoking, condiments, pastry, and new bread—(I may add, in passing that I am a life abstainer and non-smoker). He should eat slowly, take regular exercise, keep up a mild, steady course of training by using Indian clubs and other gymnastic appliances, take a cold bath a few times every week, and keep the mind as free from worry and anxiety as his daily occupation will admit. Nothing need be said as to the physical effects of cricket. No man or boy who does not keep fit may ever hope to become, or remain, a good cricketer. A clear eye, a steady hand, a watchful brain, and a cheerful temper are the qualities necessary to attain success.

The author's chief object in writing this book has been to furnish the rising generation with a reliable and useful guide to the game, combined with an interesting record of his long experience in first-class cricket. If carefully studied by young aspirants to cricket fame, it will go far towards making expert cricketers of them. It will be found to be a reliable handbook to the game of cricket, both now and in years to come.

"A Chip off the Old Block"—(L.B.W.)

The Author "coaching" his only grandson, Leslie Barlow Wilson, three years of age. Grandpa's first present was a hollow cricket ball containing money, which the baby, then not many days old, took in his left hand. This greatly amused the veteran left-handed bowler, who took it as an omen that his descendant might become a worthy successor to him in the world of cricket.

[*Photo. by R. Berry, Blackpool, 1908.*]

Cricket Miscellany.

CRICKET SONG.

Then cricketers are we—each a batter bred and born.
The birds do sing, and so do we—and rise at early morn
To field and run, and bat and bowl, against a worthy team.
There's nought can beat a cricketer's life, out in the fields so green.

(*Chorus*)   Out in the green fields, so happy and so gay,
               Out in the green fields we pass our time away ;
               Out in the green fields we cricket all the day,
               And, like the larks, we whistle in the morning !

Captain Hornby is the finest man for many miles around,
And all his men have brawny arms—their equals can't be found.
When cricket time again comes round, we all shall then be seen,
We like the open sunlight best, out in the fields so green.

(*Chorus*)   Out in the green fields, so happy and so gay,
               Out in the green fields we pass our time away ;
               Out in the green fields we cricket all the day,
               And, like the larks, we whistle in the morning !

Of all the games we e'er did love, cricket's the game for us—
With bats and balls, stumps and bails, we form the wicket glorious.
As books supply the mind with food, the all-inspiring wicket
The body keeps in glowing health. Then three hurrahs for Cricket !

(*Chorus*)   Out in the green fields, so happy and so gay,
               Out in the green fields we pass our time away ;
               Out in the green fields we cricket all the day,
               And, like the larks, we whistle in the morning !

                             —*By R. G. Barlow (1880).*

    The following verses were composed and published after the
Hon. Ivo Bligh's English team brought home "the ashes" from
Australia in 1883 :—

IVO BLIGH [1883].

Ivo Bligh had a shy
    At Australian sticks ;
Scored like fun, gave them one
    Of the neatest "licks."
Hi, Ivo ! Ho, Ivo !
    Britons breathe once more,
Whilst they "fill" to your skill
    And Leslie's spanking score !

Ivo Bligh—England's eye—
　Murdoch's fairly wiped.
Barlow's "gross" retrieves our loss;
　How he bowled and swiped!
Hi, Ivo!　Ho, Ivo!
　Stick to it you will—
Not for "crow," just to show
　England's in it still!

LET CRICKET FLOURISH!

It flushes with glow of health each manly cheek and brow;
It bids the slow and sluggish blood in kindlier currents flow.
It knits the sinews into strength, and quickens every eye;
It nerves the hand, renews the heart, and bids all sorrow fly.

THE CHIEF OF GAMES.

What conduces to health deserves recommendation—
'Twill entail a strong race in the next generation;
And of all the field games ever practised or known,
That Cricket stands foremost, each Briton must own.

THE CRICKET MATCH, FROM A WOMAN'S POINT OF VIEW.

[An Extract.]

A newly-married man returned home one day to find his wife in tears.

"What are you crying for, Mary?" he asked.

"Oh, John, I simply cannot help it!　How those poor men must have suffered!　That Jessop is a brute!"

"Great Scott!　What has he been doing?"

"Haven't you read it?　Why, it says that when he came in he started punishing the bowlers severely!　He cut Hirst twice in the first over, and he knocked Haigh all over the field. Wainwright interfered; but he didn't do much good, because Jessop drove him to the boundary, out of the way. Next, Rhodes came up to see what he could do, but Jessop ran out to him, and knocked him over the pavilion. Brown came on, and what do you think Jessop did to him? Why, he skied him, and I think he would have been killed, but, fortunately, a man ran up and caught him!"

[R. G. B. umpired in the above match—Gloucestershire v. Yorkshire, at Bristol—which took place some years ago.]

THE LANCASHIRE CRICKETERS.—CHAMPION COUNTY, 1881.

13 Matches played; 10 won, 3 drawn.

G. Nash.   J. Crossland.   J. Smith (Umpire).   R. Pilling.   A. Watson.
A. G. Steel, Esq.   Rev. V. K. Royle.   A. N. Hornby, Esq.   A. Appleby, Esq.   J. Briggs.
W. Robinson.   R. G. Barlow.   O. P. Lancashire, Esq.

[Photo. by C. Voss Bark, Clifton.]

Autographs.

The following interesting collection of Autographs of well-known Cricketers has been made by the Author during his travels as Professional Cricketer and Umpire, extending over many years.

LANCASHIRE.

A. N. Hornby

R.G.Barlow 1850   cap 29

Alec. Watson

J. T. Tyldesley

John Briggs

I. Sharp.

Jack Baker

A.G. Paul

Arthur Mold

A. C. MacLaren

LANCASHIRE.

Allan G Steel

Vernon Royle

Albert Ward

Walter Brearley

Frank Sugg.

Willis. R. Cuttell

Alexander Eccles.

L.O.S. Poidevin

J.E. Stanning

A. H. Hornby

LANCASHIRE.

A. Kermode

R. H. Spooner

J P Whiteside

W. Worsley

W. R. Gregson

H Makepeace

H Dean

Wm Huddleston

Frank Harry

Oswald S. Lancashire

W Findlay.

YORKSHIRE.

Hawke. 1860.

Jno F Brunncliffe

Geo. H. Hirst

S Haigh.

R. Moorhouse

Jt Rhodes

J. T. Brown

D. Hunter

Lees Whitehead

YORKSHIRE.

David Denton

E. Wainwright

Frank Mitchell.

Louis Hall

W. Bates

R Peel

F. Stanley Jackson

H Myers

W. H. Wilkinson.

NOTTS.

A O Jones

J. A. Dixon

William Gunn.

T. Wass

J. Oates.

J Hardstaff

Jn Shrewin

W Payton

J W Day

Geo. Gunn

NOTTS.

G T Branston

E. Alletson

M. Flowers

Rich^o Daft

Alfred Shaw

William Attewell sup 22.0

Arthur Shrewsbury.

Albert: W. Hallam

J. Iremonger

John. Gunn

SUSSEX.

Charles *[signature]*

Kumar Shri Ranjitsinhji

George Brann.

Will. L. Murdoch

Charles d A Smith

D. Newham

Ernest Harry Killick

Cyril H. G. Bland

George Rubens Cox

George Bean

SUSSEX.

H. R. Butt

H. Parris

F. W. Marlow

Edward Tate.

HAMPSHIRE.

D. A. Steele

a.S.Webb.

C.B. Llewellyn

Charles Robson.

Edward. C. Lee

Silver Cup, Silver Claret Jug, Buckle, and Diamond Breast Pin.
Presented to Barlow on different occasions. See text.

HAMPSHIRE.

E. Robson (Somerset)

W. T. Langford.

J. Newman

J. Stone.

C. B. Llewellyn (2nd signature, see p 190)

Alec. Bonell

J. H. Babcock

H. G. Smoker

J. Soar

Harry Baldwin see p 220

Tudor H. Barlin

Christopher Heseltine.

LEICESTERSHIRE.

H. G. Hazlerigg

Arnold Lyalott

Arthur Woodcock

G Gill

C. E. de Trafford

W W Odell

R. T. Crawford

C. J. B. Wood

V. F. S. Crawford (Surrey)

LEICESTERSHIRE.

Jno. H. King.

H. Whitehead.

J. Gayes

SURREY.

D. L. A. Jephson.

K. J. Key.

H. D. G. Leveson-Gower

W. Davis

A. Marshal

Edward Pooley

Fred. Stedman.

SURREY.

Dalmeny

N. A. Knox.

J H Gordon

Fred Holland

H. Strudwick

T R Rushby

W. S. Lees.

J B Hobbs

W C Smith

SURREY.

J. N. Crawford

Ernest G Hayes.

Robert Abel

W. Brockwell

T. Richardson

W. H. Lockwood

H Wood

T. Hayward

C. Baldwin.

James Street

DERBYSHIRE.

Levi G. Wright

S Herbert Iverstad

C Augustus Ollivene

H Bagshaw

J Mycroft

Lew Hay

W. Storer

Joseph Hancock

Ja. Higson

NOTTS. COUNTY CRICKET CLUB.

TRENT BRIDGE GROUND, NOTTINGHAM,

Monday, September 1, 1884, and following days.

North of England v. Australians.

NORTH OF ENGLAND.	1st Innings.		2nd Inn.	
A. Shrewsbury	b Spofforth	2	c Palmer, b Boyle	1
W. Scotton	c Blackham, b Boyle	17	b Boyle	4
W. Barnes	b Spofforth	10	c Scott, b Spofforth	17
W. Gunn	l b w, b Spofforth	2	b Boyle	11
R. G. Barlow	not out	10	b Bannerman	101
W. Bates	c Bonnor, b Boyle	7	c Palmer, b Spofforth	4
W. Flowers	c McDonnell, b Boyle	26	c Spofforth, b Bonnor	90
W. Attewell	b Spofforth	3	c Bannerman, b Bonnor	9
M. Sherwin	c Murdoch, b Boyle	1	c Blackham, b Bannerman	7
J. Selby	hit wicket, b Boyle	2	c Blackham, b Bonnor	2
R. Peate	c Murdoch, b Spofforth	6	not out	0
Byes 0, leg-byes 4, wides 0, no-balls 1		5	B 7, l-b 0, w 0, n-b 2	9
Total		91	Total	255

AUSTRALIANS.	1st Innings.		2nd Inn.	
Mr. P. S. McDonnell	b Peate	23	b Attewell	5
Mr. A. C. Bannerman	c Peate, b Attewell	0	c Peate, b Attewell	4
Mr. W. L. Murdoch	c Selby b Attewell	1	b Barlow	3
Mr. H. J. H. Scott	l b w, b Attewell	7	c Shrewsbury, b Barlow	4
Mr. G. Giffen	b Barlow	20	st Sherwin, b Attewell	6
Mr. W. Midwinter	b Attewell	0	c Bates, b Attewell	17
Mr. G. J. Bonnor	b Attewell	38	c Barnes, b Barlow	0
Mr. J. M'C. Blackham	b Barlow	3	c Gunn, b Barlow	15
Mr. F. R. Spofforth	c Selby, b Barlow	0	b Barlow	7
Mr. G. E. Palmer	not out	1	c Gunn, b Barlow	8
Mr. H. F. Boyle	b Barlow	4	not out	3
Byes 3, leg-byes 0, wide 0, no-balls 0		3	B 2, l-b 1, w 1, n-b 0	4
Total		100	Total	76

Umpires, R. Carpenter & W. F. Farrands.

Stumps drawn at 6.

Printed on the Ground by George Richards, Greyhound Street, Nottingham.

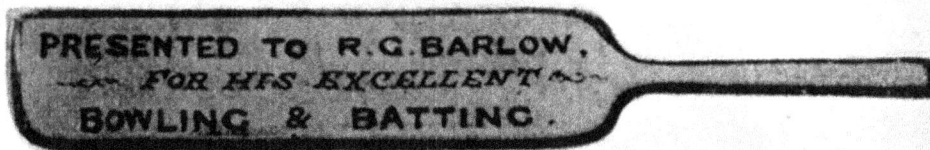

PRESENTED TO R. G. BARLOW, FOR HIS EXCELLENT BOWLING & BATTING.

THE FULL SCORE OF THE ABOVE MATCH, PRINTED ON SATIN,
Was presented to the Author, along with a few other presents named elsewhere.
The 10 wickets which he took in this match only cost him 48 runs.
The Author considers the above match to be his best all-round performance in his long career.

GRAND CRICKET MATCH
ENGLAND - V - AUSTRALIA

Played on the County Ground, Old Trafford, July 5th, 6th, and 7th, 1886.

AUSTRALIANS.	1st Innings.		2nd Innings.	
1 Mr. S. P. Jones	lbw b Grace	87	c Ulyett b Steel	12
2 Mr. H. J. H. Scott	c Barlow b Ulyett	21	b Barlow	47
3 Mr. G. Giffen	b Steel	3	c Shrewsbury b Barlow	1
4 Mr. A. H. Jarvis	c Scotton b Ulyett	45	c Lohmann b Barlow	2
5 Mr. G. J. Bonnor	c Lohmann b Barlow	4	c Barlow b Peate	2
6 Mr. J. W. Trumble	c Scotton b Steel	24	c Ulyett b Barlow	4
8 Mr. W. Bruce	run out	2	c Grace b Barlow	0
9 Mr. T. W. Garrett	c Pilling b Lohmann	5	c Grace b Ulyett	22
7 Mr. J. McC. Blackham	not out	7	lbw b Barlow	2
10 Mr. G. E. Palmer	c Lohmann b Ulyett	4	c Pilling b Barlow	8
11 Mr. F. R. Spofforth	c Barlow b Ulyett	2	not out	20
	Wds 1 byes lb nb 1		Wds. bys 3 lb nb	3
	Total	205	Total	123

Fall of the Wickets.

1	2	3	4	5	6	7	8	9	10	1	2	3	4	5	6	7	8	9	10
58	71	134	141	181	187	188	192	201	205	37	42	44	55	68	70	70	73	103	123

ANALYSIS of the BOWLING. 1st Innings. 2nd Innings.

	Overs.	Mdns.	Runs.	Wkts.	Wd.	Overs.	Mdns.	Runs.	Wkts.
Peate	19	7	30	0	..	46	25	45	1
Lohmann	23	9	41	1	..	5	3	14	0
Steel	27	5	47	2	..	8	3	9	1
Ulyett	36·1	20	46	4	1	6·3	5	7	1
Barlow	23	15	19	1	..	52	31	44	7
Grace	9	3	21	1	.	1	0	1	0

ENGLAND.	1st Innings.		2nd Innings.	
1 Mr. W. G. Grace	c Bonnor b Spofforth	8	c Palmer b Giffen	4
2 W. Scotton	c Trumble b Garrett	21	b Palmer	20
3 A. Shrewsbury	b Spofforth	31	c and b Giffen	4
4 Mr. W. W. Read	c Scott b Garrett	51	c Jones b Spofforth	9
6 Mr. A. G. Steel	c Jarvis b Palmer	12	not out	18
5 R. G. Barlow	not out	38	c Palmer b Spofforth	30
7 G. Ulyett	b Spofforth	17	c Scott b Spofforth	8
8 J. Briggs	c Garrett b Spofforth	1	not out	2
9 G. Lohmann	b Giffen	32		
10 E. Peate	st Jarvis b Palmer	6		
11 R. Pilling	c Bruce b Palmer	2		
	Wds bys 2 lb 2 nb	4	Wds bys 10 lb 1 nb	11
	Total	223	Total	107

Fall of the Wickets.

1	2	3	4	5	6	7	8	9	10	1	2	3	4	5	6	7	8	9	10
9	51	80	109	131	156	160	206	219	223	7	15	24	65	90	105	..	..	..	..

ANALYSIS of the BOWLING. 1st Innings. 2nd Innings.

	Overs	Mdns	Runs	Wkts	Overs	Mdns	Runs	Wkts	Wd
Spofforth	53	22	82	4	29·2	13	40	2	..
Giffen	32	15	44	1	24	9	31	2	..
Garrett	45	23	43	2	17	9	14	1	..
Bruce	10	7	9	0	..	..	..	..	..
Palmer	17·2	4	41	3	7	3	11	1	..

Umpires :—Messrs. West and Pullen.

Test Match
England - v - Australia 1886
Presented to R. G. Barlow for his
very fine Batting & Bowling

THE FULL SCORE OF THIS MATCH, PRINTED ON SATIN,
Was presented to the Author, along with £5.

DERBYSHIRE.

J. Hulme

J. Humphries

W Bestwick

Ernest Needham

W Chatterton

Walter Sugg

KENT.

Fred H Huish

W A Bradley

C J Burnup

KENT.

C H B Marshall

K. L. Hutchings

A P. Day

J C Hubble

F. E Woolley.

H. T. W. Hardinge

Geo G Hearne

Walter Hearne

Alec. Hearne 1863.

C Blythe

E. Humphreys

J. R Mason

ESSEX.

C McGahey

A.G. Owen.

T. M. Russell

H. Young.

W. Mead

H. Carpenter

Harry Pickett

F.G. Bull

P. Perrin

A.J. Turner.

ESSEX.

A.P. Lucas

C.E. Green

AUSTRALIA.

B. J. Wardill

Chas M Leod

Jack Worrall

Alfred Johns

J.J. Kelly

W. P. Howell

AUSTRALIA.

Joe Darling

M. A. Noble

V. Trumper

Hans. Iredale

E. Jones

Syd. Gregory

Clem Hill

Hugh Trumble

Frank Laver

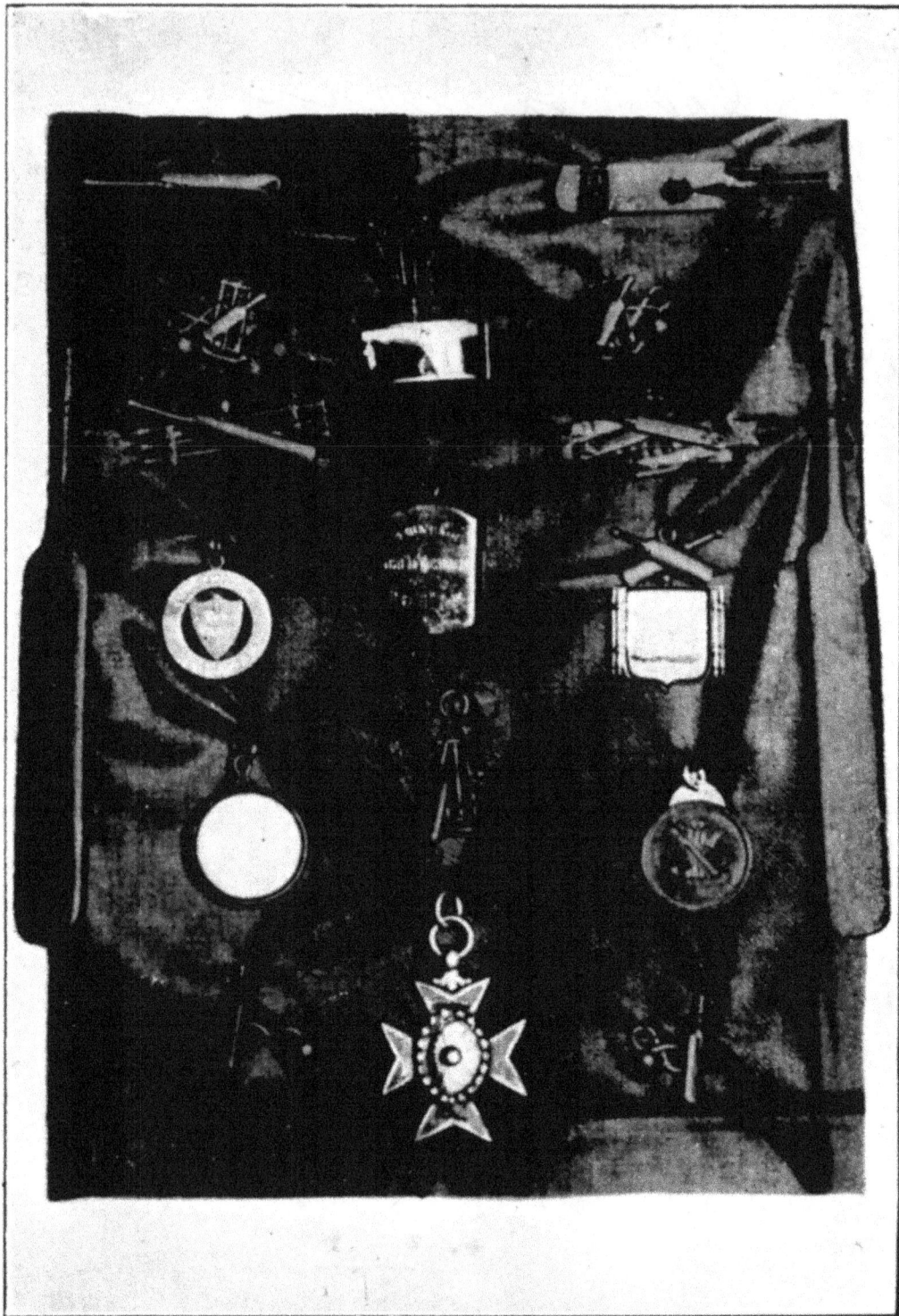

PRESENTATION MEDALS AND ORNAMENTS FOR CRICKET,
FOOTBALL, AND RUNNING,
Which the Author has received during his career.

SOUTH AFRICANS.

E. A. Halliwell

R. S. Harwood

@ Ernest Vogler

G. A. Faulkner

Cyril D. Robinson

Harry E. Smith

Percy W. Sherwell

S. D. Snooke

A. D. Nourse

SOUTH AFRICANS.

W. A. Shalders

S. J. Snooke

F. Tancred

R. O. Schwarz.

Gordon White

M. Hathorn.

James Kotze

J. Sinclair

J. Middleton

WORCESTERSHIRE.

H. K. Foster

R. E. Foster

G. Bromley Martin

Geoffrey. N. Foster

E. Arnold

George Gaukrodger

W.L. Foster

Albert Bird

Fred Wheldon

G. A. Wilson

WARWICKSHIRE.

L. F. Byrne.

Arthur A. Lilley

Walter Quaife

Walter Richards

John Devey

Herbert W Bainbridge

E. J Diver.

Frank C. Field.

Sam Hargreave.

WARWICKSHIRE.

W. S. Quaife

C Charlesworth

M.C.C.

F. E. Lacey (SECY)

F. H. Farrands

George. F. Hearne

CHESHIRE.

S. Brown

OXFORD UNIVERSITY. (CAPT. 1907.

Egerton. L. Wright.

CAMBRIDGE UNIVERSITY. (CAPT.) 1907.

M. W. Payne.

A FEW CRICKET TROPHIES

Presented to R. G. Barlow on various occasions for excellence in batting and bowling.

NORTHAMPTONSHIRE.

E. M. Pehile Crossan

L. T. Duffield

W. East

Chas. J. T. Pool.

W. H. Kingston

G. A. T. Vials.

Alec R. Thompson

G. J. Thompson

W. A. Buswell

W. Wells

M. Cox

B. C. Smith

GLOUCESTERSHIRE.

W. G. Grace
1899

E. M. Grace.

W. A. Woof

Leigh D. Brownlee

F. H. B. Champain

J. H. Board

C. L. Townsend

George Dennett

Cyril H. Sewell

GLOUCESTERSHIRE.

G. L. Jessop

Sidney A. P. Kitcat

H. J. Huggins

Harry Wrathall

F. G. Roberts   *sep 26*

MIDDLESEX.

Greg a Mac Gregor

Francis G. J. Ford

H B Hayman.

George Burton

MIDDLESEX.

A. E. Stoddart.

P. F. Warner

B. J. T. Bosanquet.

F. G. J. Ford

C. C. Page

A. J. Webbe

J. T. Rawlin

J. T. Hearne

A. E. Trott

I. D. Walker.

WEST INDIANS.

H B Gardiner Austin

J. J. Cameron M.D.

G. Challenor

George C. Learmond

C Stuart Morrison

P. S. Cumberbatch.

J W Parker

P A Goodman

Claude K. Bancroft.

Richard Ollivierre

L. Constantine

O. Layne

Sydney G Smith

GENTLEMEN v. PLAYERS. 1884.

THE BALL WITH WHICH R.G.BARLOW

TOOK THE WICKETS OF Dr W.G.GRACE

W.W.READ, AND J.SHUTER IN THREE

SUCCESSIVE BALLS. BARLOW WAS CAPTAIN

FOR THE PLAYERS IN THIS MATCH.

218

SOMERSETSHIRE.

Lionel C.H. Palairet

Sny Woods

A. E. Newton

A. E. Bailey

Len C Braund

A. E. Lewis

Wn Roe.

R. C. N. Palairet.

J. A. Phillips

Vernon. Hill

SOMERSETSHIRE.

G. B. Nichols

Edwin J Tyler

UMPIRES.

Valentine A Pitchmarsh

John Carlin

A. A. White

Walter Richards

W. A. J. West.

Arthur Millward

F. G. Roberts

R. G. Barlow

220

UMPIRES.

Jas Phillips

M Myers

M Attewell   Sep 88

John Moss

C E Richardson

Alfred. J. Atfield

C. E. Dench

A Dick Pougher

H Baldwin   Sep 92

Thomas Brown

S . Brown

BLACKPOOL CRICKET FESTIVAL, July 7th, 8th, & 9th, 1904. LANCASHIRE COUNTY v. AN ENGLAND XI.

ENGLAND XI.

W. A. J. West (Umpire). J. Iremonger. T. Richardson. E. Arnold. R. G. Barlow (Umpire).
Mr. G. L. Jessop. Mr. C. Robson. Mr. A. O. Jones (Captain). L. Braund. W. Brockwell.
R. Peel. J. Gunn. R. Abel.

[Photo. by R. Berry, Blackpool.]

The Laws of Cricket.

As Revised by the Marylebone Club 1884, 1889, 1894, 1899, 1900, 1902, and 1906.

1. A match is played between two sides of eleven players each, unless otherwise agreed to. Each side has two innings, taken alternately, except in the case provided for in Law 53. The choice of innings shall be decided by tossing.

2. The score shall be reckoned by runs. A run is scored—

   1st. So often as the batsmen after a hit, or at any time while the ball is in play, shall have crossed, and made good their ground, from end to end.

   2nd. For penalties under Laws 16, 34, 41, and allowances under 44.

Any run or runs so scored shall be duly recorded by scorers appointed for the purpose. The side which scores the greatest number of runs wins the match. No match is won unless played out or given up, except in the case provided in Law 45.

3. Before the commencement of the match two umpires shall be appointed—one for each end.

4. The ball shall weigh not less than five ounces and a half, nor more than five ounces and three-quarters. It shall measure not less than nine inches, nor more than nine inches and one-quarter in circumference. At the beginning of each innings either side may demand a new ball.

5. The bat shall not exceed four inches and one-quarter in the widest part ; it shall not be more than thirty-eight inches in length.

6. The wickets shall be pitched opposite and parallel to each other at a distance of twenty-two yards. Each wicket shall be eight inches in width and consist of three stumps, with two bails upon the top. The stumps shall be of equal and sufficient size to prevent the ball from passing through, twenty-seven inches out of the ground. The bails shall be each four inches in length, and when in position, on the top of the stumps, shall not project more than half an inch above them. The wickets shall not be changed

during a match, unless the ground between them become unfit for play, and then only by consent of both sides.

7. The bowling crease shall be in a line with the stumps; eight feet eight inches in length; the stumps in the centre; with a return crease at each end, at right angles behind the wicket.

8. The popping crease shall be marked four feet from the wicket, parallel to it, and be deemed unlimited in length.

9. The ground shall not be rolled, watered, covered, mown, or beaten during a match, except before the commencement of each innings and of each day's play, when, unless the in-side object, the ground shall be swept and rolled for not more than ten minutes. This shall not prevent the batsman from beating the ground with his bat, nor the batsmen nor bowler from using sawdust in order to obtain a proper foothold.

10. The ball must be bowled; if thrown or jerked, either umpire shall call " No ball."

11. The bowler shall deliver the ball with one foot on the ground behind the bowling crease, and within the return crease, otherwise the umpire shall call " No ball."

12. If the bowler shall bowl the ball so high over or so wide of the wicket that, in the opinion of the umpire, it is not within reach of the striker, the umpire shall call " Wide ball."

13. The ball shall be bowled in overs of six balls from each wicket alternately. When six balls have been bowled, and the ball is finally settled in the bowler's or wicket-keeper's hands, the umpire shall call " Over." Neither a " no ball " nor " wide ball " shall be reckoned as one of the " over."

14. The bowler shall be allowed to change ends as often as he pleases, provided only that he does not bowl two overs consecutively in one innings.

15. The bowler may require the batsman at the wicket from which he is bowling to stand on that side of it which he may direct.

16. The striker may hit a " no ball," and whatever runs result shall be added to his score; but he shall not be out from a " no ball " unless he be run out or break Laws 26, 27, 29, 30. All runs made from a " no ball " otherwise than from the bat, shall be scored " no balls," and if no run be made, one run shall be added to that score. From a " wide ball " as many runs as are run shall be added to the score as " wide balls," and if no run be otherwise obtained, one run shall be so added.

17. If the ball, not having been called "wide" or "no ball," pass the striker without touching his bat or person, and any runs be obtained, the umpire shall call "Bye"; but if the ball touch any part of the striker's person (hand excepted) and any run be obtained, the umpire shall call "Leg bye," such runs to be scored "byes" and "leg byes" respectively.

18. At the beginning of the match, and of each innings, the umpire at the bowler's wicket shall call "Play." From that time no trial ball shall be allowed to any bowler on the ground between the wickets; and when one of the batsmen is out, the use of the bat shall not be allowed to any person until the next batsman shall come in.

19. A batsman shall be held to be "out of his ground," unless his bat in hand or some part of his person be grounded within the line of the popping crease.

20. The wicket shall be held to be "down" when either of the bails is struck off, or if both bails be off, when a stump is struck out of the ground.

THE STRIKER IS OUT:

21. If the wicket be bowled down, even if the ball first touch the striker's bat or person :—"Bowled."

22. Or, if the ball, from a stroke of the bat or hand, but not the wrist, be held before it touch the ground, although it be hugged to the body of the catcher :—"Caught."

23. Or, if in playing at the ball, provided it be not touched by the bat or hand, the striker be out of his ground, and the wicket be put down by the wicket-keeper with the ball or with hand or arm, with ball in hand :—"Stumped."

24. Or, if with any part of his person he stops the ball, which in the opinion of the umpire at the bowler's wicket, shall have been pitched in a straight line from it to the striker's wicket and would have hit it :—"Leg before wicket."

25. Or, if in playing at the ball he hit down his wicket with his bat or any part of his person or dress :—"Hit wicket."

26. Or, if under pretence of running, or otherwise, either of the batsmen wilfully prevent a ball from being caught :—"Obstructing the field."

27. Or, if the ball be struck, or be stopped by any part of his person, and he wilfully strike it again, except it be done for the

P

purpose of guarding his wicket, which he may do with his bat, or any part of his person, except his hands :—" Hit the ball twice."

28. If in running, or at any other time when the ball is in play, he be out of his ground, and his wicket be struck down by the ball after touching any fieldsman, or by the hand or arm, with ball in hand, of any fieldsman :—" Run out."

29. Or, if he touch with his hands or take up the ball while in play, unless at the request of the opposite side :—" Handled the ball."

30. Or, if he wilfully obstruct any fieldsman:—"Obstructing the field."

31. If the batsmen have crossed each other, he that runs for the wicket which is put down is out; if they have not crossed, he that has left the wicket which is put down is out.

32. The striker being caught, no run shall be scored. A batsman being run out, that run which was being attempted shall not be scored.

33A. A batsman being out from any cause, the ball shall be " Dead."

33B. If the ball, whether struck with the bat or not, lodges in a batsman's clothing, the ball shall become " dead."

34. If a ball in play cannot be found or recovered, any fieldsman may call " Lost ball," when the ball shall be " dead "; six runs shall be added to the score ; but if more than six runs have been run before "Lost ball" has been called, as many runs as have been run shall be scored.

35. After the ball shall have been finally settled in the wicket-keeper's or bowler's hand, it shall be " dead "; but when the bowler is about to deliver the ball, if the batsman at his wicket be out of his ground before actual delivery, the said bowler may run him out; but if the bowler throw at that wicket and any run result, it shall be scored " No ball."

36. A batsman shall not retire from his wicket and return to it to complete his innings after another has been in, without the consent of the opposite side.

37. A substitute shall be allowed to field or run between wickets for any player who may during the match be incapacitated from illness or injury, but for no other reason, except with the consent of the opposite side.

38. In all cases where a substitute shall be allowed, the consent of the opposite side shall be obtained as to the person to act as substitute, and the place in the field which he shall take.

39. In case any substitute shall be allowed to run between wickets, the striker may be run out if either he or his substitute be out of his ground. If the striker be out of his ground while the ball is in play, that wicket which he has left may be put down and the striker given out, although the other batsman may have made good the ground at that end, and the striker and his substitute at the other end.

40. A batsman is liable to be out for any infringement of the Laws by his substitute.

41. The fieldsman may stop the ball with any part of his person, but if he wilfully stop it otherwise, the ball shall be "dead," and five runs added to the score; whatever runs may have been made, five only shall be added.

42. The wicket-keeper shall stand behind the wicket. If he shall take the ball for the purpose of stumping before it has passed the wicket, or if he shall incommode the striker by any noise or motion, or if any part of his person be over or before the wicket, the striker shall not be out, excepting under Laws 26, 27, 28, 29, and 30.

43. The umpires are the sole judges of fair or unfair play, of the fitness of the ground, the weather, and the light for play; all disputes shall be determined by them, and if they disagree the actual state of things shall continue.

44. They shall pitch fair wickets, arrange boundaries where necessary, and the allowances to be made for them, and change ends after each side has had one innings.

45. They shall allow two minutes for each striker to come in, and ten minutes between each innings. When they shall call "Play," the side refusing to play shall lose the match.

46. They shall not order a batsman out unless appealed to by the other side.

N.B.—An appeal, "How's that?" covers all ways of being out (within the jurisdiction of the umpire appealed to), unless a specific way of getting out is stated by the person asking.

47. The umpire at the bowler's wicket shall be appealed to before the other umpire in all cases, except in those of stumping, hit wicket, run out at the striker's wicket, or arising out of Law 42, but in any case in which an umpire is unable to give a decision, he shall appeal to the other umpire, whose decision shall be final.

48. If either umpire be not satisfied of the absolute fairness of the delivery of any ball, he shall call "No ball."

48A. The umpire shall take especial care to call "No ball" instantly upon delivery; "Wide ball" as soon as it shall have passed the striker.

49. If either batsman run a short run, the umpire shall call "One short," and the run shall not be scored.

50. After the umpire has called "Over" the ball is "dead," but an appeal may be made as to whether either batsman is out; such appeal, however, shall not be made after the delivery of the next ball, nor after any cessation of play.

51. No umpire shall be allowed to bet.

52. No umpire shall be changed during a match, unless with the consent of both sides, except in case of violation of Law 51; then either side may dismiss him.

53. The side which bats first and leads by 150 runs in a three-days' match, or by 100 runs in a two-days' match, shall have the option of requiring the other side to follow their innings.

54. The in-side may declare their innings at an end in a three-days' match at or after the luncheon interval on the second day; in a two-days match, the captain of the batting side has power to declare his innings at a close at any time, but such declaration may not be made on the first day later than one hour and forty minutes before the time agreed upon for drawing stumps; in a one-day match at any time.

ONE-DAY MATCHES.

1. The side which bats first and leads by 75 runs shall have the option of requiring the other side to follow their innings.

2. The match, unless played out, shall be decided by the first innings. Prior to the commencement of a match it may be agreed: that the over consist of five or six balls.

N.B.—A tie is included in the words "played out."

SINGLE WICKET.

The Laws are, where they apply, the same as the above, with the following alterations and additions.

1. One wicket shall be pitched, as in Law 6, with a bowling stump opposite to it at a distance of twenty-two yards. The bowling crease shall be in a line with the bowling stump, and drawn according to Law 7.

2. When there shall be less than five players on a side, bounds shall be placed twenty-two yards each in a line from the off and leg stump.

3. The ball must be hit before the bounds to entitle the striker to a run, which run cannot be obtained unless he touch the bowling stump or crease in a line with his bat, or some part of his person, or go beyond them, and return to the popping crease.

4. When the striker shall hit the ball, one of his feet must be on the ground behind the popping crease, otherwise the umpire shall call " No hit," and no run shall be scored.

5. When there shall be less than five players on a side, neither byes, leg-byes, nor overthrows shall be allowed, nor shall the striker be caught out behind the wicket, nor stumped.

6. The fieldsman must return the ball so that it shall cross the ground between the wicket and the bowling stump, or between the bowling stump and the bounds; the striker may run till the ball be so returned.

7. After the striker shall have made one run, if he start again he must touch the bowling stump or crease, and turn before the ball cross the ground to entitle him to another.

8. The striker shall be entitled to three runs for lost ball, and the same number for ball wilfully stopped by a fieldsman otherwise than with any part of his person.

9. When there shall be more than four players on a side there shall be no bounds. All hits, byes, leg-byes, and overthrows shall then be allowed.

10. There shall be no restriction as to the ball being bowled in overs, but no more than one minute shall be allowed between each ball.

INSTRUCTIONS TO UMPIRES.

These instructions, drawn up in 1892 by the Committee of the M.C.C., are intended as an appendix to the Laws of the Game. Some little alteration had to be made in 1901, the decision as to the fitness of the ground and light being now in the hands of the captains, and an important addition with regard to the treatment of the wicket after rain was made in 1902, consequent no doubt on the loss of time in the test match at Birmingham.

FITNESS OF GROUND.

Law 43.—At the commencement of a match, the Umpires may be appealed to by either side as to the fitness of the ground for play.

Should they not agree, play will not commence until they are agreed.

In case of interruption from rain, as soon as the rain has ceased, the Umpires shall, immediately, without further instruction, inspect the wicket, unaccompanied by any of the players, and decide upon its fitness. Should it prove unfit, they shall continue to inspect at intervals, until they decide that it is fit for play, when they shall call upon the players to resume the game.

The ground is unfit for play—when water stands on the surface, or when it is so wet, muddy, or slippery as to deprive the bowlers of a reasonable foothold, or the fieldsmen of the power of free movement.

The Umpires are not to be biassed by the opinions of either side, still less are they to allow themselves to be influenced by the impatience of the spectators for a resumption of the game, and are not to be induced, by the public interest in a particular match, to declare the ground fit for play, unless they would consider that ground fit under any circumstances.

FITNESS OF LIGHT FOR PLAY.

The Umpires may decide, on appeal, that there is not sufficient light for play. Should the light improve before the time for drawing stumps, they shall, without waiting for instructions, call upon the players to resume the game.

In the event of the Captains agreeing as to the condition of the ground or light, the Umpires will, so far, be relieved of their responsibility.

Law 47.—An Umpire is only justified in appealing to the other umpire when he is unable to decide, owing to his having been prevented from seeing the occurrence on which the appeal is based. He is not to appeal to the other umpire in cases on which he could give a decision, merely because he is unwilling to give that decision. If he be in any doubt, the principle laid down in Law 43, " That the existing state of things shall continue," shall be followed, and, in consequence, the decision should be in favour of the batsman.

Law 48.—The special attention of Umpires is called to this law, which directs them to call " no ball," unless absolutely satisfied of the fairness of the delivery.

Umpires should not allow themselves to be unduly influenced by appeals from such of the field who were not in a position to form a judgment on the point appealed upon, or by tricks—such as throwing up the ball, on appealing for a catch at the wicket, without waiting for the decision. Umpires, being the sole judges of fair or unfair play, should remember that such devices are obviously unfair, and are not in accordance with the spirit in which cricket should be played.

By order of the Committee of the M.C.C.

June 20th, 1892.

ADDITIONS TO " INSTRUCTIONS TO UMPIRES."

In the course of the season of 1899, the following additions to the " Instructions to Umpires " were approved by the M.C.C. Committee :—

" DECLARING."

Law 54.—(A) If a side declare its innings during the luncheon interval, it must do so within fifteen minutes after the commencement of such interval, otherwise an extra ten minutes will be allowed for rolling.

(B) If a side declare its innings closed in the morning before play commences, it must do so in sufficient time to enable the other side to choose the roller it prefers ; otherwise, an extra ten minutes will be allowed for rolling.

Passed by the M.C.C. Committee, June 16th, 1902 :—

(A) Umpires are not justified in deciding the ground unfit for play, merely because the grass is wet and the ball would, in consequence, be slippery.

(B) In order to facilitate play at the earliest possible moment in wet weather, the Umpires shall see that the footholes made by the bowlers and batsmen are cleaned out, dried, and filled up with sawdust at any time during the match, although the game is not actually in progress.

Early in the Season of 1906, the following resolution was passed by the M.C.C. Committee :—

In consequence of play being so frequently suspended on appeals against the light, the following rule will now prevail :—" The Umpires may decide, on appeal from the Captains, they having disagreed that there is not sufficient light for play."

Approved by the M.C.C. Committee, June 20th, 1907 :—

1. " That the Counties should be advised to instruct their Groundmen not to cover a pitch within 24 hours of a County Match."

2. That the New Ball Rule should read as follows :—" After 200 runs have been made with a ball the fielding side can demand a new one."

[The first recommendation is a repetition of an old ruling, the importance of which has been emphasised by a recent incident. The second is an alteration aimed at removing a possible misinterpretation.]

CODE OF SIGNALLING.

Boundaries shall be signalled by waving the hand from side to side.

Byes shall be signalled by raising the open hand above the head.

Leg-byes shall be signalled by raising the leg and touching it with the hand.

Wides shall be signalled by extending both arms horizontally.

No-balls shall be signalled by extending one arm horizontally.

The decision Out shall be signalled by raising the index finger above the head.

Umpires should wait until a signal has been answered by the scorer before allowing the game to proceed.

Besides signalling, the Umpire should " call " distinctly, for the information of the players.

On giving a decision. the Umpire should make sure that the batsman understands what the decision is.

RULES OF COUNTY CRICKET.

The Rules now governing County Cricket are as follows—Rules 6, 7, and 8 having, in order to meet the wishes of the counties, been revised by the M.C.C. Committee, in October, 1906 :—

1. A cricketer born in one county and residing in another may not play for more than one county during the same season.

2. *Qualification by Birth.*—A cricketer is always eligible to play for the county of his birth.

3. *Qualification by Residence.*—A cricketer is qualified to play for any county in which he has resided for the previous 24 months, and is residing ; but :

    (A) The mere acquirement or hiring of a tenement, unless used as a *bona fide* home, does not constitute "residence."

    (B) The occupation of a tenement during the cricket season only does not constitute "residence."

4.—Where a cricketer uses as residences in the course of the year, tenements in more than one county, or where he leaves the country for the winter months, and in all other cases where his qualification is in any doubt, it is obligatory on the county for which he wishes to play to prove his qualification to the satisfaction of the M.C.C.

5. A cricketer who has played for a county for five successive years is qualified to play for that county for the rest of his cricket career, or until he plays for some other county.

6.—A cricketer may play for the county for which he has acquired a residential qualification for two successive years immediately after he has ceased to reside in such county.

7. *Transfers.*—A cricketer already qualified for, or engaged by, a county, but wishing to qualify by residence for another county, must give notice in writing to the Cricket Club Committee of the former county before he commences such residence ; and a County Cricket Club wishing to engage, under a residential qualification, a cricketer who is already qualified for, or engaged by, another County Club, must inform the Committee of the latter before commencing negotiations with the cricketer.

8. *Appeal.*—Should any question arise under these Rules, it shall be left to the decision of the M.C.C. Committee, which shall be final ; and in the event of an infringement of Rule 7, the M.C.C.

Committee shall have special authority to fix the date when the cricketer shall become qualified by residence, or even to permanently bar his so qualifying.

THE COUNTY CHAMPIONSHIP.

After the close of each cricket season, the Committee of the M.C.C. shall decide the county championship.

It shall be competed for by first-class counties. No county shall be eligible unless it shall have played at least eight "out" and "home" matches with other counties, provided that if no play can take place, owing to weather or other unavoidable cause, such match shall be reckoned as unfinished.

One point shall be reckoned for each win,; one deducted for each loss; unfinished games shall not be reckoned.

The county which during the season shall, in finished matches, have obtained the greatest proportionate number of points, shall be reckoned champion county.

The First-Class Counties are :—

Derbyshire	Northamptonshire
Essex	Nottinghamshire
Gloucestershire	Somerset
Hampshire	Surrey
Kent	Sussex
Lancashire	Warwickshire
Leicestershire	Worcestershire
Middlesex	Yorkshire

Derbyshire, Essex, Hampshire, Leicestershire, and Warwickshire were admitted to the Championship Competition in 1895, Worcestershire in 1899, and Northamptonshire in 1905.

THE MINOR COUNTIES CHAMPIONSHIP.

At the annual meeting of the representatives of the Minor Counties, held in the Pavilion, at Lord's, on the morning of Tuesday, December 18th, 1906, consideration was given to details in connection with the grouping scheme proposed by Yorkshire, and adopted at the previous meeting. The scheme, which came into operation in the summer of 1907, divided the counties into four Divisions, according to their geographical positions, as folows :—.

NORTH.

Durham
Lancashire Second Eleven
Lincolnshire
Northumberland
Staffordshire
Yorkshire Second Eleven

MIDLANDS.

Berkshire
Buckinghamshire
Surrey Second Eleven
Wiltshire
Worcestershire Second Eleven

WEST.

Cornwall
Devon
Dorset
Glamorgan
Monmouthshire

EAST.

Bedfordshire
Cambridgeshire
Hertfordshire
Norfolk
Suffolk

Every county shall play " out " and " home " two-day matches with every other county in its division.

The counties which shall have obtained in their respective divisions the greatest proportionate number of points shall play semi-final three-day matches ; provided that if two or more counties at the top of any one division have obtained the same proportion of points, preference shall be given to that county which shall have won the greatest number of completed matches. The winners of the semi-final matches shall play a final three-day match ; and the winner of the final match shall be reckoned champion county of the Second Division.

Points in the competition shall be reckoned as follows :—Five points shall be scored for a win in a completed match. Should the match not be completed, the side leading on the first innings shall score three points. In the event of a tie the points shall be divided. Matches in which no result on the first innings shall have been attained shall not be included in the table of results.

In the semi-final and final matches each of the counties engaged shall bear its own expenses, and shall receive half the gross gate-moneys, after deducting the fees paid to the Umpires.

It was decided that in the semi-finals in 1907 the North play the East, and the Midlands play the west. The semi-finals are to be finished by the 28th of August, and the final by the 7th of September.

The following resolutions were passed :—

> " That, in the opinion of the Minor Counties' Cricket Association, no player who has in any season played in six or more matches for a first-class county should, in the same season, be qualified to play in the Minor Counties Competition, and that a copy of this resolution be forwarded to the committee of each of the first-class counties whose second elevens play in the competition."

> " In matches of the Minor Counties competition each Umpire shall be paid an inclusive fee of £4 for a two-day match, and £5 for a three-day match."

ADVISORY COMMITTEE OF THE COUNTIES.

An important meeting of the Advisory Committee was held at Lord's, on Wednesday, December 19th, 1906. The following is the official report of the meeting, which was strictly private :—

Present: The Right Hon. W. H. Long (in the chair), Messrs. C. E. Green (Essex), Lord Hawke (Yorkshire), H. K. Foster (Worcestershire), Lord Harris (Kent), J. Shuter (Surrey), G. MacGregor (Middlesex), W. E. Denison (Notts), A. J. Darnell (Northamptonshire), C. Marriott (Leicestershire), J. F. Byrne (Warwickshire), C. B. Fry (Sussex), R. H. Mallett and Dr. Earl Norman (Minor Counties), Dr. Bencraft (Hampshire), H. E. Murray Anderdon (Somerset), J. Horner (Lancashire), and the Secretary of the M.C.C.

Mr. G. L. Jessop (Gloucestershire) joined the meeting almost at its close.

The minutes of the last meeting, having been printed and circulated, were taken as read.

The proposition of Yorkshire with regard to the registration of players by the M.C.C. was introduced by Lord Hawke. The question as to the principle of registration was put by the Chairman in order to ascertain the opinion of the meeting, and a vote was taken, which resulted in eight being given in favour and eight against. On the casting vote being given by the Chairman, the resolution was carried.

Warwickshire then moved " That a player qualified by birth shall have his qualification approved and registered by the M.C.C.

immediately after he has played for the first time in a county championship match."

Worcestershire proposed to add the words " or residence " after the word " birth." The proposition and amendment were accepted by thirteen votes in favour and three against.

The proposition of Essex, " That the period for qualification of Colonial cricketers should be for not less than five years," was withdrawn in favour of the one submitted by Kent, which read as follows : " That the time for qualification be extended for the man who comes to this country for the purpose of making a livelihood out of cricket."

This proposition was rejected by eight votes to seven, the voting being : For (7)—Yorkshire, Essex, Worcestershire, Minor Counties (one representative), Leicestershire, Kent, and Notts. Against (8)—Hampshire, Somerset, Warwickshire, Northamptonshire, Lancashire, Minor Counties (one representative), Sussex, and Surrey.

The suggested proposition from Essex that the residential qualification should be for a period of three years instead of two was withdrawn.

A letter from Gloucestershire *re* gate-money in first-class matches was read, and, in the absence of Mr. Jessop, was postponed for consideration.

Mr. R. H. Mallet, supported by Lord Harris, moved " That a sub-committee, consisting of one representative from each of the following counties, viz., Notts, Lancashire, Warwickshire, Middlesex, Surrey, Yorkshire, and two representatives from the Minor Counties, should meet in January and consider the question of classification and promotion of the counties engaged in the County Competition." This was carried.

The following Rules for the registration of county cricketers were drawn up by the M.C.C. Committee, in February, 1907, but the matter remains in abeyance, the counties being much divided in opinion :—

1. In the case of cricketers claiming under Rule 5, the committee of M.C.C. will be able for itself to check the claim.

2. In the case of cricketers claiming under Rule 2, a certified copy of the cricketer's birth register must be lodged with M.C.C., if possible, before he plays for his county, but, if that is impossible, then as soon as possible after his first match.

3. In the case of cricketers claiming under the residential rules, a full statement, signed by the secretary of the county club on behalf of his committee, or in case of emergency, by the captain of the County XI., of the residential qualifications of each cricketer must be lodged annually with M.C.C.

N.B.—It will obviously save much inconvenience if county committees will lodge their claims early in the year. In the case of cricketers suddenly called on to play for their counties, M.C.C. will do their best to give a prompt response to such applications for registration, but it is obvious that this will depend to a considerable extent on the information supplied by the county clubs.

COUNTY QUALIFICATION.

With regard to county qualification, the following Rule was passed February 3rd, 1908: "A cricketer may not play for more than one county within the calendar year, the penalty for an infringement of this Rule to be disqualification for two years. A British colony, dependency, or state, shall, for the purposes of this Rule, be regarded as a county."

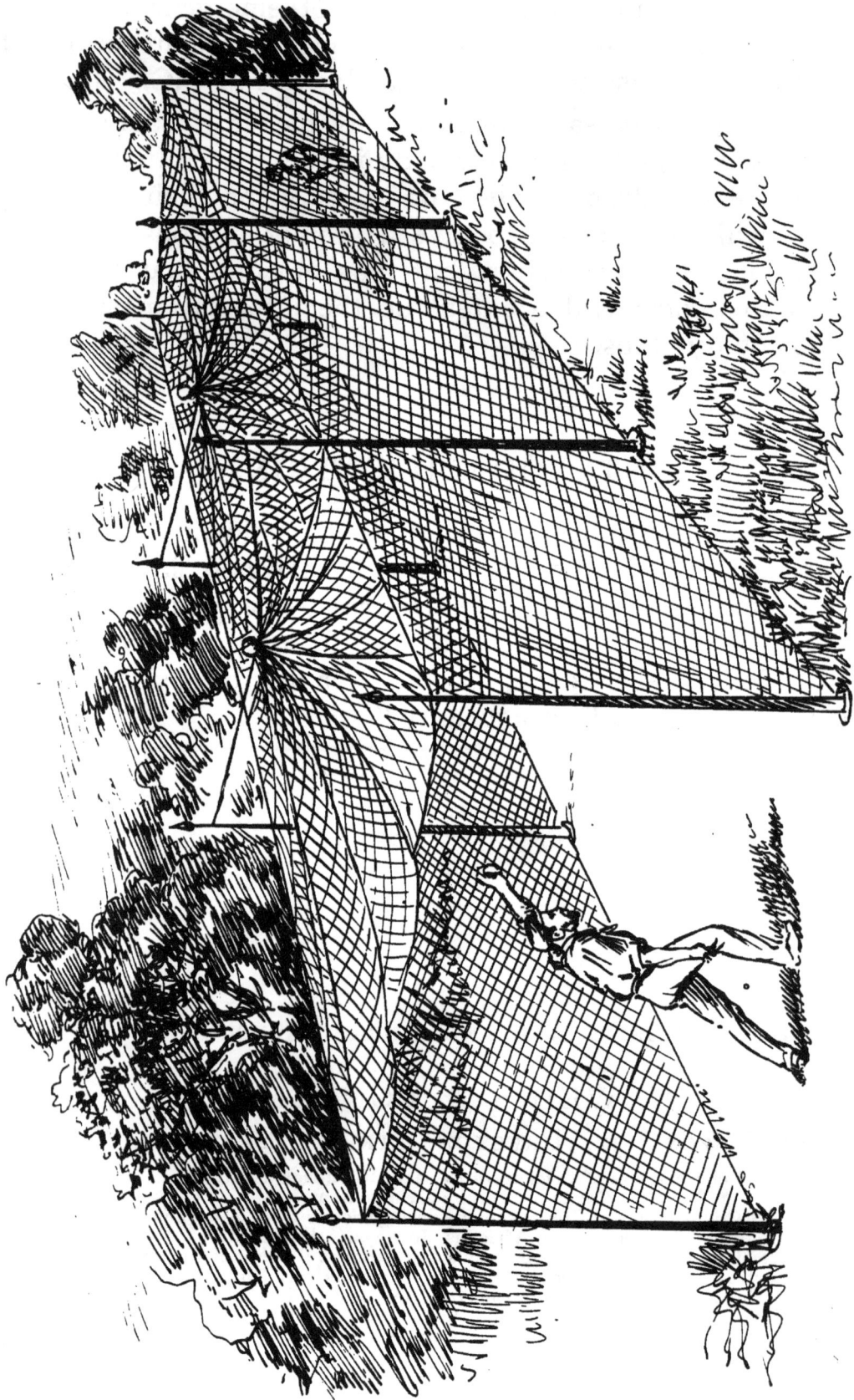

THE ABOVE IS AN ILLUSTRATION OF A CRICKET NET,

Which the Author had made for his private practice and coaching, and which proved to be extremely useful.

It was erected in the garden at the back of his house at Old Trafford, Manchester.

Cartoons.

The following seven amusing Cartoons were published in Australia after the Hon. Ivo Bligh's English team had " won the rubber " by defeating Murdoch's Australian team in two of the three Test Matches in 1882-3.

Drawn by M. C. B. Massie.

INTERNATIONAL CRICKET MATCH,

Jan. 1st, 1883.—Australians 1st and 2nd Innings.

Ivo Bligh had a shy
    At Australian sticks ;
Scored like fun, gave them one
    Of the neatest "licks."
Hi, Ivo ! Ho, Ivo !
    Britons breathe once more,
Whilst they "fill" to your skill
    And Leslie's spanking score !

Ivo Bligh—England's eye—
    Murdoch's fairly wiped.
Barlow's "gross" retrieves our loss ;
    How he bowled and swiped !
Hi, Ivo ! Ho, Ivo !
    Stick to it you will—
Not for "crow," just to show
    England's in it still !

245

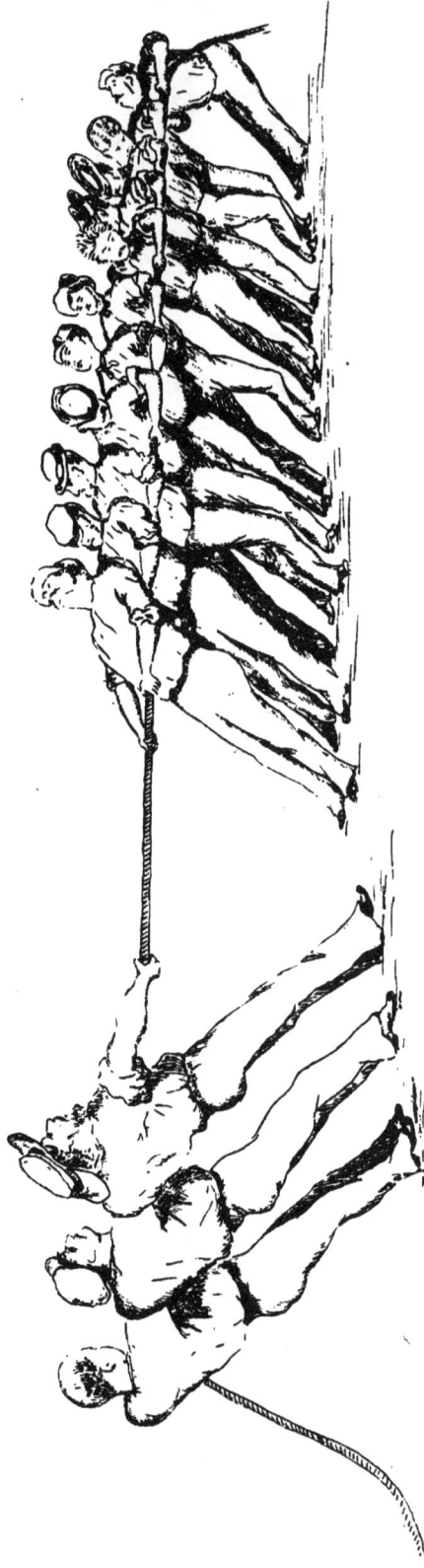

1 Wicket, 133 runs.   All out, 247 runs.

International Cricket Match,
Sydney, Jan. 27th, 1883.

Drawn by M. C. B. Massie.

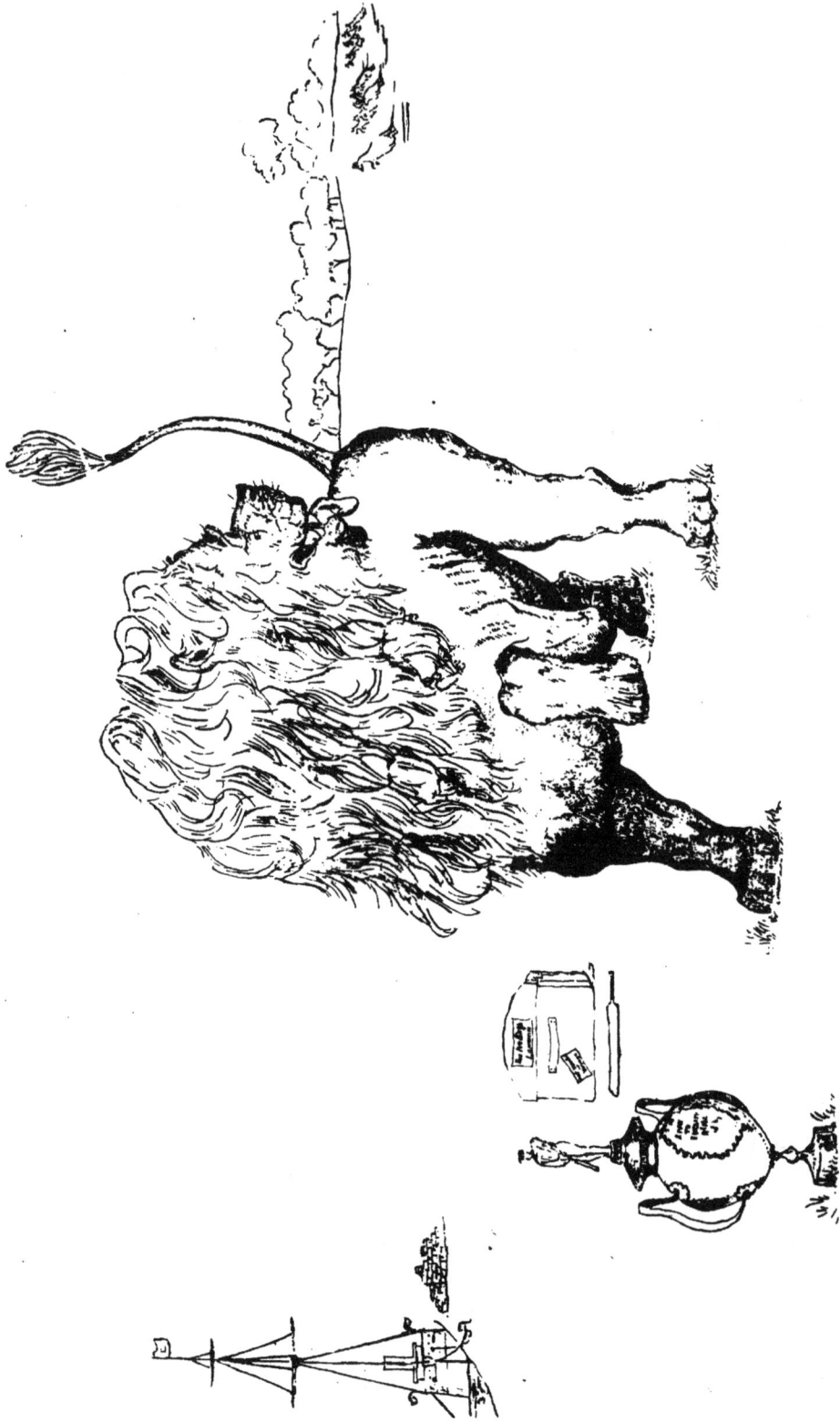

THE LION OFFERS ONE MORE CHANCE.

SYDNEY, Feb. 17th, 1883.

Drawn by M. C. B. Mussie.

To be, or not to be.

Feb. 17th, 1883.

Drawn by M. C. R. Massie

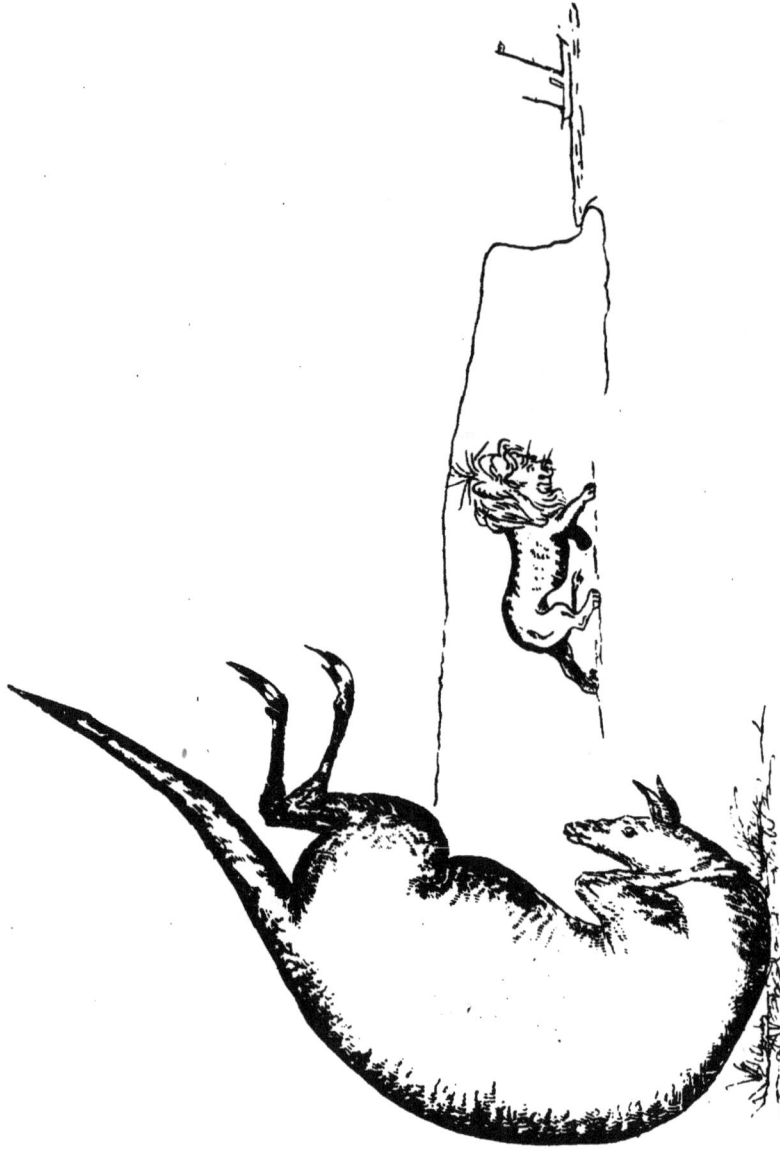

WON BY FOUR WICKETS.
SYDNEY,
Feb. 17th, 19th, 20th, 1883.

Drawn by M. C. B. Mussie.

BEATEN, BUT NOT DISGRACED.—VICTORIA VICTRIX.

March 12th, 1883.

Drawn by M. C. B. Massie.

THE ASHES GONE.

Hi, Ivo! Ho, Ivo!

Drawn by M. C. R. Massie.

www.ingramcontent.com/pod-product-compliance
Lightning Source LLC
Chambersburg PA
CBHW080512090426

42734CB00015B/3035